Better A Patriot Soldier's Grave

BETTER A PATRIOT SOLDIER'S GRAVE

THE HISTORY OF THE SIXTH OHIO VOLUNTEER CAVALRY

by
WILLIAM G. BURNETT

DEDICATED
TO
SAMANTHA
AND
MICHELLE
(SAM AND MIKE)

ACKNOWLEDGEMENT
Howard C. Aley

BETTER A PATRIOT SOLDIER'S GRAVE is the exciting story of the courageous Sixth Ohio Volunteer Cavalry written by a devotee of Civil War history for devotees of Civil War history. Only an obsessive love for his subject and a concern for others like himself who find their appetites for Civil War history insatiable, could have mustered the persistence to see this heroic effort through to completion.

William G. Burnett first came to me as a student in junior high school some forty years ago. To have been approached these many years later by a now eminently successful business man, who through four decades had nourished his love for Civil War lore, and to witness his determination to see his dream of writing such a work fulfilled, has been one of the outstanding teacher-student experiences of my career.

Being William G. Burnett, "Bill" would try to credit his former English teacher with having had a part in this effort, but the facts are that beyond suggestions, and occasional advice and encouragement along the way, this is William G. Burnett's book. He may in his generosity of spirit share credit widely among those who helped along the way, but in every page there is inextricably woven the persistence, his knowledge, and his love of the subject, that are the requisites of any book that is worth the paper on which it is printed.

Lovers of Civil War history will find this effort to have many values. It adds to the growing mass of regimental histories that continue to flesh out the bare bones histories which must be more general than specific. It tells an interesting and exciting story of a little known, but extremely important facet of the history of the War Between the States. It portrays the role of many hundreds of young men of a particular section of Ohio, known as the Connecticut Western Reserve, and follows them through the heat of battle to ultimate victory at Appomattox.

And finally, it fulfills the aspiration of many devotees of Civil War history in that it makes a contribution to the total library of that period between 1860 and 1865. Who among lovers of Civil War history has not dreamed of doing just that.

It derives its title from the observation of one of the boys of the Sixth Ohio Volunteer Cavalry, who wrote home that he would prefer to die in the field rather than compromise his principles. He, however, said it better, "Better a patriot soldier's grave, than A TRAITOR'S DISHONORABLE LIFE AT HOME."

Howard C. Aley
Ridgewood
August, 1982

Contents

A *Patriot's Prayer*
By
Dorothy E. Burnett

Muskets heavy; shoulders sore;
Ground is rough; shoes half gone;
Canteen's empty; stomach, too;
Why is it I go on and on?

Time passes on from dark to light,
Lines are thinning, comrades dead.
I march and stop and march and fight.
What is it that I see ahead?

The war has ended, victory won
With awful cost; we fought for right.
And there it lies, in setting sun,
The glorious Union, shining bright!

FOREWORD

Better A Patriot Soldier's Grave

This is the story of a crack Civil War regiment that endured nearly four long years of civil strife, the Sixth Ohio Volunteer Cavalry. Most of the boys who belonged to this unit came from Ohio's Western Reserve (counties in Northeast Ohio once claimed by Connecticut). The Western Reserve! From time immemorial the climate of the area was Abolitionist. The Jefferson Gazette observed in 1850 that "The Civil War could easily have started in Ashtabula County." And there were reasons. In December of 1850, at Hartsgrove, Ohio, an Antislavery Convention published some nineteen resolutions, one of which proclaimed, "Sooner than submit to such odious laws (The Fugitive Slave Act of 1850), we will see the Union dissolved; sooner than see slavery perpetuated, we would see war; sooner than be slaves, we will fight." Only fifty miles away from Ashtabula county, was Oberlin College, a mecca for runaway slaves, while John Brown of Harper's Ferry fame, was widely known throughout the area. Little wonder that the Sixth Regiment's manpower quota was easily filled eleven years later. Long conditioning had molded the boys' point of view.

When Abraham Lincoln, on May 16th, 1861, called for 75,000 volunteers, he touched the lives of some 1,758 men of the Western Reserve who volunteered for duty in the Sixth Cavalry Regiment (which in the beginning was known as Wade and Hutchins Cavalry).

The First Battle of Bull Run sobered the people in Northeast Ohio, convincing them that it might be a long, hard war. On September 9th, it was announced that a Company of Cavalry would be raised in Orwell, Ohio. On Saturday, September 28, 1861, Ohio's Senator Benjamin Wade and Congressman John Hutchins received orders from the Adjutant General's office to raise an ad-

1

ditional Regiment of Cavalry for three year's service in the United States Army. The fairgrounds in Warren, Ohio, was named Camp Hutchins, the location where all the companies would assemble, from Ashtabula, Orwell, Jefferson, Geneva and Madison, to name only a few of the towns from which the volunteers came.

This was the birth of a Regiment. What followed, as recorded in letters from the boys and in the weekly press, would write meaningful new pages into Western Reserve history and would become a significant part of the military history of the Civil War.

From its first contact with Confederate forces at Woodstock, Virginia, on June 2, 1862, to its participation at the site of Lee's surrender at Appomattox Court House and its mustering out at Petersburg, Virginia, they, the Sixth, would have engaged in combat no fewer than fifty one times. From Second Bull Run, Fredericksburg, Kelly's Ford, Gettysburg, Rapidan Station, Cold Harbor, Stony Creek, Five Forks and Sailor's Creek, to Appomattox on April 8-9, 1865, was a long, three-year journey, and, of course, all who set out, would not complete it. But the Regiment came through, and the record it left behind, when placed in the balance of loyalty, service, devotion to duty, and military effectiveness, is not found wanting.

By late fall of 1861, 796 men had enlisted in eight companies of the Sixth. In the beginning, each Company was named after the captain who organized it. Later the companies bore designations A through M. With men streaming into Camp Hutchins, sleeping quarters were hastily thrown up. Warren residents contributed clothing and blankets, for the cold winds of fall would soon be upon them. The recruitment program, the call for food, clothing and blankets, and the extra money circulating throughout the community, gave the War Between the States a new dimension in the Western Reserve. It was rapidly becoming a matter of clear and present danger that must eventually command the concern of all in one way or another.

Slowly but surely, the companies of the Sixth were filling up at Camp Hutchins. The final push for recruits came from the Adjutant General's office that no volunteers would be accepted after the 15th of December. Thursday, December 11th, was an eventful day at Camp Hutchins, with 800 men in handsome uniforms and under good drill, participating in a dress parade.

On Thursday, January 5th, 1862, four companies of the Sixth departed for Camp Dennison, under Major Stedman, while a like number of companies under Colonel William Lloyd left on Saturday, January 7th, leaving Camp Hutchins deserted. In later years it would be the site of many annual conventions of this famous Regiment. As the townspeople observed, "Good as were those whom Trumbull County had sent out before the war, none finer had gone from here and adjoining counties than the Ohio Sixth Volunteer Cavalry."

Following is a list of battles, engagements and skirmishes in which this Regiment bore an honorable part:

Woodstock, Va., ... June 2, 1862.
Mt. Jackson, Va.,.......... June 3, 1862.
Cross Keys, Va.,.......... June 8, 1862.
Luray Court House, Va., ...July 12, 1862.
Warrenton, Va., ...August—, 1862.
Bull Run, Va.,....... August 29-30, 1862.
Chantilly, Va., ...September 1, 1862.
Fredericksburg,
    Va.,.............. December 13, 1862.
Kelly's Ford, Va.,........March 17, 1863.
Stoneman's Raid,
    Va.,.......... April 29 to May 2, 1863.
Stevensburg, Va., ... June 9, 1863.
Aldie, Va.,............... June 17, 1863.
Middleburg, Va.,.......... June 19, 1863.
Upperville, Va.,.......... June 21, 1863.
Gettysburg, Pa.,.......... July 1-4, 1863.
Hagerstown, Md., ...July 6, 1863.
Boonsboro, Etc., Md., ... July 8-10, 1863.
Falling Water, Md.,........July 14, 1863.
Sheppardstown, Va., ...July 16, 1863.
Rapidan Station,
    Va.,........... September 13-14, 1863.
Sulphur Springs,
    Va.,................ October 12, 1863.
Auburn Mills, Va.,..... October 14, 1863.
Bristoe Station, Va. .... October 14, 1863.
Mine Run, Va.,......November 27, 1863.
Todd's Tavern, Va.......May 5-7, 1864.
Mitchell's Shop, or Jerrald's
    Mills, Va., ... May 9, 1864.
Yellow Tavern, Va., ... May 11, 1864.
Meadow Bridge, Va., ... May 12, 1864.

Hawe's Shop, or Aenon Church,
    Virginia, ... May 28, 1864.
Cold Harbor,
    Va.,........... May 31 to June 1, 1864.
Bottom Bridge, Va., ... June 6, 1864.
Trevilians' Station,
    Va.,................. June 11-12, 1864.
St. Mary's Church, or
    Ladd's Farm, Va., ... June 24, 1864.
Malvern Hill, Va., ...July 28, 1864.
Darbytown, Va., ...July 28, 1864.
Deep Bottom, Va., .. August 15-16, 1864.
Ream's Station, Va. ..... August 25, 1864.
Preble's Farm, or Davis' Farm,
    Virginia, ... October 1, 1864.
Boydtown Road,
    Va.,................ October 27, 1864.
Stony Creek, Va., ... December 1, 1864.
Hatcher's Run,
    Va.,............. December 8-9, 1864.
Hatcher's Run,
    Va.,............. February 5-7, 1865.
Quaker Road, Va., ...March 29, 1865.
Dinwiddie Court House,
    Va.,................. March 31, 1865.
Five Forks, Va., ... April 1, 1865.
Jettersville, Va., ... April 4-5, 1865.
Deatonsville, Va., ... April 5, 1865.
Sailor's Creek, Va., ... April 6, 1865.
Farmville, Va., ... April 7, 1865.
High Bridge, Va., ... April 7, 1865.
Appomattox, or Lee's
    Surrender, Va.,........ April 8-9, 1865.

CHAPTER I

January, 1862, Through June, 1862

OVERVIEW OF THE WAR

The beginning of 1862 saw both The Army of the Potomac and The Army of Northern Virginia in winter quarters.

In the west, "Unconditional Surrender" Grant captured Fort Donnelson on the Mississippi River, on February 16th.

On March 9th, the now famous battle between the Merrimack and the Monitor, ironclads, was fought to a draw, forever changing Naval warfare.

By April, the Army of the Potomac, under McClellan, was on the move to open the Peninsula campaign, and by May 17th the Union forces held the peninsula and the river approaches to the Confederate capitol, followed by the Seven Days battle, which put a stop to McClellan's march on Richmond.

Throughout the Peninsula campaign, the Confederate general, "Stonewall" Jackson, tied down 60,000 Union troops with his march and countermarch up and down the Shenandoah Valley.

OVERVIEW OF THE SIXTH CAVALRY

The skirmishes at Luray, Strasburg, Cross Keys and Woodstock marked the beginning for the Sixth. Here they had their baptism under fire.

January, 1862, Through June, 1862

As the boys of the Sixth marched to the station to board the cars (train), for Cleveland and Camp Dennison, their regimental dog, "Paddy McManus," accompanied them sharing their fortunes for a year until, as one more casualty of the Civil War, he would turn up missing. Fifty years later, when the Sixth held its golden anniversary reunion, Billy Kneal would reach into his pocket and come up with a picture of Miles McManus' dog. Rarely is a dog so well remembered by so many as was "Paddy McManus" of the Sixth Ohio Voluntary Cavalry.

The Sixth arrived at Camp Dennison on January 5th, 1862, finding the large barracks with a good kitchen and cookstoves more to their liking. Upon arrival at their new home, the boys of the unit took a vote, abolishing card playing in the barracks, profane language, and permitting dancing only once per week.

As in all army camps of all wars, the rumors flew. "The Sixth is to be disbanded." "They are to be turned into Infantry." "The government has enough cavalry." "They will be distributed among other cavalry regiments."

In the second week of January, the Second Ohio Voluntary Cavalry left for Cincinnati, where they would board boats for St. Louis. It was an emotional leave taking, with the members of the Sixth wondering when their turn would come.

Camp life was dull and monotonous with mail call the best hour of the day. Waiting patiently for assignment, they drilled and wrote letters home. Rumors circulating back home about their drinking, fighting and fraternizing with the local cortesans were greatly exaggerated. Evidence indicates that they were the best and most orderly regiment ever at Camp Dennison.

On January 23rd, 1862, the Sixth Ohio Volunteer Cavalry was presented a "stand of colors" made by the "Ladies of Warren", together with a description of every symbol in the flag:

"The azure canopy dotted with stars speaks of a freedom limited by no tyrant's sway. The helmet, hopefully promising complete political salvation, indicates protection of freedom of thought wherever our banner shall wave. The stripes of pure white betoken love to all friends; the scarlet warns tyrants and traitors. The full-fledged eagle bears in his powerful talons, arrows for the hearts of invaders, and the generous olive for yielding foes. With these he exalts in a conscious ability to carry the scroll with its motto: 'E Pluribus Unum', in triumph from mountain to sea and from ocean to ocean."

The months dragged on in the camp of the Sixth. Guarding Secesh prisoners, complaining that they had not as yet been issued mounts or arms, or been paid, some took furloughs, while others ended up in hospitals. The inactivity caused much sickness in the Union camps.

On February 2nd, 1862, death for the first time visited the Sixth Cavalry. Charles Jenkins of Company "A" died; his body was sent home.

In early March their orders at long last came through. The Sixth was ordered to Camp Chase, outside Columbus, to "guard prisoners." At Camp Chase two more members of the new regiment died. Ivory B. Saunders of Company "A" died of congestive chills on May 5th, while George Edney, also of Company "A", died on May 16th.

Finally, after six long months, the regiment was paid on May 2nd. It must have seemed even longer to the wives and children of these men who were counting upon the soldiers' earnings to keep them fed, clothed and under roof while their "menfolks" were off to war. They were paid up to March 1st, 1862, the total regimental payroll amounting to $7,620.50.

On April 26th, sabres, belts, caps and cartridge boxes were issued, and the boys were jubilant over the prospect of going into the field.

"Guard" duty continued, with many bemoaning the fact. The Sixth called them "lovely prison birds," and had not much respect for the type of men they were guarding.

Suddenly, it was their turn. On Tuesday, the 13th of May, 1862, both battalions of the regiment left Camp Chase for Camp Carlisle, Wheeling Island, Virginia, where they arrived about 11:00 A.M. Wednesday. By the next morning, orders were received from General Fremont's staff, calling for the movement of two companies to New Creek, Camp Jessie, Virginia.

It was at this time, through letters sent home that they showed their lofty ideals and sentiments.

"The late war news is as cheering to us soldiers as it can be to friends at home. The present position of our mobile armies thrills us with hope that the internal rebellion will soon be killed outright and our country once more will be free; not free in name only, either, but truly so."

"The late order of General Hunter is sanctioned and sustained by the government. We, in our humble judgment, consider this move the most important and mightiest for true freedom ever made on the American continent, and it must be the most fervent prayer of every true patriot of all our land that the spirit and letter of order #11 from Hilton Head may be carried out in every state. Then we can and will have the grandest, best and purest country and government on earth, and Abraham Lincoln a second Washington. Let us have faith, but not without works."

Order #11, of which the writer speaks, freed all the slaves in Georgia, Florida and South Carolina, but was rescinded by President Lincoln on May 19th.

By now, with horses under saddle and rumors on the issuance of their pistols and carbines, they felt they were part of the war to save the Union.

Most of the boys of this untried regiment, were new at riding horses. As one boy wrote home, "The boys have a good deal of fun seeing one another get throwed off from their horses."

On May 19th, the Sixth boarded railroad cars, arriving at Piedmont, near the Maryland line, on the 21st, riding the remaining five miles to New Creek, Virginia. At this time they entered the beautiful Shenandoah Valley, in the pursuit of "Stonewall" Jackson. The valley had become a major military highway for both armies, the Blue Ridge Mountains on the east shielding the valley and providing excellent opportunities for Southern cavalry to screen out the prying eyes that appeared at the gaps between the mountains. Further, the Shenandoah Valley, during much of the war, was a vital source of food and forage for the Confederacy.

In pursuit of Jackson, the regiment would ride through Winchester, Mt. Jackson, New Market, Cross Keys, Front Royal, Luray, Waynesboro, Culpepper Court House, Warrenton, Fairfax, Centerville, Stafford Court House and Hall's Farm.

By June 2nd, they were at Strasburg, Virginia, on the extreme right of Fremont's army, an extensive front which was considered formidable. Things were quiet except for guerilla activity, which the boys of the Sixth hated, because of Johnny Reb's ambush tactics.

On May 31st, part of the regiment went out on scout duty and had a skirmish with a part of Ashby's Confederate Cavalry. The next day Fremont's force was on the march, heading for Strasburg, where they hoped to meet Jackson. Later in the day, the regiment went out on a reconnaisance mission where they discovered very little of the enemy at their front.

That evening, an extremely heavy thunderstorm turned the roads to rivers of mud. The boys of the Sixth pursued the enemy knee-deep in mire, picking up prisoners throughout the next day. Finally coming upon the rear of the Rebel army they were pursuing, the Sixth was greeted with a shower of balls and shells which flew thick and fast. One exploded in the midst of Company "A", slightly wounding two men and several horses. After an hour of cannonading, the enemy continued its flight, burning the bridge over the Shenandoah, making immediate pursuit impossible.

The Sixth fought battles at Harrisonburg on the 6th, and at Fort Republic on the 8th, and were severely handled by the Rebels. At the end of the day, both armies retired from the field. Jackson had accomplished his goal, tying up the Union forces by the chase.

On June 16th, while out on a foraging expedition, a squad of the regiment were attacked and captured by about sixty of Ashby Cavalrymen. A messenger scout brought back the news that the whole party had been cut off and taken prisoner by the rebels.

Within minutes the bugle blew and sixty men were in their saddles ready to march under Captains Barrett, Barber and Bowe. They met the rebels at a line of woods, both the Federals and Rebels charging at each other. Many shots were exchanged rapidly. The struggle was fierce for a short time, until the Rebels retreated back into the woods. Members of the Sixth pursued some distance but the Rebels ran too swiftly to be caught by tired horses.

At the end of the melee, the Sixth had lost fifteen men, one killed and fourteen taken prisoner. Nineteen horses and two government wagons were also lost.

Those taken prisoner included Quartermaster Sergeant Theodore Woolcott, Privates H. J. Hickox, George King, Myron Patterson, Charles Hamlin, Alfred Pierce, Caleb Rising, Quartermaster Sergeant Isaac Crampton, Edwin French, Nathan Bassett, Robert White, Edwin Bailey, William H. Treat and Stephen Thorpe. A boy by the name of Boots was killed.

The Sixth had had their baptism under fire, been in the saddle for fourteen days, took fourteen prisoners and killed one of the Confederates.

As the first half of 1862 closed, the regiment rested in camp, still doing scout duty, but more importantly, took to foraging. The Union Army, as they were to do throughout the war, requisitioned (the "Secesh" called it stealing) food for themselves and their mounts throughout the Virginia countryside. They were in a lush valley and they took advantage of it. Pigs, cattle, corn, fruit and hay were taken every day from surrounding farms. Boys who had been brought up with the "Ten Commandments," thought nothing of cleaning out a farm of anything that grew since, in their opinion, the people of Virginia were Secesh and should not have seceded from the Union. Supplying the armies in the field was still in its infancy, and it seemed as if the supply trains never caught up to the marching armies. Those who didn't or wouldn't steal, much of the time would pay 30 cents to 60 cents per pound for sugar, $1.50 for coffee, 75 cents per pound for salt and 50 cents for a loaf of bread. Shortages in the South were already being seen. The boys' greenbacks (federal money) were coveted by the Southern farmers, while Confederate script was frowned upon. The boys' rations were supplemented by food sold by sutlers who had a sort of semi-official concession with the regiment, the concession said to have been usually secured through political influences in their own states.

CHAPTER II

July, 1862, Through December, 1862

OVERVIEW OF THE WAR

McClellan had a victory at Malvern Hill, but still retreated down the peninsula, and the peninsula campaign was over.

General Pope was outflanked by Jackson, and they met at Manassas Junction, the Second Battle of Bull Run, and, as in the first, the Federals were soundly defeated.

McClellan was put back in command of the Army of the Potomac and stopped Lee's invasion of the North at Antietam, Maryland.

General Burnside superceded General McClellan and managed to walk into a slaughter and defeat at Fredericksburg by the end of the year.

In the west, the Union's General Carlos Buell thwarted the invasion of General Bragg's army into Kentucky at Perryville, and at Stones River or Murfreesboro. The Confederates were again defeated.

OVERVIEW OF THE SIXTH CAVALRY

It was a busy time for the Sixth Ohio Volunteer Cavalry. They fought at Laury Court House, Warrenton, Bull Run, Chantilly and Fredericksburg, Virginia.

July, 1862, Through December, 1862

On July 4th, the regiment was encamped about five miles from Strasburg on the road to Winchester. They celebrated the 4th with dress parades, the firing of cannon and listening to speeches. Only July 5th they were on the march again. Upon reaching Laury, Virginia, they camped, but for the next few days continual skirmishing took place. In this period of time, one cavalryman, Washington Bagle, was wounded and six were taken prisoner by the rebels, two of them being Johnson McClain and James Muller. One was killed, James Caffee.

By July 15th they were posted four miles east of Luray as a rearguard to the main body of the army. On the march to their new camp, David Porter of Company D was wounded in the leg by accidental discharge of his pistol. The heat and jarring discharged firearms accidentally throughout the war. The Sixth skirmished nearly every day with guerillas. James Burns of Mecca was shot in the hand and Edwin Prentice was captured. Thus it went, in the midst of the excitement and danger every moment.

The Sixth enjoyed camp life for the next month, but on the 9th of August was ordered to Culpepper where next morning a heavy battle ensued which lasted throughout the day and brought much heavier losses to the Union side than to the Confederates. Jackson, again, had hit and retreated, giving the Union another bloody nose.

At four o'clock on the morning of August 29th, the Sixth Ohio was ordered into the saddle. They were entering the battle of Manassas, or Second Bull Run. By 10:00 A. M. the fight was going on sharply in the front, and ambulances were rapidly passing their position, bearing many wounded away from the battle front. Four hours later the battle was still raging with the roar of artillery incessant and shells bursting in every direction. Occasional volleys of musketry were heard, and above the field hung a heavy cloud of battle smoke which completely enveloped the combatants. At 4:25, the battle still raged, marked by incessant musket fire to their front. The enemy had fallen back, but the fighting continued. Next day dawned with ambulances hurrying the wounded to shelter, and an increase in action as the day wore on. With artillery shells flying in every direction, the Union infantry was sent forward to attack the enemy position only to be met by a tremendous fire of grape cannister and musketry that sent them flying backwards out of the woods in great disorder. Soon the panic spread to others and, for a time, a general stampede seemed inevitable. Straggling infantry and wagons were falling back in disorder and a scene of confusion prevailed. At this point the cavalry was ordered out, and by forming a line and beating back the stragglers, they succeeded in checking what might otherwise have been a second Bull Run panic.

Finally the Army retired in good order. The Sixth crossed Bull Run and moved to Centerville where they stayed the night.

By the morning of the 30th, a long train of carriages and ambulances arrived from Washington to convey the wounded to hospitals. Many of the wagons were loaded with bread and other necessities for the wounded.

The following day, the enemy unexpectedly made a demonstration on the regiment's right flank with a view to capturing the supply train. From 5 P. M. until darkness the fighting raged without intermission. The regiment fell back to Germantown where they were left in line and ordered to hold their horses. After passing a cold and uncomfortable night, the movement was back toward Alexandria, the regiment ordered out as pickets to cover the retreat of the army. They had now been under fire for fourteen straight days.

On the 3rd of September, the line of march passed to the left of Washington, before reporting to General Sigel at the Chain Bridge eight miles above the city. By now they were assigned to the 2nd brigade, 2nd Division, 1st Army Corps of Virginia. The 2nd Division was Sigel's.

Now it was back to camp life, patrolling, picket duty and skirmishing.

It was in late September, while on a reconnoitering mission between Bristow and Cateletts Station, that the advance guard of Companies A and K suddenly came upon a heavy force of the enemy and were engaged in a brisk skirmish. The advance guard was forced to fall back to the main body. During this action four men of Company A, Orlando Ferry, Wells Bushnell, Jacob Sager and Martin Sager, were taken prisoner. And so it went through the final months of the year.

Back home in Orwell, Ohio, other events were taking place that would strengthen the Sixth's rolls.

On October 22nd, 1862, an advertisement appeared in the Ashtabula Sentinel announcing that Captain Amandar Bingham would be at headquarters he had established at Jefferson and at Orwell, Ohio, for the purpose of recruiting four entire companies for the Sixth Ohio Cavalry. The Captain would be at Orwell on Mondays and Tuesdays and at the American House in Jefferson on Fridays and Saturdays. It was further said that any good man bringing with him thirty good men would be entitled to a Captain's commission; if twenty, a Lieutenant's commission, if eight men, a company sergeant, if ten men, a Quartermaster Sergeant Assistant.

The Sixth were now encamped four miles outside of Halls Farm for refitting, new revolvers and horses.

Endless days of patrolling followed, over the sad fields of Chantilly, Bull Run and Manassas, fields that will always be important to American history. At this time they were sad fields. The bones of horses and men were strewn thickly over them and from many a scant heaped mound a hand or foot or skull protruded, telling of the hasty burial. At Chantilly, where the rebels made their last desperate attempt to cut the Federals off from Washington, the rebel dead were buried so hastily that the first rain had washed away the scanty covering, and fleshless skeletons, by scores, lay bleaching in the sun and storm. By October 9th the boys would have moved to Centerville after a skirmish at Warrenton Station.

On October 2nd, death visited the Sixth again. Wellington Parker of Company K was killed by accidental gun discharge. And on October 20th, at a skirmish at Thoroughfare Gap, Edwin Bailey was wounded and died.

By November 2nd they were back in Centerville. On November 22nd Liberty Raymond was taken prisoner. It never seemed to end. The first week of November, now camped at Warrenton Junction, a detachment of the Sixth Ohio, while reconnoitering to their front with an equal number of Indiana Cavalrymen, scouted out to a distance of 45 miles to Fredericksburg.

14

The surprise was complete and Colonel Lloyd, the leader of the Federal force, captured 29 of the enemy and 20 horses.

The first days of December saw the boys of the Sixth camped near Chantilly, scouting out as far as Aldie at the north end of the Bull Run Mountains. They ventured on through Snickers Gap into the Shenandoah Valley where they had expected a fight. But the fight did not materialize, although some 30 Confederates were taken prisoner. On December 9th movement started for the Sixth towards Fredricksburgh. The weather had turned cold and snowy. They stopped at Potomac Run.

As Christmas came, several parties made dashes into the countryside to gather a turkey, goose or chicken or anything to make merry with gladness in the stomach. But the exceeding barrenness of all roosts and yards made their dashes generally unfruitful, leaving them with their usual dish of hard tack, pork or beef, and coffee for Christmas, with dessert of beans or rice. Not exactly what the good mothers, wives and sisters would choose as most proper and acceptable for a holiday dinner or supper.

CHAPTER III

January, 1863, Through June, 1863

OVERVIEW OF THE WAR

The new year opened with Abraham Lincoln announcing the Emancipation Proclamation. The first draft law passed on March 3rd.

Much of the activity of the winter months was Naval.

In the spring General Joseph Hooker was defeated at Chancellorsville, while General Grant was defeating the Confederates in Mississippi and launching the seige of Vicksburg.

In the last weeks of June, Lee invaded the North.

OVERVIEW FOR THE SIXTH

As the first half of the year became history, the Sixth Ohio fought at Kelly's Ford and took part in Stoneman's Raid into the heart of Virginia. They skirmished at Stevensburg, Virginia, Aldie, Middleburg and Upperville.

And the rolls of the wounded, dead and captured grew longer.

January, 1863, Through June, 1863

Eighteen Sixty-three saw the Sixth Ohio Volunteer Cavalry in winter quarters at Potomac Creek Station, Virginia, guarding the Rappahannock and going through a reorganization in preparation for the spring campaign.

Morale was at a low ebb, not only in the Sixth, but throughout the Army of the Potomac. The whipping at Fredricksburg had accomplished that. Their bough houses were but scant obstacles to the cutting winds which swept over the hills. They could scarcely stay warm even by the aid of the largest fires they could build.

In the endless patrolling, there had to be casualties. In January, Marshall Northway, William Stiles and an unknown recruit were taken prisoner.

Six new recruits joined the regiment on January 7th. The Sixth was continually under marching orders, so they had to keep three days cooked rations prepared, and had to hold themselves in readiness to move at any moment.

But with all the obstacles, camp life was much more restful and permanent than those long days and weeks in the saddle on picket duty or skirmishing. The sutler and paymaster arrived and every table groaned with simple but high-priced luxuries. Hut building grew into an art, and a great deal of pipe carving was done from the roots of trees. All in all, it was a peaceful time.

As of March 14th, all letters from home to the Sixth were to be directed: "Sixth Ohio Volunteer Cavalry, First Cavalry Brigade, Second Division, Via Washington."

Cannon was heard in the distance.

General Hooker, now in command of the Army of the Potomac, decided to outflank Lee's army, but first the Federals had to gain control of the crossing points across the Rappahannock for his infantry. One of the shallow parts of the river was at Kelly's Ford, so the Federal Cavalry was sent to take it and guard it.

Along with the Sixth Ohio, other regiments beefed up the attacking force. The First and Fifth U. S. Regulars, the Third,

Fourth and Sixteenth Pennsylvania, the First Rhode Island, the Fourth New York and the Sixth New York battery of artillery. This, then, was the lineup that faced Stuart's Cavalry on March 17th.

The first shots were fired at 6:40 A.M. A deadly rifle fire came from Rebel pickets in rifle pits, behind trees and stumps. The first attempt to cross the river was thwarted. But finally the First Rhode Island and the Sixth Ohio gained the other side, even though the enemy had placed felled trees in the river to obstruct crossing. Once on the opposite bank, a line was formed and the cavalrymen waited for the rest of the division and the artillery battery to cross, a movement which took until noon. Preparations were made to proceed toward Culpepper. Some 30 of the Sixth Ohio were thrown ahead as advance guards under Captain Norman Barrett. The remainder of the Sixth was on the right of the field. They drove the Rebels for three-quarters of a mile, until they were suddenly fired upon by enemy artillery, and then came the Rebel charge. Down they came, yelling and brandishing sabres and pistols, thinking, no doubt, that the Yankees would turn and run. But the boys of the Sixth, with sabres drawn, waited until they were within a hundred yards. The order came, "Forward," and they charged down to meet them. There was a moment of wild clamor, the ringing of sabres and the crack of revolvers and then a cheer went up from the boys. The Rebels had fled, nor did they once more that day venture their fortunes in a charge. The artillery fight continued until nearly sundown when, after driving the enemy about three miles, the division recrossed the river, having fought throughout the entire day.

The Union forces lost nine killed and 35 wounded, while the Confederates lost 11 killed and 88 wounded.

In appraising the action, General Arvil said, "It was the most gallant cavalry fight of the war." It was at Kelly's Ford that the Federal Cavalry came into its own. It had whipped Stuart, the best the Rebels had to offer.

In the Sixth, the losses were one killed, six wounded and one missing. Missing was Charles Shattuck of Company A; killed, Lucas Labis of Company G; wounded, J. P. Wood, G. P. Wilson, S. Philman, A. Smith, Henry Truesdale and Lemuel Granger.

In late March, 74 new recruits joined the regiment, and on April 8th, Abraham Lincoln arrived to review the Corps of General Sickels. The officers of the Sixth were privileged to attend.

They were now encamped at Potomac Station, and their new Brigadier, N. D. Duffie, a Frenchman by birth, was a well-disciplined officer, but great for style.

They drilled twice a day and held dress parade once a day. Careful watering and grooming kept their cavalry horses in good trim.

The Sixth left Potomac Station on the 13th of April and moved to Warrenton Station. It was at this time that General Hooker detached Stoneman, the head of the Cavalry Corps, from the main operations of the Army of the Potomac, with orders to cross the Rappahannock for a raid on the communications with Richmond —turning Lee's left flank and inflicting on him every possible injury. Stoneman's raid coincided with the battle of Chancellorsville.

Before nightfall on the evening of Tuesday, April 28th, the Sixth received orders to pack up and march to Morrisville toward which General Stoneman had set out the previous morning. After marching all night, they reached Morrisville at four o'clock in the morning, proceeding immediately to Kelly's Ford some five miles away. The entire day was spent in getting the cavalrymen and the 11th and 12th army corps across the river. General Stoneman and his escort crossed the river at 4 P.M. Some six miles farther on, the Sixth halted and encampd for the night.

Dawn of the 30th of April found them once more back in the saddle. The pack trains having been sent back, the men were required now to depend upon their own resources for subsistence. Crossing the Rapidan River at 4 P.M., the men marched until eleven, camping at Raccoon Ford on the same stream. They were ordered back to the march at 2 A.M., but it was finally 4 A.M. before the column was again in motion. They camped that night without fires.

On the first of May the regiment moved on, crossing the Orange and Fredericksburg Pike. Some of the boys captured an officer of the 4th Virginia Cavalry, returning to his regiment after having been on furlough. Unaware that any Union boys were in the area, he at first construed the capture as a prank being played on him by some of his own men.

The people throughout the countryside stared in astonishment as they were the first "Yanks" they had ever seen. They had evidently been taught to believe that the Yanks were monsters, and were surprised that they did not murder them nor destroy their property.

For the first time since their departure on Tuesday evening, May 2nd, the men were permitted to unsaddle their horses on Friday evening at 10 P.M. But Saturday morning they were off once more to Louisa Court House where they destroyed a large section of the Virginia Central Railroad. At 10 o'clock that evening, a squadron of the 1st Maryland Cavalry joined the Sixth boys and proceeded under orders down the South Anna to burn bridges and destroy fords along that stream. Working all night, the morning of May 3rd found them within 25 miles of Richmond.

At noon on Sunday, May 4th, the regiment reached a place called Squirrel Church, some 18 miles from Richmond. They were, for the time being, attached to General Gregg, who, at sundown sent 235 men under Lieutenant Colonel Smith of the 10th New York Cavalry to burn the railroad bridge across the South Anna. The Sixth accompanied the expedition. Finding the bridge too heavily guarded to permit their mission, the Colonel ordered his men to burn several buildings filled with Confederate stores, and to destroy some track and a number of smaller bridges. It was an all night task and the boys did not rejoin General Gregg's division until four in the morning. Three hours later they were back in the line of march to Thompson's Crossroads where they had left General Stoneman. They arrived at their destination at 2 P.M. having been in the saddle almost constantly for two days, and having covered not less than 100 miles. They were permitted to unsaddle on Monday evening, the second time they had done so since leaving Warrenton Junction.

Following the course of General Stoneman, the Sixth started out again on Tuesday morning, May 6th, traveling all night without stopping until 9 o'clock on Wednesday morning. But it was a short stop, only long enough to feed their horses and themselves. It rained heavily that night and because the General was eager to get across the Rappahannock before it rose too much to permit crossing, they marched all night after the crossing.

Many of the men slept in their saddles, and when the column stopped, one could hear snoring all along the line.

The Southern people along the Sixth's line of march had never before seen "Yankees" and did not know what to make of them. They had supposed themselves safe from invasion. As for the blacks, they were perfectly wild with joy, some of them would dance, some would sing and cry. Some of the Southern people who had been taught that the Yankees would kill all their children, consequently tried to conceal the youngsters from the strange troops. By this time, many of the negroes were following the column. But it was back to base camp and a rest.

Stoneman's raid had destroyed millions of dollars worth of Confederate property, and although it cut Lee's communication for a short time only, its moral effect was considerable.

Back at Beulton Station, the paymaster arrived in mid-May. As the boys would say in later years, when the paymaster arrived, there was sure to be a battle. It was not uncommon for a soldier to be paid only every six months, so the event was received with much joy.

It was now time for Lee's turn at invasion. For various reasons; food for the army, much needed supplies, and an advance on Washington, his three corps jumped off on June 3rd. Between the two armies, the rival cavalries sparred and skirmished, each commander trying to get news of the enemy's position and deny to the enemy news of his own.

There was a skirmish at Stevensburg, Virginia, on June 9th. Continually in the saddle, they had another brush with the Confederate pickets at Aldie, Virginia, on June 17th. They moved on to Middleburg, where they again fought a small skirmish on June 19th. Peter Potter was wounded in this engagement.

On the nights of the 19th and 20th, pickets from the Sixth Ohio were out in front and were but 60 rods from the Confederate pickets. On Saturday morning, the 21st, the Sixth joined with infantry and artillery in moving forward, pushing the enemy some six miles to Upperville at the foot of the Blue Ridge. Stuart's cavalry made a determined stand at that point, his entire force being concentrated there. The fight lasted until sundown and was a succession of desperate charges, first upon one side and then upon the other.

Captain Northway's regiment was the first to enter Upperville, the Rebels having decided to make a stand beyond the town. An effort by the Second New York Cavalry was thwarted and the Sixth, which was in the Second's rear, was immediately deployed to the field, Captain Northway having been ordered by the General to charge with his squadron upon the Rebs who were massed beyond the road. Captain Northway was assured by the General that he need have no fear, for he would have adequate support. Consisting of Companies A and D, Northway's men drew sabres and advanced on the enemy who were some half a mile ahead. They charged with but 20 men against a whole Rebel regiment massed in the road.

Just before coming upon the enemy, Northway noted a little hollow which made him and his men invisible for the moment, and the enemy believed from the shouting and yelling which reached their ears that a much larger force was advancing than actually was. The Confederates at first began to retreat, but when they saw how few men were arrayed against them, they rallied and poured a perfect hailstorm of bullets into the little band. On they went, however, although it seemed that no earthly being could get through that fire alive. They dashed upon them and for a moment there was a little of the sharpest work the Sixth had ever seen.

Finding that he and his men were not supported, and knowing that his little force must either be killed or captured unless they could escape, Northway ordered his men to fall back. They went out on the double quick and in not very good order. But the retreat was not without loss. Five men were captured and four wounded, Captain Barrett among them, although the sabre wound he suffered in his face did not take him out of action.

Sergeant Mortimer Baker suffered a flesh wound in the arm, William Drake had a slight facial wound and Corporal John Allison of Colebrook suffered a slight sabre cut in the hand. Captured were Orderly Sergeant A. W. Stiles, Corporal John Granger, Private Johnson McLean, Daniel Losey and John Zimmerman.

In addition to the five captured and the four wounded, the Sixth lost eight horses. The losses for the entire regiment were sixteen wounded, among them Corporal Fayette Babcock, and one killed. Sergeant Horace Drew, Thomas Covert, Samuel Rex, Wells Bushnell and, in fact, all of the boys who were there, went in bravely. Lester Blood had been killed by Rebel sharpshooters earlier in the day.

Finally they gave Stuart a sound thrashing and drove him through the gap. As the fighting continued, Major Stanhope had his arm badly shattered, Lieutenant John Roberts was wounded in the right thigh, and Sergeant Schaffer of Howland had his right arm broken.

According to newspaper accounts at the time, some of the boys were hospitalized at Georgetown and the rest at Lincoln Hospital. As one of the participants was said to say, "Our regiment fights like the deuce. If there is anything that wants fighting, we are put in."

CHAPTER IV

July, 1863, Through December, 1863

OVERVIEW OF THE WAR

The significance, the drama and the magnitude of the battle at Gettysburg, Pennsylvania, on July 1st, 2nd and 3rd, 1863, were of such proportions that historians have often been hard put to adequately describe what transpired there. One writer has described it as "doubtless the finest military spectacle ever witnessed west of the Atlantic." But no matter what else may be said of Gettysburg, that battle, the greatest of the war, marked the beginning of the end. The tide had turned with the bloody fighting at Seminary Ridge, Little Round Top, Culp's Hill and the Wheat Field, but by no means would it be down hill all the way from that point on. The nearly 90,000 Union troops who fought those battles left 3,155 dead. The 75,000 Confederates left 3,903 dead, and between them, their wounded totalled more than 33,000. Lee turned back once more toward the Potomac, but Meade's cautiousness resulted in a slow follow-up, with Confederate cavalrymen covering the retreat. There were fights at Manassas Gap and Chester Gap in the Blue Ridge in late July. As the month came to an end, Lee was back near Warrenton, Virginia, crossing the Rappahannock into a triangle formed by the Rapidan River, at Culpepper. But in between the victory at Gettysburg, the fall of Vicksburg in early July, and capture of General John Hunt Morgan's cavalrymen who had penetrated northward to New Lisbon, Ohio, New

York City had seen some 500 of its people die in anti-draft riots that reached alarming proportions.

August and September were comparatively quiet in Virginia, except for cavalry fights. While fighting was limited in Virginia in October there was more movement.

As General Meade advanced, Lee withdrew behind the Rapidan, planning, when General Hooker's two Union corps moved west, to move around Meade's flank. On October 9th, Lee swung west and north of the Rapidan. Meanwhile, Meade, leaving Culpepper on October 11th, arrived at Centerville on the 14th. There was an engagement at Bristoe's Station on the 14th, and other rearguard actions.

November found Meade on the offensive in the Mine Run Campaign. A plan whereby the Army of the Potomac was to cross the Rapidan on Lee's right and attack the Confederates from the east before they could regroup after their action at Centerville. They found Lee in strong entrenchments in the Wilderness on the west bank of Mine Run, having been warned by Stuart's cavalry of Meade's crossing at Germanna Ford on the 26th.

Christmas found a stalemate on the Virginia front. Nearly three long years of war had dragged by and some sixteen more months of conflict lay ahead.

All hopes for "A six-months war," "It will be over soon," "We will soon be home," had long since fled. The war, despite Confederate defeat in the west, and the loss of much territory, was still a reality and it promised to continue to be that for a long time to come. Despite their losses, Confederate armies were intact. They had demonstrated what they could do, and the North could plainly see that much remained to be done.

OVERVIEW FOR THE SIXTH OHIO

For the last six months of 1863, the Sixth Ohio was in no less than ten engagements. They saw action at Gettysburg on July 4th; Hagerstown, Maryland, on July 6th; Boonsboro, Maryland, July 8th-10th; Falling Water, Maryland, July 14th; Sheppardstown, Virginia, July 16th; Rapidan Station, September 13th-14th; on October 12th, Sulphur Springs, Virginia; October 14th, Auburn Mills, Virginia, and Bristoe Station, Virginia and Mine Run, Virginia, on November 27th. The boys had a very busy time of it.

July, 1863, Through December, 1863

Leading up to the battle at Gettysburg, the Sixth crossed the Potomac River at Edward's Ferry on the 27th of June, and for the first time in more than a year they stood on loyal soil. On Sunday, the 28th, they reached Frederick about noon and then proceeded toward Mount Airey, a station on the Baltimore and Ohio Railroad, some 30 miles outside Baltimore.

Learning that Stuart's Cavalry was in the area, the Sixth made their way to Westminster and on to Manchester in pursuit of the famous Cavalryman. The next day, June 30th, found them across the state line at Hanover Junction, Pennsylvania, but they encountered no rebels. Returning by way of Manchester, they came once more to Westminster. The Sixth was on the right wing of Meade's army, guarding the roads so that the confederate Cavalry would have no chance of turning the Union right.

And so the panorama began.

When Lee was informed that the new General of the Army of the Potomac, Meade, had concentrated his army at Frederick, Maryland, on his flank, he hastened to concentrate his three marching columns at the handiest place, which was a town called Gettysburg, Pennsylvania.

On July 1st, the outnumbered Federals were driven through town to formidable positions on Cemetery Ridge. On July 2nd, Lee struck at both flanks, but could not dislodge the Union Blue. On July 3rd, Lee attacked the center of the line in an all-out effort to crush the defenses. The attack was gallant but doomed. Demonstrations by Stuart's cavalry on Meade's right flank were unsuccessful and by nightfall the battle was over.

On July 4th, Lee began his retreat, and the boys of the Sixth were back in action.

On the morning of the fourth, they left Westminster for Emmitsburg, a distance of 23 miles, but the enemy was gone. At sundown, the Sixth joined General Kilpatrick's division and proceeded through the gap in the mountains toward Waynesboro. At midnight they fell upon a Rebel train of a hundred wagons guarded by a thousand men. The division fell upon them in the middle of a rainstorm. The frightened teamsters tried to run off with their wagons, but wheel locked with wheel and the road was soon impassable. The cavalrymen captured the guard and burned the entire train. The wagons contained some arms, but mostly they were loaded with plunder extracted from farmers of Pennsylvania; boots, shoes, hats, caps, clothing of all kinds, cooking utensils, school books and so forth. Soon it was all reduced to ashes.

On Sunday, July 5th, they reached Smithburg on the Hagerstown Pike where they were attacked by Stuart who had been following them. A brisk artillery fight ensued.

On July 6th, the Sixth, together with Kilpatrick's forces engaged Stuart's cavalrymen at Hagerstown. The division was nearly surrounded by superior forces and so fell back to Antietam Creek, the Sixth protecting the retreat. One man was wounded from the Sixth. There they remained the night before proceeding to Boonsboro the next day.

Reports on July 7th that a rebel force 150,000 strong was approaching the town (Boonsboro) proved false, but on the following day, the 8th, the boom of rebel cannon was very real, and it signaled the presence of mounted cavalry, infantry and artillery, which the Sixth engaged. The ground was not favorable for cavalry movements, so the boys dismounted and fought them on foot. They drove the Confederates about two miles, killing and wounding many, and captured three artillery pieces. The regiment was in the fight from 2:00 P.M. until dark and the boys went in with a will.

In a letter home, one of the participants of this skirmish said, "General Kilpatrick has great confidence in our regiment, and whenever there is any wavering in our lines, the Sixth Ohio is called for. The other night he sent several miles to the rear of the column to get a squadron to charge one of the enemy's batteries. His old regiment, the Second New York, and ours usually fight together . . . and where we go, the Secesh 'just climb', as the boys say."

They were now guarding the gaps in the mountains so the Rebels would not escape.

On July 14th, the Sixth advanced through Williamsport, Maryland, amid cheering crowds. Although the main target, Stuart's cavalry corps, was gone, they captured between 1,500 to 2,000 prisoners, the Confederate rear guard.

On July 16th they marched from Boonsboro to Harpers' Ferry, crossing the river at one o'clock P.M. After resting two hours they took the line of march and relieved General Geary who was surrounded at Sheperdstown.

At this time many of the nine-month enlistees of the regiment went home, and they were promised 500 draftees to fill their rolls. Colonel Duffie, formerly of the Sixth, had been promoted to General, taking command of the cavalry under Burnside. It was said that he had requested that the First Rhode Island, the First Massachusetts and the Sixth Ohio be assigned to him. But, as one Sixth cavalryman remarked, "Our regiment won't get away from here now for it has got its name up too high."

At the beginning of August they were stationed at the mouth of Thoroughfare Gap, in the Bull Run Mountains, guarding it from the passing of the Rebels. Some of the greatest losses for the Sixth, during its history, did not come in actual battle, but in doing its daily duty of picket and patrolling.

And so it happened on September 1st, while on picket duty at Orleans, ten miles toward Manassas Gap. From this village on the Rappahannock River, a patrol of 49 men and officers inclusive, under command of Major J. John Cryor, were sent out six or seven miles to Barbers' Crossroads.

The same route had been patrolled for several days but nothing heretofore had occurred of a serious nature and, as usual, the patrol passed along through the usual places before returning without discerning anything out of the way. As they were ready to return to camp, a glimpse was had of the graybacks who, all at once, from a dense pine thicket, opened a tremendous volley, sending lead like hail all along and through the whole column.

It was so sudden and unlooked for, it was a wonder the command were not nearly all killed, or at least thrown into utter confusion and all taken prisoner at once, for they were surrounded by hundreds. The column coolly stood their ground and returned terrible fire upon the concealed foe as well as they could, but as ill-luck would have it, many of the pieces misfired. It was no fault of the boys, however, but, of course, it caused a little confusion. Simultaneously with the first fire of the guerillas, for such they proved to be, a large squadron of Rebels dismounted in the thicket, dashed in ahead of the column and another made a dash in front from another source of concealment to divide their force.

Sergeant William Barrett, in command of the advance (Lieutenant Sheppard having been cut off) gave the command, "Draw Sabres," and instantly the glistening weapons were flying in the air, and the boys were dashing with terrible power through the ranks of three times their number, luckily without loss.

Their main thoughts were to rejoin their comrades, who were with Major Cryer and were being pressed back toward camp. Rallying, they charged like infuriated tigers, back through the confused and frightened Rebels, and then dashed out into the fields and pressed forward.

The roads and field were full of graybacks for three miles and the crack of carbines and pistols and the clash of sabres was constant, mingled with the savage yells of the guerillas.

After fighting their way over three miles, Sergeant Barrett, thinking all were past, made a dash with his weary, jaded command, to regain the road back to camp. But here again, they encountered a fresh lot of the hated guerillas, who ordered the little band to halt and surrender.

"Never!" was the ready answer as the bloody sabres flew into the air. "Charge, boys, charge the devils!" rang out upon the clear air, and again they came down upon the trembling, hesitating traitors and soon they had passed them. But now, not so luckily. Sergeant Shaffer was shot through the body and Sergeant William Barrett, who had so bravely led his noble band, was shot through the shoulder and fell from his horse. The boys could not bear to leave so brave a comrade on the field and sought to save him and bring him off, but that was more than could be done safely for the guerillas were well mounted and gathered so fast that the band could not get away and were obliged to surrender at last.

Major Cryer, though badly wounded, finally reached camp

with a part of his patrol. The Rebels suffered severely, but the Sixth suffered, too. Yet it was surprising to all that such an escape was made with the overwhelming odds of six to one. Only the coolest and most determined bravery could have done what this little band did that day, once they were completely surrounded. At another time, Sergeants Shaffer and Barrett leaped their horses from a ledge ten feet high, striking fair and right side up, twenty feet from its base.

When the Rebels started to leave the action, a major, old, with long curling flowing hair, commanding the Rebel force, ordered Sergeant Barrett to mount and go along, but the Sergeant refused. He threatened to kill him there, but the threat was to no avail. The Sergeant would not go. The old major left him after taking from his pockets, and also from others, what money and valuables they had.

The ambulances were soon on the ground and brought in the dead and wounded. Sergeant Shaffer, who was shot through the body, died at one o'clock that night. He did not think he was going to die, but lay chatting cheerfully with a brother soldier until half past twelve o'clock when, turning on his side, he fell into an easy sleep, and in half an hour his noble spirit had passed beyond all worries and strife. Samuel J. Ford was killed instantly at the first fire. Two of the wounded were taken prisoner; Taylor and L. F. White.

KILLED OR WOUNDED

Major Cryor	wounded in the knee
Pvt. Samuel J. Ford	Co. B killed
Sgt. Frank Shafer	Co. G killed
Sgt. William Barrett	Co. G killed
Emory Lackey	Co. B wounded
L. F. White (prisoner)	Co. D wounded
Pvt. Allen Taylor	Co. B wounded

PRISONERS

Lt. Sheppard, Co. I	Pvt. James Rourke, Co. G
Sgt. Ralph Fowler, Co. G	Pvt. Seldon Sears, Co. G
Cpl. George Williams, Co. G	Pvt. Richard S. Cooley, Co. G
Cpt. Lemuel Granger, Co. G	Pvt. Shannon Harmon, Co. G
Pvt. William Shible, Co. G	Pvt. Dave Bush, Co. B
Pvt. John A. Cameron, Co. G	Pvt. Peter Moore, Co. B

Pvt. Robert Barrett, Co. G

Pvt. Robert McClain, Co. G

Pvt. Frank Kinnoman, Co. G

Pvt. Robert Lowry, Co. D

Pvt. George Hays, Co. D

Pvt. John Burns, Co. B

Bugler Norman Brown, Co. D

Pvt. Patrick Cox, Co. D

Pvt. Wm. R. Davidson, Co. D

Pvt. Charles Tucker, Co. D

After this bad day, a brigade went out on a reconnaisance through Upperville, and out as far as Middleburgh, near Aldie, but nothing was seen of any account.

It was now September 12th and the whole division under General Gregg crossed over the Rappahannock with four days rations.

Though a great loss had occurred to the Ohio Sixth on September 1st, morale was high with the victories over the summer months. Insofar as the boys were concerned as to the complete rightness of their cause, there was no question.

Their politics were pro-Lincoln in the majority of cases, and anti-Vallandigham, who was running for governor of Ohio. Vallandigham, who was pro-southern, had become the symbol of treason and treachery to all Ohio boys throughout the Union armies.

It was the 13th of September. Sunday dawned rainy and cheerless. At three o'clock in the morning came the order, "Saddle up and get ready to march." With cups of steaming coffee hastily gulped down, the boys leaped into the saddle to head for Hazel River, some seven miles distant. The rain subsided and in due time the regiment reached the river and crossed it, but the enemy, despite reports that he was at hand, was nowhere to be seen. But, moving toward Culpepper Court House, it was not long before the heavy boom of artillery announced that the head of the column had contacted the enemy and was already engaged in battle. This was the beginning of the battle of Rapidan Station, Virginia. Confirmation of the heat of the activity came in the form of an order for ambulances to go forward, "on the double quick." The farther the column advanced, the more clearly the evidence of a sharp conflict stood out. A wounded officer lying by the roadside, a surgeon kneeling over him attempting to dress his wounds. Trees marked by bullets. Pushing on into the town, the regiment joined with Generals Buford and Kilpatrick. A mile beyond town, the rebel guns found their mark as shells began crashing through the very midst of the regiment. Captain Northway saw the horse shot out from under Sergeant Jacob Templin of Company L, blood gushing from the steed's mouth as it fell. Scrambling from beneath the dying animal, the sergeant seized another mount which was running loose and rode headlong into the fight. Shells continued to fall in the midst of their ranks, and horses and men were struck and went down.

The ranks became partly broken, but the men rallied and re-formed in the column of a squadron while tree tops and branches severed by the fire from rebel guns fell around them.

An order from the Brigade Commander saw the boys form a line. "Draw Sabre," rang out, followed by the command, "Forward." With sabres gleaming in the sun, the regiment made its way across a wide field which was divided by a deep ditch. Some horses, failing to negotiate the ditch, fell and rolled over upon their riders. The charge went on with the enemy running like sheep. Without much hope of catching them, the Sixth halted and reformed their shattered line. With nightfall, a heavy thunderstorm swept over the countryside, converting little streams into raging torrents waist deep. Having been ordered to dismount and join the skirmishers of the First Pennsylvania, the regiment left their horses in the charge of a portion of the men, while the rest advanced to their new positions. At 11:00 P.M. they rejoined the remainder of the regiment and lay down in the rain to catch a moment of rest before the stirring duties of another day.

The next morning dawned wet and dreary. Those who had rations hastily consumed them; those who had none went without. Setting out shortly after daybreak, the men soon came upon still smouldering rebel camp fires. Halting three miles from the river, the Sixth Ohio, First Massachusetts and First Rhode Island were sent forward to reconnoiter. Part of the Sixth was deployed on both sides of the road as skirmishers. Within a mile of the river they came upon rebel pickets. Moving forward, they found that the rebels had a heavy line of skirmishers supported by columns of cavalry, infantry and artillery. Two guns were visible on one side of the river. The opposite side was bristling with field pieces. A brief respite followed an hour of skirmishing whereupon the order to advance came once more.

Supported by the First Massachusetts, a squadron of the Sixth advanced, but had no sooner started when the enemy batteries opened fire. Shells screamed and burst; solid shot whistled and crashed in front and in the woods to the rear. The First Massachusetts was obliged to retire because no column could live in such a fire. The Sixth continued its advance to within 400 yards of the enemy with artillery fire flying over their heads and striking far to their rear. Suddenly, the rebels charged down upon them. The men rallied to the right and left, but because they were a mere handful compared to the enemy's charging column, they were ordered back over a wide ditch, there to await the onslaught.

Yelling and swinging sabres, the enemy charged. The boys stood quietly with carbine and revolvers, waiting the order to fire. When within 100 yards, they gave them a volley and some of the rebels doubled up and rode to the rear. For a few moments the crack of carbines and revolvers was incessant and the rebels retired without driving the little band an inch. In action a short while later with the aid of the First Massachusetts, the rebels were driven from the field in disorder. The boys of the Sixth held their position until nightfall when they were relieved by the First Maryland. A charge by the rebels, while the relief was underway, did not gain any advantage. In this action, Lieutenant Oliver C. Russell was shot through the arm. He and Corporal Albert Champion were both hospitalized with wounds. It was after this action that four more men were hospitalized from the Sixth, but probably due to sickness; Arthur Holdridge, Joseph Jackson, Thomas Covert and Salmon Rose.

The action at Rapidan Station won commendation from General Gregg and Colonel Sargent, the former saying that he never saw men fight better. It was said the regiment stood as the best fighting regiment in the division.

The opposite was said of the Fourth New York Cavalry which was prohibited from carrying their colors until some single service earned them the right to do so. This punishment was on account of their so-called cowardly conduct in allowing one of their squadrons to be captured without an attempt to prevent it.

Beginning October 4th, for nearly a week, the men of the Sixth were constantly on the move. Marches of 30 miles a day were common. Then on October 12th, at Sulpher Springs, Virginia, the rebels attacked with infantry, cavalry and artillery. They succeeded in driving the Sixth, as there were but three or four regiments to oppose them. The next day they moved about 15 miles. But what lay ahead was even more devastating at crossroads called Auburn Mills and Bristoe Station, Virginia.

On the morning of October 14th, at daylight, came a forward attack by the rebels which commenced with the driving in of the Sixth's pickets. In the division, the Sixth was the only one saddled, so it was ordered out as skirmishers. But soon the action became general and there was fire from left and right, and from the front. Cannonading was heavy and severe, and the musketry was rapid and incessant. It was evident that the rebels were trying to cut them off by turning their right flank. But shortly the firing on the right suddenly ceased, and it was learned that the Second Corps had captured two rebel regiments and a battery. The cessation was, however, short lived. Suddenly two lines of infantry came out of the wooded area. The boys of the Sixth, on horseback, were only targets and were suffering severely from their fire. Captain Bowe was mortally wounded, Lieutenant Bingham in the wrist, while Captain Rickart suffered lesser wounds. Corporal Stroup of Company I was killed in the heated action which finally saw the Sixth cavalrymen dismount, finally driving the rebels off. The rebels suffered severely in this day's encounter, losing two batteries of artillery and four regiments, besides killed and wounded.

It was during the movements of the Sixth in October that they voted for the November elections, a privilege which was not denied any boys in uniform. In all state elections, Abraham Lincoln was given a vote of confidence, while in Ohio, Clement C. Vallandigham, a fiery opponent of Lincoln, was defeated soundly. In the Sixth Ohio, nary a vote was cast for this so-called scoundrel at this time.

From the middle of September to the middle of October, it had been a month of incessant riding and fighting. No permanent camp was to be had. Sometimes they had nothing to eat, and sleeping in the saddle was not uncommon. A month of lying down in the rain, without shelter, sometimes with a blanket and sometimes not. They were short of forage for the horses, and many times it was three to four days before the horses were fed. But they all withstood the discomforts that beset them.

For the next month, the Sixth did their usual patrol duty and got a well-earned rest.

On the day before Thanksgiving, 1863, Meade decided to move around Lee's right flank and strike across a small stream called Mine Run. The Sixth did some skirmishing in this action, but it all went for naught. Meade saw that the rebel fortifications were too much and ordered a retreat, and so ended the year of 1863.

The year-end saw the firing of cannon in Washington, D.C., signalling the placement of the headpiece atop the Statue of Freedom above the Capitol Dome. The headpiece, facing north towards freedom, with its back toward slavery.

The war was now 32 months old. After the hard summer and fall campaigns, the diseased and wounded of the army filled the hospitals of the North and South alike. The military hospitals in Washington were numerous, numbering six in all. A large number of tents could be seen pitched nearby each hospital where the overflow sick and wounded were cared for. Many of the Sixth Ohio were in these hospitals. The previous year's campaign had worn the regiment down to the point that they not only needed refitting with weapons and horses, but with new men. Most of them would be draftees from this point on.

Official figures for 1863 show that ten men were killed in action in the ten companies of Sixth OVC, the regiment losing 163 men in all during the war's third year. Sixty-three men died of wounds and disease; 58 were discharged upon expiration of their terms of service; five officers resigned, one officer was transferred, and the remaining lost were captured.

It was now the second Thanksgiving and Christmas that most of these boys had spent away from their loved ones. While their relatives in such towns as Orwell, Ashtabula and Chardon read the casualty lists with trepidation, the boys that were so close to death most every day prayed that the same death would not appear at home to their own loved ones they had left behind. But it was not to be. Loved ones did die in their absence, which made the campaigning even more difficult since they could not be home with the bereaved wives, parents, brothers and sister. Although there were many deaths among the relatives of the boys of the Sixth during their tenure with the regiment, none was more touching than the death of Edith August Covert. Thomas Covert, Private, Company A, Sixth Ohio Volunteer, received word in early November of his loss. The Ashtabula Sentinel of November 11th, a weekly newspaper, carried the death notice:

"DIED IN ORWELL, OCTOBER 30: of Scarlet Fever, Edith August, daughter of Thomas and Phoebe Ann Covert, age six years.

"On her downy coffin pillow,
Lay the darling little head,
Lay the precious sleeper softly
In her strange and lonely bed.
Never more shall pains keen arrows
Pierce that sweet and tender form.
She is safe from every evil,
Safe from every earthly storm;
Jesus loves these little children,
He has borne her o'er the flood,
And has laid our treasure safely
In the bosom of her God."

And so it went. The four horsemen of the Apocalypse: Death, Pestilence, Disease and War rode on.

CHAPTER V

January, 1864, Through June, 1864

OVERVIEW OF THE WAR

By January, 1864, hopes both in the North and in the South for an early termination of the war had long since faded. Gettysburg and other actions in the north had given the Union a sense of guarded optimism; while in the South, despite the fact that territorial losses were notable, the Confederate Army had demonstrated its strength and had won victories that were impressive.

The action that transpired on the battlefields during January was confined to lesser battles, although for those who engaged in them, fatalities and wounds were as real as if they had occurred in major conflicts.

There were confrontations at Jonesville, Virginia (January 3rd), and Medley, West Virginia (January 29 - February 1st), but these were, in the total picture, of somewhat minor significance.

There was a quickened tempo in February spurred by the daring cavalry jaunt to within five miles of the Confederate capital by Brigadier General Judson Kilpatrick and Colonel Ulric Dahlgren. It cost the young colonel his life.

Albemarle County, Virginia, saw a dashing young blonde Brigadier General by the name of George Custer charging through the countryside, and out of the labyrinthine tunnels of the despised Libby Prison at Richmond, more than 100 Union prisoners made good their escape. But by mid-month a prison that would become symbolic of suffering and agony had started accepting prisoners; Andersonville in Georgia.

March saw a new figure at the head of all the Union armies. He was Ulysses S. Grant who, on March 9th, had been named Lieutenant General, and on the following day assumed his new command. Whatever else could be said of him, Grant was recognized as a fighting leader. At his side was General George Meade in command of the Army of the Potomac.

The following month saw General Philip Sheridan assuming command of the Cavalry of the Army of the Potomac, hopefully to lead the Union Cavalry to levels of accomplishment heretofore surpassed by the horsemen of the Confederacy.

By May, the die had been cast that, once more, Richmond was to be the prize sought by the Army of the Potomac, hopefully this time, a prize to be sought and won. Plans called for attacks by Sigel in the Shenandoah Valley, Banks at Mobile, Johnston in Georgia and Butler to attack Richmond from south of the James River. Grant and Meade, leading the Army of the Potomac, were to strike straight ahead. Those were the plans, but they did not materialize.

Banks never got started, Sigel's retreat was not long in coming, and the forces under Butler soon ground to a halt. Yet, there was action enough. As Grant started on May 3rd across the Rapidan River and into the wilderness west of Chancellorsville, Lee's Army of Northern Virginia dashed eastward to head him off. The Confederates stood up to strong Union pressures on May 5th, but on the 6th the Federal assault had become intense, until midmorning when Longstreet now being in position, the Union forces eased off.

Upon the discovery by General John Brown Gordon of a hole in the Federal line, only the cover of darkness prevented him from seriously jeopardizing the Union forces. May 5 - 7 saw the Battle of the Wilderness in which Union losses were 2,246 dead and 12,037 wounded, with Confederate dead and wounded adding up to about 7,750. In all, more than 162,000 men were engaged in the conflict.

Thirteen days of bloody struggle lay just ahead at the Bloody Angle, from whence Grant issued his famous assertion that he intended to fight it out along his present line, if it should take all summer. Casualties were high, higher for the North than for the

South, but perhaps much costlier to the Confederacy because of the greater difficulty of replacement in the South.

Under newly appointed cavalry commander General Phil Sheridan, who had inspected and reviewed the Sixth on April 18th, some 10,000 men headed toward Richmond on May 8th, but Sheridan was frustrated in his efforts to reach the Capital of the Confederacy, and he rejoined General Grant some sixteen days later. Generals Butler and Sigel also failed in the Shenandoah Valley.

May ushered in a summer of great activity which would see a direct attack on Cold Harbor, June 1st through the 3rd, with more than 107,000 Federals (their losses in killed and wounded totalled some 12,000) moving ever closer to Richmond, but the Capital remained in Confederate hands.

A grinding summer lay ahead, and June marked only the beginning. There were hot actions at Cold Harbor with a three-day struggle, engaging 108,000 men with losses by death and wounded amounting to some 12,000 among the Union forces. Grant was suddenly looked upon by some as "The Butcher" after the 3rd, the worst of the three days of action. Union boys charging into the Confederate earthworks left them confused and decimated.

But better days lay ahead when Grant stealthily shifted across the James River at Petersburg. Richmond could have fallen had Grant pressed an attack instead of getting his army across the river, but the Confederate capital still stood. The nation was in turmoil. The long casualty lists from Virginia nourished talk of a negotiated peace, and there were nasty attacks on the President who was looked upon as too lenient. On the 28th of June, a law which had for 14 years stood on the books and precipitated much of the agony of the pre-war days was repealed. It was known as the Fugitive Slave Law.

Late June saw the beginning of the siege at Petersburg.

OVERVIEW OF THE SIXTH CAVALRY

In January, 1864, some 200 of the men of the Sixth Ohio Volunteer Cavalry re-enlisted as veterans so that by the time the results of the recruiting by officers for their various companies were in, later in the spring, the regiment was nearly up to its maximum number. When the regiment broke camp and left winter quarters on May 3rd, 1864, it was with high hopes, if not confidence, that the war would be over within 60 days.

With Grant, on his sidle to Richmond, and with Sheridan's Cavalry Corps, the Sixth took part in nine engagements in the first six months of 1864.

They fought at Todd's Tavern, Virginia, on May 5 - 7, Mitchell's Shop, or Jerrald's Mills, on May 9th, Yellow Tavern, May 11th and Meadow Bridge, May 12th.

Then it was on to Hawes Shop, or Aenon Church, May 28th, and then the road led to Cold Harbor, May 31st and June 1st. Skirmishes with the rebel cavalry also took place at Bottom Bridge, June 6th, Trevilian's Station June 11-12 and St. Mary's Church or Ladd's Farm, June 24th.

All in all, it was a busy six months, and the cost came high for the regiment.

January, 1864, Through June, 1864

As the year opened, the regiment made a reconnaisance mission across the Blue Ridge Mountain which resulted in a skirmish with the Confederates before the Union boys returned to camp on January 4th. It was a time that many of the enlistments in the Army were running out, and yet the government needed to keep these veterans for the campaigning ahead.

While in winter quarters, the Sixth had 241 re-enlistments, almost three-fourths of the regiment. The reactions of family and friends back home to the re-enlistment by the boys in the Sixth Ohio was always a matter of concern to the cavalrymen, but their dedication to the task at hand saw re-enlistment as yet another way of saying, "Better a patriot soldier's grave, than. . . . "

Although they were dedicated, there were other assets to signing up for another three years. They received $402.00 from the

State and Federal government, and the promise of a furlough, many of the boys being sent home during the winter.

In many cases the boys felt they could not go through another campaign without going home, and they might be drafted if they were mustered out.

So, many of the Sixth were discharged and mustered back in the same day. Along with the veterans staying with the Sixth, draftees were now joining the regiment in large numbers.

Following acceptance and the formation of groups of men into Companies, the new draftees and veterans were required to take the oath of allegiance and to read the articles of war. The latter act was required to be repeated twice each year thereafter, as prescribed by the tenth article of war.

By now, the third year of the war, it became very unpopular to be at home for men between the ages of 18 and 50, so much so that a popular song of the day was, "I Am Bound to be a Soldier's Wife or Die an Old Maid."

Chevrons of red and blue braid, worn on the left sleeve, designated the veteran volunteers, a designation which the boys wore with genuine pride. Altogether there were some 200,000 in the Armies of the North who belonged to this important group. Their ultimate contribution to the triumph of northern arms cannot be overestimated.

The winter of 1864 was extremely cold with very little action except for patrolling and picket duty. But there were still casualties for the Sixth.

While on picket duty on the Warrenton Road in the first part of February, Private George Bigelow was shot and killed. Lieutenant Oliver Russell, of Company A, was also shot but did recover from his wounds.

On February 10th, 1864, the Western Reserve Chronicle of Warren, Ohio, reported the death, on December 30th, 1863, of Elijah Champlin of the Sixth Ohio Volunteer Cavalry, at the Confederate Prison at Richmond.

The official roster of the Sixth Cavalry contains the names of ten boys who died at Andersonville; nine at Salisbury Prison in North Carolina; one at Libbey Prison. Numerous other deaths were recorded at other unidentified Confederate prisons.

And now started Grant's move south.

On Friday, April 29th, the regiment was ordered to be ready to march at 9:00 A.M. that day with four days' rations and two days' forage. By Tuesday, the Sixth was the regiment in advance, and all of the boys must have wondered how many saddles would be emptied in this new campaign.

The following day, the Sixth was fired upon by rebel pickets who promptly fell back, with boys of the regiment pursuing them. Three of the Confederates were captured. In passing over the Chancellorsville battlefield, the Sixth was engaged in skirmishes throughout the day.

On May 5th, advancing as far as Todd's Tavern, with the Third Division in advance, a sharp engagement ensued during which the rebels drove back the Third, and part of the Sixth relieved them, eventually winning out, but with heavy losses.

By Friday, May 6th, the cavalrymen were on half rations and their horses on half forage. Saddled up long before daylight, the rising sun was greeted by a continuous roar of musketry that lasted for hours, hundreds of men being wounded and killed. The enemy was driven ahead of the Sixth throughout the day. Stubborn enemy resistance was encountered the following day when the battle was renewed and continued until nightfall. Six of the regiment were wounded, none killed. On Sunday morning the regiment was called in from picket duty before daylight and was overtaken by infantry at Todd Tavern. There was some cavalry fighting, but the regiment was not engaged except in supporting a battery.

Drawing three days' rations the next morning, the Sixth acted as rear guard for the day as the regiment started for the rear of Lee's army, their objective point being behind Richmond.

At Mitchell's Shop, or Jerrald's Mills, rebel cavalry under General Stuart, including Lomax, Wickham, and later Gordon's brigades, charged the rear of the Sixth time and again with great fury, compelling the Union men to face about and return their fire. The assault was renewed by the Confederates as often as they were repulsed. Darkness finally ended the struggle. Four men were either killed, wounded or captured. The death was that of Captain James Abell. Charles Stedman and Sergeant F. M. Baker were wounded. Enemy losses were said to have been very heavy.

Before crossing the South Anna River on Tuesday, May 10th, the Sixth was shelled at a cost of two of its horses. But after burning the Beaver Dam railroad station, three hundred Union troops, most of them infantry who had been captured in Wilderness fighting, were rescued. After burning one of General Lee's supply trains, the regiment bivouacked sixteen miles from Richmond.

Next day, May 11th, near Yellow Tavern, while pressing toward Richmond, the Sixth was pressed on the flanks and at the rear by a desultory fire which it returned in like manner, capturing, that afternoon, one general and some two hundred men. A heavy rain about five o'clock in the afternoon made the all night march a most uncomfortable one, delaying the fulfillment of the hope that the fortifications of Richmond might be invested before daylight. The boys did not know it as yet, but the famous James Elwell Brown Stuart had been wounded that day and would die the next day in Richmond. This was a great blow to the Confederacy. He would be sorely missed in the coming campaigns.

At daylight the Sixth was four miles out of Richmond, close enough to hear the town clock proclaiming the hour of seven, surrounded by enemy who had been warned of their approach, and who had planted nine torpedoes in the road over which the advancing Union men must march.

The torpedoes were connected by a cord, the far end of which was held by a "Johnnie Reb" stationed at the far side of an adjoining field. His orders were to pull the string and explode the torpedoes when he saw the Division Commander, General Gregg, and his staff passing over them. The advance guard discovered the trap and an officer was stationed there to direct the advancing column around it. General Gregg's arrival resulted in the torpedoes being dug up by rebel prisoners.

The rebels made a stand on May 12th at Meadow Bridge but were soon overcome by the Union boys who passed on through Mechanicsville and camped for the night near Gaines' Mills.

Out of rations, out of forage, the regiment was completely exhausted from the continuous marching and fighting since the campaign opened.

They passed through a portion of the Wilderness and over the blood stained ground of Spotsylvania Court House. It was a dreary place. The long lines of the abandoned earthworks, the houses, fences and trees thickly scarred with shot and shell, the piles of fresh earth denoting graves, while here and there a decaying body of some soldier yet unburied gave a melancholy twist to the scene.

But despite their exhaustion and the fatigue of their horses, the men slept on their sidearms on the night of Friday the 13th, and the horses remained saddled. Arriving at Bottom Bridge, a wooden structure on the Chickahominy River, on Saturday, they discovered that the Confederates had already been there, for the planking of the bridge was floating on the river where they had thrown it. Not far from the bridge a field gun had been implanted which gave the rebels control of the already impassable span. The bridge floor was soon replaced with fence rails, brush wood and earth which, when packed down, made the bridge passable. The field gun, meanwhile, had been rendered ineffective and the Sixth Ohio and the First New Jersey Cavalry made their way over the river.

Next day, making their way toward the James River, the boys were fired upon by a Union gunboat, whose crew assumed them to be Confederates. The Signal Corps soon corrected the misunderstanding, and a Sergeant Hayes, having somehow realized some corn meal, the boys had their first nourishment other than parched corn in several days. Cooked with salt and water, it tasted very good.

From Haxall's Landing on the 16th, the boys heard heavy cannonading upriver which they assumed to be Butler's army attacking Fort Darling. Drawing two days' rations, the boys started out at ten o'clock in the morning, only to be ordered back, and they remained inactive until setting out on an all night march to rejoin Grant's army.

During the many halts made throughout the night, the men fell asleep in the saddle or briefly sprawled on the ground. Many lost their hats while sleeping in the saddle. Crossing the Chickahominy at Jordan's Ford, the regiment went into camp three miles west of New Kent Courthouse.

As they waited, saddled, for orders the next morning, Captain Harper of the brigade staff rode up and ordered the horses unsaddled and the men to go into camp.

A foraging expedition by mess officers Phillips and Hayes

yielded only a straw hat and some flowers. The next day was better, when a foraging party went to Old Church Tavern, returning at nine at night with two bags of shelled corn and two chickens.

On the 21st, Captain Norman A. Barrett, with 100 men of the regiment, set out to destroy a railroad bridge. They rejoined the regiment when that mission had been accomplished and all started off toward Fredericksburg.

The march seemed endless. On through Lynn, King Phillip's Courthouse, Aylettesville, Bowling Green and on to Chesterfield Station, where finally they rejoined the Army of the Potomac. Wagons, rations, forage and mail awaited the unit.

Action awaited the regiment on Saturday morning, May 28th, after further marching that was very trying for the men and horses. Cannonading started at ten in the morning, and the regiment was relieved of picket duty and ordered hurriedly to the front, where they found the brigade already engaged near Aenon Church. Quickly dismounting, the boys engaged in a hot fight on foot, driving the rebels back and holding the ground until dark, but the cost of the gain was high. Captain Northway, Simon Grubb (Company B), Billy Borta (Company G), Sergeant Robertson, Dan Brown, Billie Harris, Tanner and an unidentified cavalryman, all of Company I, lay dead on the field.

Ordered to support the First Division, which was engaged with the enemy, the boys lay waiting all day and night in a wheat field. One of the men built a fire at night over an unexploded shell which burst and wounded Captain Loveland.

On Wednesday, June 1st, the Sixth reached Cold Harbor, the boys camping on the identical spot on which they had camped when on the Richmond raid. The horses had just been fed and the boys were making coffee when the enemy opened up with gunfire from an infantry division, an assault which was speedily repulsed. There was sporadic action over the next several days until on Sunday, June 5th, when the boys were relieved by the Third Division, whereupon the Sixth started toward New Castle. Arriving at about 6 P.M. after crossing the Pamunkey River on pontoons, they camped about a mile from the town. Some sixty new mounted recruits joined the unit.

On Monday, June 6th, there was a skirmish at Bottom Bridge, but it was indecisive. On the same day the regiment was ordered to draw 12 days' rations, and to make the three days' rations already on hand do for five days. This always meant there were going to be some long marches.

On June 11th they met the enemy in force at Trevelian Station on the Gordonsville and Richmond Railroad. They had a very hard fight, but succeeded in driving the rebels back. Custer's brigade lost heavily, especially the Seventh Michigan Cavalry. The Sixth had two wounded, but captured four hundred prisoners, mostly of Jeb Stuart's Cavalry.

The following day, much of the time was spent in tearing up enemy railroad tracks, the First Division bearing the brunt of the fighting. The Confederates shelled the Union boys furiously throughout the night before the latter withdrew to rejoin the army, their purpose in destroying the railroad having been accomplished.

It was hot, and the heat had a telling effect upon the men and their horses. Some days it was an almost continuous march from sun-up until breaking for camp at night. On Wednesday, the 15th, it was on across the Potomac to Spottsylvania Court House where evidence was seen on every hand of the fierce battle that had been joined there. The houses were full of shell holes, and the town was heavily fortified. There were foraging expeditions which some days yielded adequately and other days less than that.

The rate of progress on the march was slowed because of the number of prisoners that were on foot. On the afternoon of the 17th, the Eighth Pennsylvania Regiment dismounted and the prisoners were allowed to ride their horses. Some of the boys did not relish the idea. Colonel Stedman of the Sixth Ohio walked and let a prisoner ride his horse. Such were the not infrequent evidences of compassion that were demonstrated between men who were enemies, but yet shared the common bond of being men!

The regiment was detailed, together with the Eighth Pennsylvania, to escort wagon trains and the wounded, the prisoners and a lot of contraband to West Point, Virginia, on Sunday, June 19th. Once West Point had been reached and the prisoners and wounded put aboard boats, the regiment went into camp, remaining there until the 21st, ferrying wagons and ambulances across the river and awaiting their turn to cross, which did not come until 11:00 P.M.

Friday, the 21st, found them in contact with the enemy at St. Mary's Church, where they skirmished all day, the boys of the Sixth fighting mounted. Adjutant Baldwin and four men were killed. Twenty-two were wounded and eleven missing. The regiment lost upwards of 100 horses killed and wounded.

The following day, Saturday, June 25th, saw the Union boys driven back, the first time during the summer's campaign, and then only because they were greatly outnumbered. Against their two brigades of cavalry, the rebels had two cavalry brigades and 1500 dismounted men. The Sixth became the rear guard. Probably no regiment in the army so excelled in this duty. From what they had been through, the boys were completely fagged out, and the horses jaded from the prolonged period of marching and fighting.

Falling back, they reached the James River at a point below Harrison's Landing, crossing the river on the 27th of June. On the 28th the boys camped at Fort Powhatten, and on the 29th halted six miles from Petersburgh. The next day they moved to Warwick Swamp, formed a line and drove in the rebel pickets and went into camp for the night. Heavy cannonading could be heard from Petersburgh.

The Sixth Ohio was completely used up. Again, it was time for refitting.

CHAPTER VI

July, 1864, Through December, 1864

OVERVIEW OF THE WAR

Petersburg was under siege, and the efforts were once again reminiscent of Vicksburg. Negro troops suffered most heavily in an action, known as the Battle of the Crater, that found 4,000 Union boys killed or wounded following a charge into Confederate lines from which they could not extricate themselves. That was at the end of July, but earlier there had been actions in the Shenandoah Valley, and of course, the siege of Atlanta was underway. Hood would turn his back on the city on September 2nd and Sherman would move in. The armies glowered at each other at Petersburg, with Grant taking the Weldon Railroad and having a skirmish at Reams Station. The siege would drag on for nine months. In October there were fights at Darbytown, Hatcher's Run (Burgess' Mills), Fisher's Hill and Strasburg.

The last big battle of the Shenandoah Valley at Cedar Creek (or Middletown) saw the Confederates driven from the field on October 19th. Some 30,000 Union forces were engaged with 18,000 Confederates. Losses in killed, wounded and missing ran to 5,500 among Union forces; 2,900 for the Confederates.

Up north in Vermont an experience brought the war home to New Englanders as General Morgan's foray into Ohio had done the previous year. The little town of St. Albans was suddenly "invaded" by a small group of Confederate raiders who swept in and out of Canada, robbed the bank and shot up the place, retiring at once after the foray. Always in quotation marks, the incident has been referred to as the northernmost "battle" of the Civil War. That was on October 19th.

In November, Abraham Lincoln was re-elected President, defeating General McClellan by about half a million votes. The electoral vote gave Lincoln a much more meaningful victory: 212 to 21, clearly a mandate to prosecute the war to a victorious conclusion. Eight days after the election, on November 16th, General William Tecumseh Sherman started his historic "March to the Sea," an expedition in pillage and destruction which brought the war home to the South in a new dimension and which would, by many of their descendants, not be forgotten.

There were other evidences in the North of the discontent and impatience that was being felt there. Eleven hotels were set afire, along with Barnum's great American Museum in New York City, on November 25th, although most of the fires were somewhat less than devastating. Rumors of conspiracy were widespread, and there was talk of capturing Chicago, freeing Southern prisoners and, most menacing of all, withdrawing some northwestern states from the Union. These were trying days, and the Copperheads; so-called by the Unionists who said that these Peace Democrats who opposed Abraham Lincoln reminded them of the poisonous snakes with the copper colored heads; were to a great extent making them so.

December found General Philip Sheridan having pretty much his own way in the Shenandoah Valley. Sherman was ravaging his way to Savannah, Fort McAllister falling at mid-month. A telegram from General Sherman to the President tendered him the city of Savannah, together with 150 heavy guns and 25,000 bales of cotton, as a Christmas present. The year came to a costly end with General Thomas' attack on Nashville with some 50,000 troops. On the 15th and 16th of December he won one of the most smashing victories of the entire war. Of the Union's 49,773 soldiers engaged, 387 were killed, 2,562 wounded and 112 missing. Some 23,000 Confederate troops were engaged, of whom nearly 4,500 were killed, wounded or missing. There are wide discrepancies in figures relative to those missing or taken prisoner in this engagement.

The year ended with clear-cut victories for the North in Georgia and in the West, but the North still faced Lee at Petersburgh.

49

OVERVIEW OF ACTIONS OF THE SIXTH CAVALRY

The summer of 1864 was one of significant activity to the Sixth Ohio Volunteer Cavalry. Into the minds of those of its men who survived the actions that ensued between July and the end of December would be burned forever the events that transpired at Malvern Hill, Darbytown, Deep Bottom and Ream's Station in Virginia during the heat of July and August. And fall would see still more action at Preble's Farm (also known as Davis' Farm), Boydtown, Stony Creek and Hatcher's Run. It was a time to be remembered.

July, 1864, Through December, 1864

In retrospect, Civil War historians are in generally widespread agreement as to the relative ineffectiveness of Union cavalry during the first two years of the war. It appears that it was not until shortly before the battle at Gettysburgh did the mounted arm of the Union forces find itself.

By this time, the summer of 1864, the Confederate cavalry compared unfavorably with that which they had in the beginning of the war. Then the riders were the wealthy and educated young men of the South who took into their service their best horses. The previous experience of these men in the saddle and with firearms rendered them formidable foes.

But, by now their ranks were thinned by the dead and wounded. There were few good horses left, and very little hope of obtaining them. While these lines may in part explain the declining effectiveness of the Southern cavalry, it is interesting to note the explanations given for the poor showing of Union cavalrymen at the outset of the war. It is generally understood that General Winfield Scott and others did not, in 1861, see a very important role for cavalrymen in the wooded terrain in which it was believed much of the war would be fought. It was Scott's opinion

50

that the regular cavalry would be sufficient and that there was no need for volunteers. Much of the work assigned to the five cavalry regiments available in January, 1861, and the six that were added in April, once the war had broken out, was that of headquarters' guards and orderlies. The first cavalrymen were no match for their southern adversaries.

The regular army held that three years was the time required to make a cavalryman of a raw recruit, but as late as the Peninsular Campaign of 1862 more than half of the Federal cavalrymen had been in service only about six months. However, a new day lay ahead of the Union cavalry in 1864. Once Sheridan had taken command of the cavalry in 1864, it was extensively used and it invariably won when sent into battle.

The heat in Virginia was intense that summer of 1864, and the boys of the Sixth Ohio suffered from it.

They were camped on the north bank of the James River in early July, but its brief respite was suddenly broken by orders to break camp and move. Starting a little before dark and traveling all night, the regiment, by noon of the following day, was on the left flank of the Confederates, east of Petersburg.

On the 26th of July they left camp near Lighthouse Point. Marching all night, the Sixth crossed the Appomattox River and rested on the banks of the James till noon, at which time the Second Corps had crossed over. They followed the Sixth, moving to their right. They camped in line of battle until night, about one mile from the river. On the morning of the 27th they started on reconnaisance by Malvern Hill near the Chickahominy. The boys were passing the pickets of the Reserve Brigade to the left of Malvern Hill when firing commenced and grew rapid between the pickets and a force of Johnnys.

They engaged them at once, the Sixth Ohio and the First Pennsylvania being the only ones to dismount and fight on foot. The Rebs advanced their lines and they were found to be infantry in heavy force. The fight raged fiercely; the discharge of muskets and carbines became more rapid and subsided into a continuous roll.

Soon the Rebs came charging forward on the Pennsylvania boys with fixed bayonets. This was too much for them. They fell back, thus exposing the flank of the Sixth, so they, too, fell back in a most hasty manner as the Rebs on their left were beyond them.

They brought out their wounded and fell back rapidly, but in good order.

About this time the First Division flanked the rebels on their right, driving them back in confusion and capturing between two and three hundred prisoners, also three stands of colors. The Division lost one piece of artillery, the horses being shot away.

The regiment was now under the command of Lieutenant Colonel Barrett, Colonel Stedman being in ill health.

They fell back on the 30th in the direction of the old camp, hoping for rest as they had had none for four days and nights.

Turning to the right, they went to the rear of the army near Petersburg, and thence 15 miles out to the left on a reconnaisance which they quietly made until near Warwick Swamp (Darbytown), where they found two regiments of Confederate cavalry picketing.

Part of the Sixth was in the advance, so they did the fighting. The Rebs had an excellent position, but a brigade of the Sixth flanked in front of them until the Rebs were glad to make a hasty retreat. Their losses were not severe at this place as the men were under cover of the woods.

That night the Sixth fell back a few miles and just before daylight went into camp.

The Sixth, in the two-day engagement, lost Martin Sager, Company A, killed. Lieutenant Colonel Barrett, Lieutenant Wood, Company D; Lieutenant Cryer, Company M; Sergeant Bishop, Company B; Corporal Reed, Company C; Allen Barr, Company D; Wilson Kinkaid, Company D; Robert Force, Company D; Orderly Sergeant Simmons, Company F; Thomas Leeny, Company I; Sergeant Wilcox, Company M; William Dimmick, Company B, wounded. Missing was Sergeant Horace Cole, Company K, and Amos Ramilla, Company D.

Somewhat mauled, the regiment was permitted to encamp behind the works at Petersburgh for several weeks, during which time its activity was confined to light picket duty.

The wounded of the regiment were sent to City Point where, at one time, they could accommodate 6,000 sick and wounded. From this point the disabled were shipped to Washington, Baltimore, New York and other places north. Some ended up being discharged, some came back to the regiment after convalescence, while others were assigned to the "Invalid Corps," doing light garrison duty in the forts and guarding the railroads.

In the month of August, 1864, as Grant continued to lengthen his lines to the left, the Sixth was in a skirmish at Deep Bottom on August 15th and 16th, with the rebels attempting to protect Lee's left flank and keep the remaining railroads open.

They were at Reams Station on August 25th. They had started out on August 21st when Hancock recrossed the James and proceeded south with two divisions and Gregg's troopers, the Sixth Ohio included, for a follow-up strike at the vital supply line near Reams Station about five miles below Globe Tavern and ten above Stony Creek. They reached their destination on August 23rd, and by the close of the following day, had torn up three miles of track beyond it. By the 25th, A. P. Hill with his Confederates fell upon the blue troopers so fast that the infantry had little time to get set. It became a rout, and the boys in blue retreated back to their own lines.

An incident of little note in the history of the Sixth Ohio happened on September 16th. Hampton's cavalry, some 5,000 strong, came around Grant's flank and coolly drove off 2,000 head of beef cattle that had been herded in the rear of the army. The Sixth, with other units, pursued the Confederate cavalry for the purpose of heading them off. They met them about ten miles out and fought them from two in the afternoon until ten at night, but they found them too strongly posted and the Union troops fell back, hoping to draw them into a position of their choosing. They couldn't see it and the Rebs would not come out. So, waiting until ten the next morning, the boys returned to camp.

It was later learned that General Kautz's cavalry, who followed on the rear of the raiders, recaptured all the cattle so that the rebels were but little benefited by their foray.

The loss in the Sixth in this skirmish was one killed, Private Clark Ellis of Company C, and three slightly wounded. It was a slight loss at most.

October 1st found the regiment preparing for a general engagement. This action at Preble's Farm (Davis Farm), started at 3:00 P.M. with a grand assault in which the enemy was partly successful. Fifty-six of the Sixth OVC were killed, wounded or missing following the first assault, but the Sixth rallied and hand-somely repulsed the enemy's further assaults. The Sixth left the field as victors.

Following this action, the regiment returned to Prince George and remained until the 11th. From there they went into camp.

On the evening of October 26th, 1864, the regiment was ordered to be ready to march with light saddles at 11 o'clock that night. It was a clear, starlit night, but rather chilly. Three days' rations and one hundred rounds of ammunition had been issued the men, which meant that there was business ahead.

The Sixth was at the time near Hancock Station on the Milton Railroad, connecting the army with City Point, and was assigned the duty of a picket line guarding the army's rear and flank. Gregg's division of cavalry was, meanwhile, holding the line from the James River to the extreme left of the line.

The Third Brigade was a newly formed outfit that consisted of the First Maine, the 21st Pennsylvania and the Sixth Ohio Regiment under the command of Colonel Smith of the First Maine. The Sixth led the advance of both the cavalry and infantry.

They drove in the enemy pickets with the advance of the cavalry column, before daylight, routing their reserve and capturing their position, a strong line of works at the bridge across Hatcher's Creek. After a sharp skirmish, dismounted and pressing on alone before breakfast, they captured the telegraph line from Petersburgh to Stoney Creek Station. The boys captured eleven wagons, part of them loaded with tobacco, fifty mules, a signal station of the enemy with six glasses (telescopes), fourteen flags and lanterns, along with all the camp equipment of the party of sixteen men, four of whom were captured, the others escaping on their horses.

Another skirmish followed in which both sides used their artillery and the enemy was driven from its position to another fortified position.

Then the cavalry connected with infantry which had moved up by a shorter route, and things began to have the appearance of a battle on a grand scale. But no collision took place until evening when the enemy charged with great vigor. A portion of the Second Corps captured two guns and a number of prisoners, but afterward they were bloodily repulsed with a loss of several hundred captured. At the same time, a severe attack was made on the Union cavalry on the rear flank with the hope of breaking through and capturing their ammunition train, but in this they were foiled, but not without a severe engagement by the Sixth in which they fought dismounted, as usual. They lost Captain E. S. Austin, killed, shot through the head while mounted. With sabre drawn he was gallantly urging his men to hold their ground with pistols, their carbine ammunition having become exhausted.

The Sixth was soon reinforced and the enemy was driven back several miles, the progress of the advancing Sixth being slowed by the barriers which were constantly thrown in its way. Coming upon a stream of major size, across which there were strong earthworks, the Sixth was soon ordered into a field out of sight of the enemy, having been relieved by another force of Union boys.

The regiment had sixteen casualties:

Captain E. S. Austin, Company B, killed
Corporal John Kerr, Company G, killed
Corporal Isaac Emerson, Company C, killed
2nd Lieutenant J. E. Templeton, Company D, severely wounded
Private J. O. Packard, Company D, severely wounded
A. B. F. Wilson, Company D, severely wounded
William Lucas, Company D, badly wounded
Jacob Kaiser, Company D, slightly wounded
James C. St. Clair, Company E, mortally wounded
John D. Bryant, Company E, mortally wounded
James Drake, Company H, mortally wounded
Conrad Frank, Company H, badly wounded
William Porter, Company H, slightly wounded
William Stowe, Company I, severely wounded
Michael Mulvihill, Company M, severely wounded

On October 28th the cavalrymen returned to camp near Fort Stephenson. It was now time for national elections, and the boys of the regiment anxiously awaited returns from Pennsylvania, Ohio and Indiana. They had already had their regimental election on October 13th, voting 200 for Lincoln (the Union party), and 11 for McClellan (the Democratic party). There was only one vote from Ashtabula County for McClellan. Like the state elections the year before, the boys of the Sixth OVC were fighting the enemy in front with their sabres and in the rear with the ballot box.

At three o'clock on the morning of December 1st, the cavalry-men started out on a reconnaisance which by daylight had brought them to the enemy's pickets. The force they encountered at Stony Creek was totally unprepared and a Confederate rout ensued.

Good news came to the boys the early part of December. Among prisoners returned following a prisoner exchange at Savannah, Georgia, all of whom had arrived at Annapolis, were three men from the Sixth Ohio Volunteer Cavalry: E. C. Northway, Company A; T. Hayward of Company K; and E. B. Collingwood (company not identified).

As a raiding party led by Generals Warren and Gregg on the Weldon Railrod, the 13th Pennsylvania Cavalry from Army Headquarters, and "The Half Dozenth Ohio" were ordered to make a demonstration and capture an enemy position on the Vaugn Road where they had previously battled on the 1st and 27th of October.

In the first encounter which occurred on December 8th, the attack, led by the Pennsylvania 13th, failed due to darkness falling and a stream of some proportions separating the cavalrymen from the earthwork which they sought to take. Six or seven men of the Pennsylvania cavalry were wounded but none of the Sixth.

They were greeted next morning by several inches of snow and sleet on the ground, and, being in the saddle at 4:00 A.M., through the darkness they advanced once more on the position they had sought the evening before, this time supported by an infantry division. The boys of the Sixth were in the advance on this occasion, and eventually they were successful in out-maneuvering the enemy and flushing them from behind their earthworks. The rebels held them until the next day when they attacked the two regiments and the boys in blue fell back with the intention to draw them on. Thus the engagement was ended.

On December 11th the cavalrymen set out to meet Generals Warren and Gregg, whom they joined at Hawkinsville, Virginia, returning with them to camp.

Five days later, the regiment was relieved and returned to camp to spend the remainder of the year repairing their winter quarters. The conflict, which some had felt ever since joining in October, 1861, would be over within six months, was, as December 1864 dwindled into January 1865 at long last within sight of truly being over, but the end was not as apparent now that it was less than 100 days away, as it seemed to have been nearly four years earlier. . . .

The regiment by now had been through 36 engagements since its inception, had taken more than 1,000 prisoners, two twelve-pound guns and two battle flags, but their losses had been great.

CHAPTER VII

January, 1865, Through April 14, 1865

OVERVIEW OF THE CIVIL WAR

The end of the War which had been hoped for, expected, wished for and fought for over a period of thirty months was at long last but a short time in the future, but like a patient, terminally ill, the month, week, day or hour of the end was still not apparent. Whatever hope still existed in the South was without foundation, and Jefferson Davis made the overture that he would enter into peace negotiations if it would bring peace to both countries. But because the war was fought to preserve the Union, Abraham Lincoln's contention that there was only one country made such negotiations impossible.

Robert E. Lee was named Commander-in-Chief of all the Southern armies on January 19th by the Confederate Congress. His formal appointment by Davis followed on the 6th of February. On the 28th of January, Davis appointed a three-man commission to hold informal meetings with Abraham Lincoln. On the first of February, Sherman would head northward out of Savannah, cutting a swath of destruction north.

On the battlefield in the late winter there was comparatively little action. Petersburg was still beset by siege lines and there was activity in the Shenandoah Valley. Columbia, the capital of South Carolina, was taken on the 17th of February, and Charleston, held by many to have been the birthplace of the secession, was cut off and occupied without a struggle on the 18th.

On the 3rd of February, Abraham Lincoln and Secretary Seward talked with Alexander Stephens, Vice President of the Confederacy, and his commission, but the attitude of the Southerners regarding independence as a nation reduced the efforts to futility.

While Sheridan was making one last blow in the Shenandoah Valley in March, the siege at Petersburgh continued. Late in the month Grant sent Sheridan eastward pushing past Dinwiddie Court House toward a junction of roads at Five Forks.

It was suddenly spring, and Whitman's lilacs were blooming in the dooryard. Abraham Lincoln, about whom Whitman would write, "When lilacs last in the dooryard bloomed," would, next day, April 4th, be walking the streets of Richmond.

The supplies which Lee's hungry army was to get at Amelia Court House on April 4th were not there and the Army of Northern Virginia was being harrassed around the edges by swarms of Union troops. At Sailor's Creek, Ewell's Corps was cut up and captured. That was on the 6th of April. On the evening of the next day, correspondence between General Ulysses S. Grant and General Robert E. Lee got under way with Lee asking for terms and proposing that peace be treated for. Grant, however, had neither the authority for, nor the disposition to treat for peace. Unconditional surrender was his only course.

On the 9th of April, Lee unsuccessfully attacked Sheridan's cavalry and a flag of truce appeared. The interview that followed at Appomattox Court House at 3:45 P.M. in the McLean farmhouse brought the war perceptibly toward the end.

Grant ws tendered the care of 28,356 men of the great Army of the Confederacy and the arms were stacked and flags furled, but they were permitted to retain their side arms and their horses. Their acceptance of peace was no longer a matter of choice.

The last major center of the Confederacy fell on April 12th, when Mobile, Alabama, went down. Two days later, the American flag went up over Fort Sumter in Charleston harbor.

But on the morning of the next day, flags throughout the Union were lowered to half mast, for although the war was over . . . in Washington, D.C. . . . Abraham Lincoln lay dead . . . another fatality of the conflict.

OVERVIEW OF THE ACTIONS OF
THE SIXTH OHIO CAVALRY

Action by the Sixth Ohio Volunteer Cavalry in the spring of 1865 was launched on February 3rd when a march over familiar ground ended in a battle at Hatcher's Run, which was of such severity that numerous casualties were encountered.

There were subsequent actions at Quaker Road, Dinwiddie Court House and the battle of Five Forks, at which the fate of the Confederate Capital was sealed. Pursuing Lee, the regiment saw action at Jettersville, Deatonsville, Sailor's Creek, Farmville and High Bridge, Virginia.

On April 9th, the Sixth had the distinction of opening the Battle at Appomattox Court House.

Following the action at Appomattox, the Sixth was detailed to escort General Grant from Appomattox to Burkesville Station where he entrained for Washington to meet Abraham Lincoln who had only hours to live. The Sixth, meanwhile, marched back to Petersburg where it remained until summoned to march through Virginia to North Carolina. Johnson's surrender saw it returning once more to Petersburg from whence it was sent in detachments to different counties composing the "Sub-district of the Appomattox," under the command of Brevet Brigadier General C. B. Smith.

In August, the regiment was ordered to Cleveland, Ohio, where it was mustered out of service.

January, 1865, Through April 14, 1865

There was talk of peace throughout the trenches in January. But most of the boys of the Sixth were inflexible as to the nature of any peace that should be reached between the two sides, and, in fact, their's was a reflection of the position taken by Abraham Lincoln. When the Confederate armies were disbanded, and national authority was recognized throughout the South, together with acceptance of the 13th Amendment abolishing slavery, there would be peace. Until then, there would be no peace.

Being paid became a problem since some of the boys of the Sixth had not been paid in six months. There were rumors that the paymaster was "scandalizing" their money. There was talk that their regiment alone owed the sutler over $2,000, and more talk that it could be over three. It would not be until the first part of March that the boys would get their back pay.

For the Sixth, it was a cold and wet January and February in 1865.

From February 5th through the 7th, there was frequent skirmishing over familiar ground at Hatcher's Run which was of such severity that numerous casualties were encountered. It was a continuous move to the left, westward, trying to capture control of the South Side Railroad.

There was constant picket duty, with casualties not always by the enemy. On March 10th, after getting in from picket duty, Leroy Chase of Company L accidently hit the doorsill with his carbine while entering his tent, shooting himself in the breast. He lived but a few minutes.

The Sixth skirmished with the rebel cavalry at Quaker Run on March 29th, but it was of little consequence.

The Sixth Regiment came upon General Sheridan's Cavalry Corps in and around Dinwiddie Court House on the morning of March 31st, after having bivouaced there for two nights because of a rainstorm that had made the already bad roads almost impassable.

On that morning of the 31st, General Charles Smith's Brigade, to which the Sixth was attached, had been ordered to move some seven miles in a northwesterly direction from the Court House to Fitzgerald's Crossing on Chamberlain's Creek.

The brigade was dismounted and soon erected breastworks of rails across the road leading to the ford. On the Confederate side of the creek the ground was high, while for some sixty rods to the rear of the Sixth the ground was level before beginning to rise at the edge of some timber. Half a mile distant was yet another ford. Captain Stiles was ordered to take a squadron consisting of Companies B and E to the left to guard that ford, while pickets were sent out for their protection. There was considerable distance between the right and left of the brigade, and the elevation was such that any movement by Stile's men was immediately apparent to the rebels. Stiles was supplied with a mounted orderly to carry dispatches back and forth and was under orders not to leave the position until ordered to do so.

On the opposite side of the creek, enemy cavalry and infantry were in strong force. Stiles and his men had not long been in position when the rebels forced a passage across the creek at the ford, driving the boys backward rapidly because of the heavy firing. Stiles dispatched a request to General Smith for orders, but none were forthcoming, which caused Stiles to realize that he and his men were completely cut off from the brigade and that their situation in the enemy's rear was a serious one.

Resolving, regardless of orders, to fall back and try to save the detachment from capture, Stiles called the pickets in and formed the boys by fours, ready to march. But soon they heard the firing coming nearer and they thought that their boys were driving the enemy back. Forming his men into squadron front, he sent out pickets to report if the enemy were likely to envelop his boys in falling back.

It was not long until the Johnnies came out of the timber, entering the open ground in much confusion, their left flank about 100 yards distant on the right, and on lower elevation. Stiles wheeled his command around and fired several volleys into them at short range, adding much to their confusion, causing them to give rapidly over toward the highway without returning fire. The enemy made a hasty return to their breastworks across the creek from which they once more opened fire on Stile's men. But Stiles and his men soon came out into the open field in pursuit and, when they were about halfway between the timber and the position they had recently left, three of his men dropped down behind a large boulder where they were completely screened from the enemy's view and his fire.

Because Stiles' men were short of ammunition, few shots were exchanged until late afternoon when supplies were brought up by horseback despite the poor condition of the roads.

Tiring of their position behind the boulder where they had been lying on wet ground, the three made a break for the timber, but were promptly forced to cover by enemy fire. Several later attempts produced the same result. Finally, late in the afternoon, they seemed determined to reach the timber at all hazards, and once more started out. About halfway to his destination, one was struck and lay perfectly quiet upon the ground. Seeing their fallen comrade, the other two immediately rushed to his side. As they bent over his prostrate form, the enemy ceased firing, rose up in their works and, lustily cheering them, permitted them to carry the comrade back without further molestation.

In the afternoon the enemy commenced firing and charged down the road at the ford on the right, and succeeded in driving the brigade back rapidly.

As Stiles' men retook the position they had left in the morning and communication was established, Stiles received the same orders he had gotten earlier regarding not moving unless ordered to do so. This time, however, he was not provided with a mounted orderly. It was evident that the boys were falling back rapidly, and by the firing, Stiles judged they must be nearly back at the Court House.

Once more they were in a serious position, and he finally called in the pickets and formed his men in line.

They started marching by fours and because the forest was dense and swampy, progress was slow. Ordering them to break ranks and get back as best they could, Stiles, a good bit exhausted from the long day, suddenly found himself entirely alone, and after much walking and running, arrived at a line of rail breastworks above which the Union colors were flying. Luckily, all of his men arrived back into the lines without anyone being lost. In this action of the Sixth at Dinwiddie Court House, there was one man killed and several wounded. April 2nd dawned fair and warm in the Capital of the Confederacy, and on that Sunday when beleaugered Richmond was in imminent danger of Ulysses S. Grant's final assault, Jefferson Davis, President of the Confederate States of America, joined his fellow Episcopalians at St. Paul's church for morning worship. Davis was seated alone in his pew when a special courier from General Lee sought him out and handed him an official dispatch in which the General advised the

President that he leave Richmond at once. The lines around Petersburg had been broken by Union troops and both Petersburg and Richmond must be evacuated without delay.

Some had already left the city, among them Jefferson Davis' family. The story of those memorable days between Petersburg and the fall of Richmond has been thoroughly documented by the definitive historians, but each man sees the world through his own eyes, and 26-year-old Alcinus Fenton, Captain of Company D of the Sixth Ohio Cavalry, set down what he saw and heard in those memorable days between April 3rd and the fall of the Confederate Capital.

Fenton, in a paper appearing in the proceedings of the 34th Annual Reunion of the Sixth Ohio Volunteer Cavalry, observed that General Lee saw two things with clear vision. First, if he fought a great battle outside his fortifications anywhere in the vicinity of Petersburg or Richmond, his army was doomed to defeat. Second, he had hopes that by a hurried evacuation and a rapid move southward, the archives of the Confederacy might be saved and there was a possibility that he might form a junction with General Joseph Johnson's Army.

"The War is over! We can unsaddle and bivouac tonight with no pickets out!" Thus did Chief Bugler Carlos F. MacDonald of the Sixth Ohio Volunteer Cavalry note in his diary the conclusion of the war at Appomattox Court House. In a running account of the Appomattox Campaign covering a fourteen-day period between Monday, March 27, and Sunday, April 9, the young bugler, who in his later years would become one of the great physicians of his time, wrote his own reactions to the history that was being made around him, and that, indeed, he was helping to make.

Following a review of the brigade by General Henry E. Davies on March 27th, the regiment broke camp the next day and went out on picket duty relieving the Second New York Cavalry. There was evidence on every hand that an important campaign was about to be undertaken.

At 3 o'clock in the morning of the 29th, the Division broke camp and MacDonald's regiment marched to Ream's Station and on to Dinwiddie Court House. There they unsaddled and went into camp for the night. The Cavalry Corps was now all together under the command of General Philip Sheridan. At 10:00 P.M.

that night it began to rain heavily, soaking the ground so thoroughly that it was impossible to sleep on it. They were forced to stand around their camp fires throughout the night. Movement was impossible next day because the rain continued without cessation. Although they were saddled and ready to move throughout the day, the order to unsaddle and bivouac for the night came at 9:00 P.M.

It was still raining on Friday morning when the order to move came at 9 o'clock, and a march toward Fitzgerald's Crossing saw MacDonald's regiment, commanded by Major Matthew Cryer, out in front of the brigade. Approaching the crossing, the regiment found the enemy strongly positioned on the opposite side of the creek, a fordable stream known variously as Chamberlain's Bed, Cat Tail Creek, or Stony Creek. A few shots were exchanged before dismounting and forming a battle line along the creek bank.

About this time a mounted battalion of the First Maine Cavalry attempted to cross the stream and were repulsed by a countercharge of the enemy, which consisted of a superior force of both cavalry and infantry. The infantry charged with a vigorous fire which was returned by the cavalrymen of the Sixth who, nevertheless, were forced to give ground. The First Maine, too, had fallen back, and at this point the rebels charged them but were met with Henry carbines carrying sixteen shots. At the same time MacDonald's regiment was delivering a raking fire which emptied many Confederate saddles. Both the First Maine and the cavalrymen of the Sixth countercharged and accounted for a large number of Confederate casualties. Having regained their former position, the cavalrymen continued to fire throughout much of the day until their ammunition was fairly exhausted. Ordered to fall back toward Dinwiddie Court House, the dismounted cavalrymen fired as they went, finally meeting Custer's Division in line of battle. There they found and remounted their horses.

Eleven men had been wounded, four were missing and Corporal Lambert was killed. MacDonald observed that it was a surprisingly small casualty count in view of the many hours the cavalrymen had been engaged. Bugler MacDonald was struck high on the left breast just below the collar bone by a nearly spent ball which, nevertheless, knocked him down. MacDonald noted in his diary that before going on the firing line, he had taken his horse to the rear and turned some $40 and his watch over to a non-commissioned officer named Joe Young, instructing him to send them home to his mother in event anything happened to him.

The next morning heavy firing was heard from the direction of Petersburg by the men of the Sixth who were on picket duty near Dinwiddie Court House. The glancing blow Carlos MacDonald had suffered the day before from a ball that came through the breastworks the Union had erected of old fence rails, had turned his chest black and blue and was sore and tender to the touch.

On Sunday afternoon, MacDonald's regiment escorted a wagon train several miles in a northwesterly direction, passing along the way a long line of Confederate fortifications and several thousand prisoners. They bivouaced that night in an old rebel camp.

On Monday, MacDonald wrote in his diary, "We saw the Second Corps and learned from them that Petersburg is captured. A little later we learned that Richmond is ours. Hurray! The troops are cheering."

Moving in a westerly direction up the Appomattox River, the regiment continued next day with foraging, a major activity of many of the men because their meat supply had been exhausted. "This country seems to be full of bacon," MacDonald wrote. "I went out and got all the bacon my horse could carry."

Upon reaching the Danville Railway, some of the men tore up some three miles of track. It was here that they met Sheridan and the Fifth Corps. Ordered to dismount, the Cavalry were sent into a firing line, but when no enemy appeared, they were recalled and proceeded to Amelia Station where the men, exhausted, and their horses "jaded," camped for the night.

On April 5th the word spread that Lee's army was in front of them and the Fifth Corps, having thrown up strong earthworks during that night, a hot fight was anticipated. At noon they were ordered out on the double-quick to protect the First Brigade which was bringing in a battery of Confederate artillery and a large number of prisoners just captured. A desperate effort was made by the rebels to recapture their losses, but to no avail. The action cost the Sixth one man killed and three wounded. That night they bivouaced without unsaddling, and slept on their arms.

Next day, marching in a southwesterly direction, the cavalry-men, setting out at daybreak, came in sight of the enemy's wagon train in the forenoon and immediately charged it, but deep mud, thick woods and a heavy line of rebel infantry prevented its seizure. Another charge in the afternoon yielded about a thousand prisoners and eight generals, among them "brave, little blue-eyed General Malone." Among the numerous wagons that were burned were several of General Lee's headquarters wagons.

Out of the booty, Carlos MacDonald said, "I got several signal flags and a Confederate officer's uniform." Two Union cavalry-men were wounded in the action, but there were no fatalities. The night was spent in guarding prisoners.

On Friday, MacDonald's regiment got behind the rest of the division because it was escorting its prisoners to army headquarters. Crossing the Lynchburg Railroad about ten miles above Burksville at noon, they arrived at Farmville, a little village of about 2,000 population, at 3:30 in the afternoon. There they crossed the river and joined the division which was engaged with the enemy. The First and Second Brigades had been driven back from the wagon train which they had reached. The regiment re-crossed the river and followed the railway back to Prospect Station where they unsaddled and spent the night.

At seven o'clock the next morning "Boots and Saddles" sounded, but it was 1:00 A.M. before the boys started to move, and it was noon when they reached Pamplin Station, having foraged along the way. After a halt of about two hours at the station, the men advanced to within about two miles of Appomattox Court House. "Our Brigade was sent out on a road with orders to hold it," Carlos MacDonald wrote in his diary, "for Lee's army would have to pass that way, if any." Four trains of cars, loaded with clothing and forage were captured.

On Saturday, April 9th, Carlos MacDonald closed his diary entry with the ominous note, "A great battle is imminent." But that battle did not materialize. "Our regiment was sent out in advance between midnight and 2:00 A.M. as far as the enemy's pickets," he wrote next morning, "where we put up rail fence breastworks and waited until daybreak, soon after which the firing began and the enemy advanced a long and heavy line of infantry. Our Brigade fell back slowly under orders, until we came upon our infantry, some of them being colored troops, formed a line in the woods. We fell in behind them."

The infantry advanced promptly, driving the enemy back to their lines of the previous night, when they hoisted a white flag and the firing ceased.

"We heard that Lee had come into our lines with a flag of truce about 9:00 A.M. I went up to the front and saw what was left of Lee's army, and a house a little east of Appomattox Court House where Grant and Lee were conferring. Later we learned that Lee had surrendered his army of 30,000 men. And then those words that for four long years the boys of the Sixth Ohio Volunteer Cavalry, hundreds of thousands of their fellow soldiers, and millions of Americans had so eagerly awaited:

THE WAR IS OVER! "

That night, at long last, they unsaddled and bivouacked with no pickets out. . . .

Epilogue

In referring to the Sixth Ohio Cavalry and its role in the Civil War, a writer for the Western Reserve Chronicle, with an ill-disguised pride in its accomplishment, wrote in October, 1916: "We may say for the Sixth that they have not equalled the claims of the historians of one of Ohio's Cavalry Regiments, that they put down the Rebellion alone, in marching and counter-marching some 27,000 miles, and in fighting little battles at Five Forks and Appomattox Court House."

But the writer was perhaps being as objective as he knew how when he wrote: "Like most of the regiments from every state, in their early experience, it had its troubles. It drilled and guarded Confederate prisoners for months at Camps Dennison and Chase, near Columbus, and like Private Maguire, it got tired of 'trainin' and trainin' and trainin'.' While General McClellan was making up his mind to fight or not to fight, in the early months of 1862, with that wonderful Army of the Potomac which he had created, but could not use." "The Regiment was about eight months old before it reached the command of General John Fremont on May 29, 1862, near Moorefield, Va. with its two battalions. Its first battalion had been permanently detached and sent to the plains of the Great West, and a dozen or more of the officers had wearied of preparedness and the prospects for a fight, and sent in their resignations. But they were not of a class much missed. The first years of the war had weeded out thousands of officers who never should have been commissioned, not alone in Ohio, but in all states." "The Regiment was handicapped for a year and a half before any steps had been taken to replace its lost battalion, and by an inefficient Colonel who resigned on April 2, 1863, leaving the way open for Major Stedman who became a real and much loved colonel until his three-year term had expired. He was the only one of his rank ever worthy of the name, in command. "The regiment was fortunate in its original captains, save two or three, who were spoiled by the assignment to recruiting service, much to the regret of the regiment. "With rare exceptions, the company commanders were competent, able and courageous leaders, and some of those promoted as the original captains were killed or discharged by expiration of term, were also fine officers."

The events of the final minutes of the Civil War, as they ticked by at Appomattox, have been told and retold in dramatic fashion and are to be found in minute detail in countless histories of the Great Rebellion. The concentration of Confederate battle flags which caused one Federal officer to recall that it seemed

69

there were more battle flags than soldiers; the musket fire at first sporadic, followed by much heavier musket fire and the heavy booming of artillery; Sheridan in his saddle, giving orders to his cavalrymen to come up into the line and to his officers, orders to bring up their infantry as quickly as possible; the chicken coop which literally exploded when struck by a Union shell, releasing countless chickens in the midst of hungry, tired men who had not eaten in 24 hours; and finally, the emergence from the Rebel lines of a lone gray clad mounted officer galloping madly toward the Union lines, a white flag flying from the tip of the staff he carried . . . these have all been covered in depth in the shelves of volumes that bring the Civil War to life once more, and are there for all who wish to relive those historic moments in minutest detail.

But there is a vast unrecorded mass of detail that never found its way into words, much less into print. Despite all that has been written and published, there comes to light from time to time, letters and diaries and memoirs long lost from view, that lend substance to the point of view that there are as many versions of the War Between the States as there were men who fought in it. Between Camp Hutchins and Appomattox Court House, a total of 1,736 men belonged to the Sixth Ohio Volunteer Cavalry. Like all their fellow soldiers, North and South alike, each saw the conflict in terms of his own experiences. What has been set forth in the preceding pages represents the observations, the thoughts, the feelings and experiences of some of them. Certainly in old trunks, wrapped in browning newsprint in cobwebbed attics, in safe deposit boxes, safes, dresser drawers and other places supposedly of safekeeping, much more remains to be put into the domain of the readers whose appetite for details of the irrepressible conflict is understandably insatiable. And certainly, from time to time, these gems will surface and lend their enchantment to what has already been written. But regrettably, with each man, honored or unsung, there has long since been buried his own personal narrative of the War Between the States, for each in his own way, in his own time and in his own place started from some Camp Hutchins and made his way toward Appomattox Court House and, hopefully, into the heart of every American who knows what it means to have preserved this last best hope on earth.

And as the boys of this Regiment who remained grew old, they would remember why they enlisted; why they fought: "Better a Patriot Soldier's Grave, than a Traitor's Dishonorable Life at Home."

OHIO

6th CAVALRY

This is a representation of our best judgement of what the flag of the 6th Ohio Volunteer Cavalry looked like, based on the description given by the ladies of Warren upon presentation of the "stand of colors", and the tattered remains of the only flag of the 6th O.V.C. that we were able to locate.

C. C. Taylor, Warren, O.

M. W. King, 1861

Lieutenant Colonel Wm. O. Collins

Dr. Carlos F. MacDonald
President 1911

Lieut. Oliver C. Russell, Co. A.

Major Delos R. Northway

Captain Eusebrus S. Austin

Col. Stedman

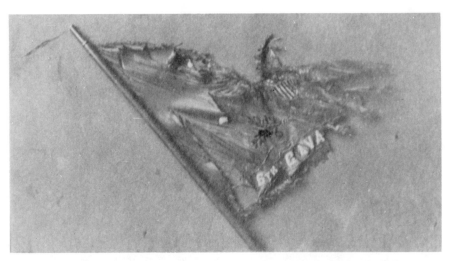

The only remnant of the Regimental Flag that could be found.

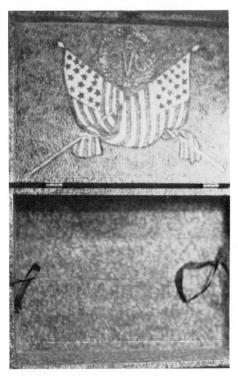

The inside of a 6th O.V.C. supply box

Back Row left to right: Isaac Gibbons, Akron, Ohio; Charles Bennett, Newton Falls; H. C. Pardee, Deerfield.

Front Row left to right: L. A. Lyons, Petersburg, Fla.; David Foulk, Ravenna

The Union Cavalry insignia

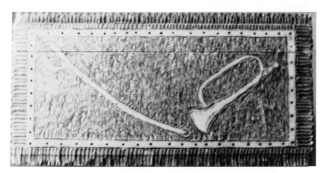

Another Cavalry insignia

The front of the program of one of
the 6th O.V.C. Reunions

T. A. Wilcox
At the age of 18, taken in 1862

Lt. H. M. Adj. Baldwin

C. C. Baker

Stiles

Lieut. J. E. Wood
Co's D and G

JWMB

77

Adjt. A. Ward Fenton
1864

JWMB

6TH OHIO VET. VOL. CAVALRY
1861–1913

MAJOR
MATTHEW H. CRYER

A Reunion Badge — 1913

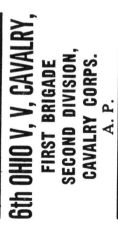

6th OHIO V, V, CAVALRY,
FIRST BRIGADE
SECOND DIVISION,
CAVALRY CORPS.
A. P.

OHIO MEMORIALS,
GETTYSBURG,
September 14, 1887

21st ANNUAL REUNION
WILLOUGHBY, O.,
OCTOBER, 4, 1887.

BRIGADE

The 6th Ohio Volunteer Cavalry gathered at barracks such as this in 1861 before they went to war. This drawing depicts the actual barracks in Warren, Ohio, built on the fairgrounds

6th REGIMENT OHIO VOLUNTEER CAVALRY

FIELD AND STAFF

Mustered in from October 2 to December 12, 1861, by Albert G. Dod, Captain 15th Infantry, and John R. Edie, Major 15th Infantry, U. S. A., and others, Mustering Officers. Mustered out August 7, 1865, at Petersburg, Va., by L. H. Bowen, 1st Lieutenant and Acting Commissary of Musters, Mustering Officer, Department of Virginia.

Names.	Rank.	Age.	Date of Entering the Service.	Period of Service.	Remarks.
William R. Lloyd........	Colonel	....	Oct. 10, 1861	3 yrs.	Mustered as Lieut. Colonel; promoted to Colonel Dec. 19, 1861; resigned April 2, 1863.
William R. Steadman......	...do...	47	Oct. 1, 1861	3 yrs.	Mustered as 2d. Lieutenant; promoted to Major Oct. 21, 1861; to Lieut. Colonel Aug. 3, 1863; to Colonel Jan. 1, 1864; mustered out Oct. 6, 1864 on expiration of term of service.
Frank C. Loveland.......	...do...	23	Oct. 26, 1861	3 yrs.	Mustered as private Co. D; appointed Sergeant Dec. 4, 1861; promoted to Regt. Com. Sergeant March 1, 1862; to Sergt. Major June 1, 1862; to 2d Lieutenant Feb. 6, 1863; wounded May 31, 1864, at Cold Harbor, Va.; promoted to Captain Co. B July 25, 1864; to Lieut. Colonel April 8, 1865; to Colonel July 30, 1865; mustered out with regiment Aug. 7, 1865.

SIXTH REGIMENT OHIO VOLUNTEER CAVALRY.

Names.	Rank.	Age.	Date of Entering the Service.	Period of Service.	Remarks.
Edward E. Steadman......	Ch'f Bug.	17	Aug. 14, 1862	3 yrs.	Promoted from private Co. L May 1, 1863; discharged Dec. 17,1863, on Surgeon's certificate of disability.
Horace Blattenberg......	Sad.Ser.	24	Nov. 19, 1861	3 yrs.	Promoted from Saddler Co. D Dec. 31, 1861;discharged Oct. 16, 1862, by order of War Department.
Max Elben...............	...do...	33	Oct. 9, 1861	3 yrs.	Promoted from Saddler Co. I Jan. 1, 1862; discharged Sept. 17,1862, by order of War Department.
Joseph Young............	...do...	22	Nov. 28, 1861	3 yrs.	Promoted from Saddler Co. C May 1, 1863; mustered out June 27,1865, at Petersburg,Va.,by order of War Department; veteran.

COMPANY A.

Mustered in from October 2 to December 6, 1861, at Camp Hutchins, Warren, O., by A. Bingham, C.R. Rowe, and John S. Mathews, U.S. Mustering Officers. Mustered out Aug. 7,1865, at Petersburg,Va., by L.H.Bowen, 1st Lieutenant and Acting Commissary of Musters, Mustering Officer Department of Virginia.

Names.	Rank.	Age.	Date of Entering the Service.	Period of Service.	Remarks.
Amandar Bingham.........	Captain	49	Oct. 2, 1861	3 yrs.	Mustered as 2d Lieutenant;promoted to Captain Oct.14,1861;to Major Oct.1, 1862.
Delos R. Northway.......	...do...	26	Oct. 4, 1861	3 yrs.	Mustered as private; promoted to 1st Lieutenant Oct.14,1861;to Captain Oct. 1,1862;wounded June 21,1863,at Upperville,Va.;promoted to Major May 9, 1864,but not mustered;killed May 28, 1864,in action at Aenon Church,Va.

Names.	Rank.	Age.	Date of Entering the Service.	Period of Service.	Remarks.
Henry M. Baldwin.........	Adjutant	26	Oct. 28, 1861	3 yrs.	Promoted to Sergt.Major from 1st Sergeant Co. G Nov.1,1862; to 1st Lieutenant and Quartermaster Dec. 1, 1862; appointed Adjutant April 1, 1863; promotoed to Captain May 9, 1864, but not mustered; killed June 24, 1864, at St. Mary's Church, Virginia.
Alcinus W. Fenton........	...do...	22	Oct. 5, 1861	3 yrs.	Promoted to Sergt. Major from Corporal Co. A April 1, 1863; wounded Oct. 14, 1863, at Aubern Mills,Va.;promoted to 2d Lieutenant Co. C May 9, 1864;to 1st Lieutenant and Adjutant Nov.12,1864; wounded Dec. 9,1864, at Hatcher's Run, Va.;promoted to Captain Co. D. Jan.31, 1865; veteran.
William M. Davis.........	...do...	22	Nov. 6, 1861	3 yrs.	Promoted from 1st Sergeant Co. G Jan. 31,1865;promoted to Captain July 30, 1865, but not mustered; mustered out with regiment Aug.7,1865; veteran.
William F. Reynolds......	Bat.Adj't.	24	June 4, 1861	3 yrs.	Appointed 1st Lieutenant and Batt. Adjutant Dec. 11,1861;resigned March 24,1862.
Marshall H. Haskell......	...do...	....	Oct. 3, 1861	3 yrs.	Appointed 1st Lieutenant and Batt. Adjutant Dec. 20,1861;resigned April --, 1862.
Charles R. Hunt..........	R.Q.M.	....	Oct. 2, 1861	3 yrs.	Appointed from civil life;resigned July 15,1862.
Joel A. Clark............	...do...	20	Oct. 21, 1862	3 yrs.	Promoted from 2d Lieutenant Co. B Nov. 12,1864;promoted to Captain Jan.31, 1865,but declined promotion;discharged June 10,1865.

ROSTER OF OHIO TROOPS

Names.	Rank.	Age.	Date of Entering the Service.	Period of Service.	Remarks.
Charles W. Babcock.......	Sergeant	35	Oct. 4, 1861	3 yrs.	Mustered as private;appointed Sergeant Oct.14,1861;mustered out June 27,1865, at Petersburg,Va.,by order of War Department; veteran.
William H. Drake.........	...do...	20	Oct. 5, 1861	3 yrs.	Wounded June 21,1863, at Upperville, Va.;appointed Corporal March 1,1865; Sergeant June 1,1865;mustered out with company Aug.7,1865; veteran.
William C. Stiles........	...do...	18	Aug. 15, 1862	3 yrs.	Appointed --;mustered out May 31,1865, by order of War Department.
Henry A. Canfield........	...do...	23	Oct. 5, 1861	3 yrs.	Appointed Corporal July 1,1862;Sergeant April 1,1863;wounded March 8, 1864, at Spottsylvania Court House, Va.;discharged Jan.14,1865,on Surgeon's certificate of disability; veteran.
Horace H. Drew...........	...do...	23	Oct. 5, 1861	3 yrs.	Appointed Corporal July 1,1862; Sergeant Jan. 1,1863;wounded May 9,1865, at Irwinsville,Ga.;transferred to Veteran Reserve Corps March 30,1865; mustered out Aug.25,1865 at Washington, D.C.,by order of War Department;veteran.
John C. Granger..........	...do...	26	Oct. 26, 1861	3 yrs.	Appointed Corporal Oct.15,1862;wounded June 21,1863, at Upperville,Va.;appointed Sergeant Aug.1,1863;mustered out Dec. 6,1864,at Columbus,O.,on expiration of term of service.
Stephen C. Thorpe........	...do...	31	Oct. 5, 1861	3 yrs.	Mustered as private;appointed Sergeant June 1,1865;prisoner of war;mustered out June 27,1865, at Petersburg, Va., by order of War Department;veteran.
Orlando W. Ferry........	Corporal	24	Oct. 5, 1861	3 yrs.	Appointed Oct.14,1861;promoted to Hospital Steward Jan.1,1863.

SIXTH REGIMENT OHIO VOLUNTEER CAVALRY

Names.	Rank.	Age.	Date of Entering the Service.	Period of Service.	Remarks.
James S. Abell..........	Major	34	Oct. 9, 1861	3 yrs.	Promoted from Captain Co. I May 9, 1864, but not mustered, as he was killed May 9, 1864, at Hawe's Shop, Va.
Matthew H. Cryer.........	...do...	23	Oct. 16, 1863	3 yrs.	Promoted from Captain, Co. C April 8, 1865; resigned June 3, 1865.
William B. Reznor........	Surgeon	.....	Nov. 10, 1861	3 yrs.	Appointed from civil life; mustered out Nov. 9, 1864, on expiration of term of service.
Alphonzo D. Rockwell.....	...do...	.....	April 18, 1864	3 yrs.	Appointed Asst. Surgeon from civil life; promoted to Surgeon Dec. 7, 1864; mustered out with regiment Aug. 7, 1865.
James C. Marr............	As.Surg.	.....	Dec. 3, 1861	3 yrs.	Assigned from civil life; resigned Sept. 3, 1862.
Zenas A. Northway........	...do...	.....	Nov. 15, 1861	3 yrs.	Appointed Hospital Steward ——; promoted to Asst. Surgeon July 4, 1862; died Sept. 27, 1864, at City Point, Va.
Augustus P. Knowlton.....	...do...	.....	May 26, 1863	3 yrs.	Appointed from civil life; discharged Dec. 18, 1863, on Surgeon's certificate of disability.
Cuno Kibele.............	...do...	.....	Mch. 25, 1865	3 yrs.	Appointed from civil life; mustered out with regiment Aug. 7, 1865.
Richard J. Wright........	Adjutant	22	Oct. 2, 1861	3 yrs.	Transferred from 72d Regiment O.V.I Oct. 18, 1861; promoted to Captain Co. L Feb. 17, 1863.

85

SIXTH REGIMENT OHIO VOLUNTEER CAVALRY.

Names.	Rank.	Age.	Date of Entering the Service.	Period of Service.	Remarks.
Winthrope Pelton.........	Vet.Surg.	40	Dec. 11, 1861	3 yrs.	Promoted to Veterinary Surgeon from Capt. Stanhope's Company, Dec. 31, 1861; discharged Oct. 16, 1862, by order of War Department.
Thomas Kinghorn..........	...do...	32	Oct. 18, 1861	3 yrs.	Promoted from Farrier Co. A Dec. 31, 1861; discharged Oct. 16, 1862, by order of War Department.
Robert Kinghorn..........	...do...	28	Oct. 14, 1861	3 yrs.	Promoted from Farrier Co. A May 1, 1863; mustered out Oct. 14, 1864, by order of War Deparment.
Ira H. Morey.............	Ch'f.Bug.	28	Oct. 21, 1861	3 yrs.	Promoted from Bugler Co. I; discharged Nov. 6, 1862, by order of War Department.
John Morey...............	...do...	32	Oct. 21, 1861	3 yrs.	Promoted from Bugler Co. I Dec. 31, 1861; discharged Oct. 12, 1862, by order of War Department.
Carlos F. McDonald.......	...do...	18	Nov. 1, 1862	3 yrs.	Promoted from Corporal Co. B Feb. 1, 1864; mustered out with regiment Aug. 7, 1865.
Edward E. Steadman.......	...do...	17	Aug. 14, 1862	3 yrs.	Promoted from private Co. L May 1, 1863; discharged Dec. 17, 1863, on Surgeon's certificate of disability.
Horace Blattenberg.......	Sad.Ser.	24	Nov. 19, 1861	3 yrs.	Promoted from Saddler Co. D Dec. 31, 1861; discharged Oct. 16, 1862, by order of War Department.

Names.	Rank.	Age.	Date of Entering the Service.	Period of Service.	Remarks.
William W. Steadman......	Hos.St'd.	21	Aug. 21, 1861	3 yrs.	Transferred from Cotter's Battery and promoted to Hospital Steward Dec. 17, 1861; discharged Oct. 16, 1862, by order of War Department.
Samuel A. Dryden.........	...do...	21	Dec. 4, 1861	3 yrs.	Transferred to 2d Battalion Sept. 20, 1862.
Frank E. Crosby..........	...do...	25	Oct. 5, 1861	3 yrs.	Promoted from Corporal Co. A Oct. 1, 1862; discharged Oct.16, 1862, by order of War Department.
Orlando W. Ferry.........	...do...	24	Oct. 5, 1861	3 yrs.	Promoted from Corporal Co. A Jan. 1, 1863; to 2d Lieutenant Co. F Nov. 12, 1864; veteran.
Caleb A. Rising..........	...do...	26	Oct. 31, 1861	3 yrs.	Promoted from private Co. D. Jan. 1, 1862; mustered out Nov. 12, 1864, on expiration of term of service.
Hiram A. Walling.........	...do...	21	Oct. 5, 1861	3 yrs.	Promoted from private Co. A Dec. 1, 1864; commissioned 2d Lieutenant April 8, 1865; 1st Lieutenant May 31, 1865, but not mustered on either commission; mustered out with regiment Aug. 7, 1865; veteran.
Charles G. Steadman......	...do...	18	Mch. 17, 1864	3 yrs.	Promoted from private Co. B Dec. 1, 1864; commissioned 2d Lieutenant April 8, 1865; 1st Lieutenant May 31, 1865, but not mustered on either commission; mustered out with regiment Aug. 7, 1865.

SIXTH REGIMENT OHIO VOLUNTEER CAVALRY.

Names.	Rank.	Age.	Date of Entering the Service.	Period of Service.	Remarks.
John R. Parshal.........	R.Q.M.	26	Oct. 5, 1861	3 yrs.	Promoted to Q.M.Sergeant from Corporal Co. A Nov.1,1862;to 1st Lieutenant and Quartermaster Aug.2,1863;mustered out Oct.12,1864,on expiration of term of service.
Uriel H. Hutchins.......	B.Q.M.	....	Oct. 28, 1861	3 yrs.	Supposed to have been discharged;no official notice received.
William H. Woodrow......	...do...	....	Nov. 5, 1861	3 yrs.	Transferred to 11th Regiment O.V.C. Sept.20,1862.
Charles B. Bostwick.....	...do...	....	Dec. 12, 1861	3 yrs.	Resigned May 16, 1862.
Charles C. Baker........	R.C.S.	19	Oct. 7, 1861	3 yrs.	Promoted from Sergeant Co. C Aug. 3, 1863; mustered out Nov.27,1864, on expiration of term of service.
Dwight H. Cory..........	...do...	21	Oct. 8, 1861	3 yrs.	Promoted to Regt.Com.Sergeant from Corporal Co. A Oct.1, 1862; to 1st Lieutenant and Commissary of Subsistence Nov.12,1864;promoted to Captain May 31,1865,but not mustered;mustered out with regiment Aug.7,1865;veteran.
Eusebius S. Austin......	Ser.Maj.	24	Oct. 5, 1861	3 yrs.	Promoted from private Co. L Dec. 16, 1861; to 2d Lieutenant Co. B Oct. 20, 1862.
Oliver H. Simmons.......	...do...	20	Nov. 4, 1863	3 yrs.	Promoted from 1st Lieutenant Co. F Aug.15,1864;to 1st Lieutenant Co. M Nov.12,1864.
James E. Darwent........	...do...	22	Jan. 2, 1864	3 yrs.	Promoted from 1st Sergeant Co. M Dec. 1,1864;to 1st Lieutenant Co.B April 8, 1865.
David W. McIntosh.......	...do...	28	Oct. 15, 1862	3 yrs.	Promoted from 1st Sergeant Co. E May 5, 1865;promoted to 1st Lieutenant May 31, 1865,but not mustered;mustered out June 27,1865,at Petersburg,Va.,by order of War Department.

SIXTH REGIMENT OHIO VOLUNTEER CAVALRY.

Names.	Rank.	Age.	Date of Entering the Service.	Period of Service.	Remarks.
Walker, William.........	Private	31	Oct. 2, 1862	9 mos.	Drafted; mustered out July 29, 1863, at Warrenton Junction, Va., on expiration of term of service.
White, Robert A.........	...do...	26	Oct. 5, 1861	3 yrs.	Transferred to Veteran Reserve Corps ——; from which mustered out May 6, 1865, at Auger Hospital, Va., by order of War Department; veteran.
White, Scott............	...do...	19	Oct. 1, 1862	9 mos.	Drafted; mustered out July 29, 1863, at Warrenton Junction, Va., on expiration of term of service.
Wilson, William........	...do...	23	Mch. 24, 1864	3 yrs.	
Wolcott, Orin..........	...do...	39	Oct. 5, 1861	3 yrs.	Captured Oct. 1, 1864, at Yellow Tavern, Va.; died Feb. 15, 1865, in Salisbury Prison, North Carolina.
Yokes, Thomas..........	...do...	21	Oct. 12, 1863	3 yrs.	Mustered out June 27, 1865, at Petersburg, Va., by order of War Department.
Young, William E.......	...do...	28	Aug. 5, 1861	3 yrs.	Discharged Oct. 28, 1862, at Washington, D.C., on Surgeon's certificate of disability.
Zimmerman, John........	...do...	19	Oct. 2, 1862	9 mos.	Drafted; captured June 21, 1863, at Upperville, Va.; died Aug.24, 1863, at Annapolis, Maryland.

ROSTER OF OHIO TROOPS.

Names.	Rank.	Age.	Date of Entering the Service.	Period of Service.	Remarks.
William O. Collins........	Lt.Col.	....	Dec. 19, 1861	yrs.	Transferred to 11th Regiment O.V.O. Sept. 20, 1862.
Norman A. Barrett........	...do...	29	Oct. 11, 1861	3 yrs.	Promoted to Major from Captain Co. D Aug. 3, 1863; promoted to Lieut. Colonel Jan. 1, 1864; mustered out Oct. 12, 1864, on expiration of term of service.
George W. Dickinson......	...do...	24	Oct. 15, 1862	3 yrs.	Promoted to Major from Captain Co. B July 25, 1864; promoted to Lieut. Colonel Nov. 12, 1864; resigned Feb. 20, 1865.
John O. Ferrell..........	Major	37	Oct. 10, 1861	3 yrs.	Mustered as private; promoted to Major Oct. 20, 1861; transferred to 11th Reg't O.V.C. Sept. 20, 1862.
Richard B. Treat.........	...do...	....	Oct. 23, 1861	3 yrs.	Appointed from civil life; resigned May 22, 1862.
Amandar Bingham..........	...do...	49	Oct. 2, 1861	3 yrs.	Promoted from Captain Co. A Oct. 1, 1862.
John Henry Cryer.........	...do...	26	Oct. 7, 1861	3 yrs.	Promoted from Captain Co. C Aug. 3, 1863; wounded ——; discharged Feb. 22, 1864, on Surgeon's certificate of disability.
Benj. C. Stanhope........	...do...	....	Oct, 3, 1861	3 yrs.	Promoted from Captain Co. B, 2d Regiment O.V.C., April 1, 1863; died June 25, 1863, of wounds received June 17, 1863, in action at Aldie, Va.
James C. Richart.........	...do...	32	Nov. 6, 1861	3 yrs.	Promoted from Captain Co. G Jan. 1, 1864; mustered out Nov. 9, 1864, on expiration of term of service.

Names.	Rank.	Age.	Date of Entering the Service.	Period of Service.	Remarks.
Porter S. Sinan..........	1st Lieut.	34	Oct. 5, 1861	3 yrs.	Mustered as private;promoted to 2d Lieutenant Oct. 14,1861;to 1st Lieutenant Oct. 1,1862;commissioned Captain May 9,1864, but not mustered;mustered out Oct. 14,1864,on expiration of term of service.
Charles G. Miller........	2d Lieut.	23	Nov. 6, 1861	3 yrs.	Promoted from 1st Sergeant Co. G May 9,1864; prisoner of war;commissioned 1st Lieutenant Nov.12,1864, but not mustered;mustered out Mch.3,1865,by order of War Department; veteran.
Oliver C. Russell........	...do...	26	Oct. 4, 1861	3 yrs.	Mustered as private;appointed 1st Sergeant Oct.14,1861;promoted to 2d Lieutenant Oct.1,1862;wounded Sept. 14,1863; at Rapidan Station,Va.; wounded in picket skirmish Feb.8,1864, in Virginia;discharged July 12,1864, on Surgeon's certificate of disability.
Albert W. Stiles........	1st Sergt.	34	Oct. 5, 1861	3 yrs.	Mustered as private;appointed Sergeant Oct.14,1861;wounded June 21,1863, at Upperville,Va.;promoted to 1st Sergeant July 1,1863;to 2d Lieutenant Co. D May 9,1864; veteran.
Wells A. Bushnell........	...do...	22	Oct. 5, 1861	3 yrs.	Appointed Corporal Oct.14,1861;Sergeant Jan.1,1863;1st Sergeant July 1,1864; promoted to 1st Lieutenant Co. E Jan. 31,1865; veteran.
Charles P. McElligott....	...do...	24	Nov. 1, 1861	3 yrs.	Appointed Corporal Jan.1,1863;Sergeant July 1,1864;1st Sergeant Feb.6,1865; promoted to 2d Lieutenant Co. F April 8,1865; veteran.

91

SIXTH REGIMENT OHIO VOLUNTEER CAVALRY

Names.	Rank.	Age.	Date of Entering the Service.	Period of Service.	Remarks.
George Taylor............	1st Sergt.	21	Oct. 26, 1861	3 yrs.	Appointed Corporal April 1,1863;wounded June 24,1864,at St.Mary's Church,Va.; appointed Sergeant March 1,1865;1st Sergeant April 28,1865;commissioned 2d Lieutenant July 30,1865, but not mustered;mustered out with company Aug. 7,1865; veteran.
James T. St. John........	Q.M.S.	45	Oct. 5, 1861	3 yrs.	Mustered as private;appointed Q.M.Sergeant Oct. 14,1861;discharged July 8, 1863,at Philadelphia,Pa., on Surgeon's certificate of disability.
Francis M. Baker........	...do...	23	Oct. 8, 1861	3 yrs.	Appointed Corporal Oct. 14,1861;Sergeant July 1,1862;Q.M.Sergeant --; wounded June 21,1863, at Upperville, Va.;wounded and captured May 9,1864, on Sheridan's Raid, Virginia;promoted to Captain Co. E, 196th Regiment O.V.I., March 23,1865; veteran.
Thomas M. Covert........	...do...	24	Oct. 4, 1861	3 yrs.	Appointed Saddler Oct.14,1861;Q.M.Sergeant March 1,1865;mustered out June 27,1865, at Petersburg, Va.,by order of War Department; veteran.
George R. Northway......	Com.Ser.	27	Oct. 4, 1861	3 yrs.	Mustered as private;appointed Sergeant July 1,1862;Com.Sergeant Oct.15,1862; wounded May 28, 1864, at Hawe's Shop, Va.;discharged June 2,1865,on Surgeon's certificate of disability; veteran.
William J. Gray.........	Sergeant	38	Oct. 5, 1861	3 yrs.	Mustered as private;appointed Sergeant Oct.14,1861;promoted to 2d Lieutenant Co. E Feb.6,1863.
Alonzo A. House.........	...do...	37	Oct. 17, 1861	3 yrs.	Mustered as private;appointed Sergeant Oct.17,1861;discharged Oct.9,1862, at Columbus,O.,on Surgeon's certificate of disability.

ROSTER OF OHIO TROOPS

Names.	Rank.	Age.	Date of Entering the Service.	Period of Service.	Remarks.
Charles W. Babcock......	Sergeant	35	Oct. 4, 1861	3 yrs.	Mustered as private;appointed Sergeant Oct.14,1861;mustered out June 27,1865, at Petersburg,Va.,by order of War Department; veteran.
William H. Drake.........	...do...	20	Oct. 5, 1861	3 yrs.	Wounded June 21,1863, at Upperville, Va.;appointed Corporal March 1,1865; Sergeant June 1,1865;mustered out with company Aug.7,1865; veteran.
William C. Stiles........	...do...	18	Aug. 15, 1862	3 yrs.	Appointed --;mustered out May 31,1865, by order of War Department.
Henry A. Canfield........	...do...	23	Oct. 5, 1861	3 yrs.	Appointed Corporal July 1,1862;Sergeant April 1,1863;wounded March 8, 1864, at Spottsylvania Court House, Va.;discharged Jan.14,1865,on Surgeon's certificate of disability; veteran.
Horace H. Drew...........	...do...	23	Oct. 5, 1861	3 yrs.	Appointed Corporal July 1,1862; Sergeant Jan. 1,1863;wounded May 9,1865, at Irwinsville,Ga.;transferred to Veteran Reserve Corps March 30,1865; mustered out Aug.25,1865 at Washington, D.C.,by order of War Department;veteran.
John C. Granger..........	...do...	26	Oct. 26, 1861	3 yrs.	Appointed Corporal Oct.15,1862;wounded June 21,1863, at Upperville.Va.;appointed Sergeant Aug.1,1863;mustered out Dec. 6,1864,at Columbus,O.,on expiration of term of service.
Stephen C. Thorpe.......	...do...	31	Oct. 5, 1861	3 yrs.	Mustered as private;appointed Sergeant June 1,1865;prisoner of war;mustered out June 27,1865, at Petersburg, Va., by order of War Department;veteran.
Orlando W. Ferry........	Corporal	24	Oct. 5, 1861	3 yrs.	Appointed Oct.14,1861;promoted to Hospital Steward Jan.1,1863.

SIXTH REGIMENT OHIO VOLUNTEER CAVALRY

Names.	Rank.	Age.	Date of Entering the Service.	Period of Service.	Remarks.
Jacob A. Sager............	Corporal	20	Nov. 5, 1861	3 yrs.	Appointed April 20,1864;wounded May 28,1864,in action at Hawe's Shop,Va.; discharged March 27,1865,on Surgeon's certificate of disability; veteran.
Dwight H. Corey..........	...do...	21	Oct. 8, 1861	3 yrs.	Appointed Oct.14,1861;promoted to Regt.Com.Sergeant Oct.1,1862.
Aleinus W. Fenton........	...do...	22	Oct. 5, 1861	3 yrs.	Appointed Oct.14,1861;promoted to Sergt.Major April 1, 1863.
Frank E. Crosby..........	...do...	25	Oct. 5, 1861	3 yrs.	Appointed Oct.14,1861;promoted to Hospital Steward Oct.1,1862.
John R. Parshal..........	...do...	26	Oct. 5, 1861	3 yrs.	Appointed Oct.14,1861;promoted to Regt. Q.M.Sergeant Nov.1,1862.
James A. Joiner..........	...do...	24	Oct. 5, 1861	3 yrs.	Appointed Oct.14,1861;accidentally wounded Aug.27,1864;near Ream's Station,Va.;died Aug.31,1864;veteran.
Zacariah Herendene.......	...do...	18	Dec. 26, 1863	3 yrs.	Appointed March 1,1865;mustered out June 27,1865,at Petersburg,Va., by order of War Department.
Lyman Gale..............	...do...	18	Oct. 22, 1861	3 yrs.	Captured June 16,1864,at Petersburg, Va.;appointed June 1,1865;mustered out June 27,1865,at Petersburg,Va., by order of War Department;veteran.
James R. Wilson.........	...do...	18	Feb. 24, 1864	3 yrs.	Appointed May 1,1865;mustered out with company Aug.7,1865.
Liberty Raymond.........	...do...	20	Oct. 8, 1861	3 yrs.	Appointed April 1,1863;mustered out Oct.13,1864,at Columbus,O.,on expiration of term of service.
Joseph Jackson.........	...do...	23	Oct. 5, 1861	3 yrs.	Appointed Aug.1,1863;mustered out Oct.5,1864,on expiration of term of service.
George Sheldon.........	...do...	34	Oct. 5, 1861	3 yrs.	Appointed --;discharged March 11,1863, by order of War Department.

ROSTER OF OHIO TROOPS.

Names.	Rank.	Age.	Date of Entering the Service.	Period of Service.	Remarks.
Allen L. Parker..........	Corporal	22	Oct. 5, 1861	3 yrs.	Appointed July 10,1864;mustered out Oct.5,1864,on expiration of term of service.
Arthur Holderidge........	...do...	22	Oct. 26, 1861	3 yrs.	Appointed June 1,1865;mustered out June 27,1865,at Petersburg,Va.,by order of War Department; veteran.
Fayette Babcock..........	...do...	24	Oct. 8, 1861	3 yrs.	Appointed Oct.15,1862;died Sept. 20 1864, at Washington,D.C.; veteran.
John Bell................	...do...	24	Oct. 12, 1861	3 yrs.	Appointed Jan.1,1863;mustered out Oct.12,1864,on expiration of term of service.
Albert C. Champion.......	...do...	....	Sept.12, 1862	3 yrs.	Appointed Feb.1,1863;wounded Sept.14, 1863,at Rapidan Station,Va.;discharged April 20,1864,on Surgeon's certificate of disability.
John Allison.............	...do...	28	Oct. 5, 1861	3 yrs.	Appointed April 1,1863;wounded June 21, 1863,at Upperville,Va.;mustered out Oct.5,1864, on expiration of term of service.
Henry F. Sager..........	Bugler	24	Nov. 5, 1861	3 yrs.	Discharged Oct.30,1862,at Washington, D.C.,by order of War Department.
Addison Harrington.......	...do...	....	Dec. 10, 1861	3 yrs.	Discharged Nov.1,1862,at Washington, D.C.,by order of War Department.
Thomas Kinghorn..........	Farrier	32	Oct. 18, 1861	3 yrs.	Promoted to Regt. Veterinary Surgeon Dec.31,1861.
Robert Kinghorn..........	...do...	28	Oct. 14, 1861	3 yrs.	Promoted to Regt. Veterinary Surgeon May 1,1863.
Alman C. Brockaway.......	...do...	20	Oct. 19, 1861	3 yrs.	Mustered out June 27,1865,at Petersburg, Va.,by order of War Department;veteran.
John Doyle...............	...do...	26	Jan. 18, 1864	3 yrs.	Mustered out June 27,1865,at Petersburg, Va.,by order of War Department.

95

SIXTH REGIMENT OHIO VOLUNTEER CAVALRY

Names.	Rank.	Age.	Date of Entering the Service.	Period of Service.	Remarks.
Benjamin Bingham.........	Wagoner	44	Oct. 6, 1861	3 yrs.	Promoted to 2d Lieutenant Co. E Feb. 10, 1863.
Babcock, Parmenio M.......	Private	19	Mch. 31, 1864	3 yrs.	Mustered out June 27,1865,at Petersburg, Va.,by order of War Department.
Bailey, Edwin.............	...do...	20	Oct. 8, 1861	3 yrs.	Died Oct. 22,1862,at Washington, D.C.
Ball, Edwin O.............	...do...	35	Dec. 6, 1861	3 yrs.	Wounded Oct.1,1864,at Waynesboro,Va.; mustered out Dec.13,1864,on expiration of term of service.
Ball, Orange A...........	...do...	30	Oct. 5, 1861	3 yrs.	Acting Hospital Steward since June 3, 1864, mustered out Oct.5,1864, on expiration of term of service.
Barber, Alfred...........	...do...	24	Oct. 15, 1861	3 yrs.	Mustered out June 27,1865,at Petersburg, Va.,by order of War Department;veteran.
Bassett, Nathan M........	...do...	29	Oct. 5, 1861	3 yrs.	Mustered out Oct.5,1864,on expiration of term of service.
Basworth, Daniel.........	...do...	35	Oct. 2, 1862	9 mos.	Drafted; mustered out July 29, 1863, on expiration of term of service.
Bazer, Gotleib...........	...do...	32	Feb. 29, 1864	3 yrs.	Mustered out June 27,1865,at Petersburg, Va.,by order of War Department
Berry, Lyman A...........	...do...	29	Oct. 5, 1861	3 yrs.	Transferred to Veteran Reserve Corps Sept.1,1863,from which mustered out Oct.4,1864, on expiration of term of service.
Bigelow, Daniel J........	...do...	18	Oct. 26, 1863	3 yrs.	Wounded May 28,1864,at Hawe's Shop, Va.;discharged April 18,1865 on Surgeon's certificate of disability.
Bigelow, George A........	...do...	19	Oct. 5, 1861	3 yrs.	Killed Jan.27,1864,while on picket near Warrenton, Va.; veteran.
Biggin, William H........	...do...	26	Oct. 5, 1861	3 yrs.	
Biggin, Job..............	...do...	19	Oct. 5, 1861	3 yrs.	Mustered out Oct.5,1864,on expiration of term of service.

ROSTER OF OHIO TROOPS

Names.	Rank.	Age.	Date of Entering the Service.	Period of Service.	Remarks.
Biggin, Thomas...........	Private	24	Oct. 5, 1861	3 yrs.	Mustered out Oct. 5,1864, on expiration of term of service.
Bingham, Salusbury F.....	...do...	20	Feb. 28, 1865	1 yr.	Mustered out with company Aug.7,1865.
Blood, Erastus R.........	...do...	28	Oct. 4, 1861	3 yrs.	Promoted to Captain Co. H, 5th Regiment U.S.Colored Troops,Sept.21,1863,from which he resigned Aug.28,1864.
Carey, John..............	...do...	18	Feb. 24, 1864	3 yrs.	
Carter, George D.........	...do...	37	Oct. 5, 1861	3 yrs.	Discharged Dec.26,1862,on Surgeon's certificate of disability.
Casebeer, Alvin B........	...do...	30	June 28, 1864	3 yrs.	Mustered out June 27,1865,at Petersburg, Va.,by order of War Department;veteran.
Case, Asa................	...do...	45	Oct. 5, 1861	3 yrs.	Discharged May 3,1864,at Camp Chase,O., on Surgeon's certificate of disability.
Chaffee, Simon U.........	...do...	32	Oct. 5, 1861	3 yrs.	Discharged Nov.7,1862,at Washington, D.C.,on Surgeon's certificate of disability.
Cleflen, Martin..........	...do...	22	Dec. 16, 1863	3 yrs.	Wounded Oct.1,1864,at Hatcher's Run, Va.;transferred to Veteran Reserve Corps.
Collins, John............	...do...	26	Dec. 22, 1863	3 yrs.	
Craft, Watson............	...do...	18	Oct. 22, 1861	3 yrs.	Mustered out Oct. 22,1864,on expiration of term of service.
Crosby, Albert C.........	...do...	20	Sept. 2, 1862	3 yrs.	Mustered out May 30,1865,at Petersburg, Va.,by order of War Department.
Curtis, Martin...........	...do...	20	Oct. 2, 1862	9 mos.	Drafted;mustered out July 29,1863,on expiration of term of service.
Dewyant, Michael.........	...do...	18	Feb. 12, 1864	3 yrs.	Wounded June 24,1864,at St. Mary's Church,Va.;discharged May 31,1865,at Alexandria,Va.,on Surgeon's certificate of disability.

97

SIXTH REGIMENT OHIO VOLUNTEER CAVALRY

Names.	Rank.	Age.	Date of Entering the Service.	Period of Service.	Remarks.
Dilworth, Samuel..........	Private	38	Jan. 7, 1864	3 yrs.	On detached duty Aug.7,1865; no further record found.
Dimich, Jonathan C.......	...do...	51	Oct. 5, 1861	3 yrs.	Discharged May 27,1862, on Surgeon's certificate of disability.
Drew, Albert.............	...do...	19	Oct. 5, 1861	3 yrs.	Captured Nov.2,1863,near Sulphur Springs,Va.;died April 30,1864, at Baltimore, Md.
Dunfee, Edward..........	...do...	25	Dec. 29, 1863	3 yrs.	
Easterwood, George W.....	...do...	27	Feb. 24, 1864	3 yrs.	Transferred to Veteran Reserve Corps Sept.16,1864;no further record found.
Eastwood, Abram..........	...do...	37	Feb. 20, 1864	3 yrs.	Mustered out June 27,1865,at Petersburg, Va.,by order of War Department.
Eberling, John...........	...do...	17	Oct. 1, 1862	9 mos.	Drafted; mustered out July 29,1863,on expiration of term of service.
Edney, George...........	...do...	24	Oct. 5, 1861	3 yrs.	Died May 18, 1862, at Camp Chase, O.
Elliott, Joseph.........	...do...	20	Dec. 21, 1863	3 yrs.	
Evans, Daniel...........	...do...	35	Oct. 5, 1861	3 yrs.	
Feidler, Charles........	...do...	32	Oct. 5, 1861	3 yrs.	Discharged Aug.21,1862,at Fort McHenry, Md.,on Surgeon's certificate of disability.
Fenton, Arthur E........	...do...	22	Oct. 22, 1861	3 yrs.	Mustered out Nov.2,1864,at Columbus, O.,on expiration of term of service.
Fenton, Lucius.........	...do...	24	Oct. 5, 1861	3 yrs.	Wounded May 8,1864,at Spottsylvania Court House,Va.;transferred to Veteran Reserve Corps April 20,1865;from which mustered out Aug.25,1865,at Washington, D.C.,by order of War Department;veteran.
French, Edwin..........	...do...	26	Oct. 5, 1861	3 yrs.	Discharged Dec.1,1862,at Chantilly, Va.,on Surgeon's certificate of disability.

Names.	Rank.	Age.	Date of Entering the Service.	Period of Service.	Remarks.
Goodrich, Payson E........	Private	17	Feb. 28, 1865	1 yr.	Mustered out July 18,1865,at Petersburg, Va.,by order of War Department.
Grover, William O.........	...do...	24	Oct. 12, 1861	3 yrs.	Mustered out Oct.12,1864,on expiration of term of service.
Harker, Henry.............	...do...	32	Jan. 12, 1864	3 yrs.	Mustered out to date Aug.7,1865,at Columbus,Ohio,by order of War Department.
Hazell, Warren J..........	...do...	21	Feb. 20, 1864	3 yrs.	Captured June 16,1864,near Petersburg, Va.;mustered out June 11,1865,at Camp Chase,O.,by order of War Department.
Higgins, Benjamin.........	...do...	34	Oct. 2, 1862	9 mos.	Drafted; mustered out July 29,1863,on expiration of term of service.
Holdridge, Henry..........	...do...	26	Oct. 5, 1861	3 yrs.	Wounded May 12,1864,at Meadow Bridge, Va.;mustered out Oct.5,1864,at Columbus, O.,on expiration of term of service.
Hopkins, Michael..........	...do...	20	Feb. 8, 1864	3 yrs.	
Hoyt, Augustus O..........	...do...	28	Oct. 5, 1861	3 yrs.	Discharged April 4,1864,at Warrenton, Va.,on Surgeon's certificate of disability.
Halbert, Alonzo...........	...do...	....	Oct. 28, 1861	3 yrs.	Died Feb.7,1863,at Philadelphia, Pa.
Hutchinson, Chancey G.....	...do...	25	Mch. 8, 1865	1 yr.	Mustered out June 27,1865,at Petersburg, Va.,by order of War Department.
Jenkins, Charles H........	...do...	19	Oct. 21, 1861	3 yrs.	Died Feb.5,1862,at Camp Dennison,O.
Joiner, Francis M.........	...do...	18	Dec. 28, 1863	3 yrs.	Mustered out with company Aug.7,1865.
Joiner, William R.........	...do...	22	Feb. 28, 1865	1 yr.	Mustered out with company Aug.7,1865.
Kehres, George...........	...do...	....	Oct. 14, 1861	3 yrs.	
Krohl, Linus, Jr..........	...do...	27	Oct. 21, 1861	3 yrs.	Discharged April 9,1862,at Camp Chase, O.,on Surgeon's certificate of disability.

SIXTH REGIMENT OHIO VOLUNTEER CAVALRY

Names.	Rank.	Age.	Date of Entering the Service.	Period of Service.	Remarks.
Losey, Daniel..........	Private	....	Oct. 17, 1861	3 yrs.	Wounded June 21,1863,at Upperville, Va.; May 28,1864,at Hawes Shop,Va.; mustered out Oct.17,1864,on expiration of term of service.
Marsh, Morris..........	...do...	39	Oct. 5, 1861	3 yrs.	Mustered out June 27,1865,at Petersburg, Va.,by order of War Department;veteran.
Moses, Henry..........	...do...	29	Nov. 1, 1861	3 yrs.	Discharged Aug.17,1862,on Surgeon's certificate of disability.
Moses, William R.......	...do...	45	Oct. 5, 1861	3 yrs.	Discharged July 18, 1862,by order of War Department.
McLane, Johnston......	...do...	18	Oct. 21, 1861	3 yrs.	Wounded Jan.27,1864;mustered out Oct. 5,1864,on expiration of term of service.
McLaren, John W........	...do...	20	Feb. 25, 1864	3 yrs.	Mustered out June 27,1865,at Petersburg, Va.,by order of War Department.
Nevins, Frederick B.....	...do...	22	Oct. 18, 1862	9 mos.	Drafted;mustered out July 29,1863,on expiration of term of service.
Northway, Francis M.....	...do...	19	Oct. 5, 1861	3 yrs.	Mustered out Oct.5,1864,on expiration of term of service.
Northway, Edward C.......	...do...	21	Oct. 5, 1861	3 yrs.	Captured May 9,1864,at Mitchell's Shop, Va.;died Dec.1,1864,at Annapolis,Md.; veteran.
Northway, Pennington J...	...do...	22	Oct. 5, 1861	3 yrs.	Discharged Dec.22,1862,at Stafford Court House,Va.,on Surgeon's certificate of disability.
Northway, Marshall C.....	...do...	24	Oct. 1, 1861	3 yrs.	Captured Oct.1,1864,at Yellow Tavern, Va.;mustered out June 15,1865,at Camp Chase,O.,by order of War Department; veteran.
Northway, Sherman B......	...do...	20	June 26, 1863	3 yrs.	Captured May 28,1864,at Hawe's Shop, Va.;mustered out June 11,1865,at Camp Chase,O.,by order of War Department.

Names.	Rank.	Age.	Date of Entering the Service.	Period of Service.	Remarks.
Northway, Miron E.........	Private	18	Jan. 1, 1864	3 yrs.	Discharged Dec.27,1864,at Cleveland, O.,on Surgeon's certificate of disability.
Plumb, Charles Squire....	...do...	31	Nov. 11, 1863	3 yrs.	Mustered out with company Aug.7,1865.
Pool, Nathan.............	...do...	23	Feb. 28, 1865	1 yr.	Mustered out June 27,1865,at Petersburg, Va.,by order of War Department.
Randall, Daniel..........	...do...	20	Oct. 5, 1861	3 yrs.	Wounded May 9,1864,on Sheridan's Raid, Va.;mustered out Oct.5,1864,at Columbus, O.,on expiration of term of service.
Randall, James R.........	...do...	27	Oct. 12, 1861	3 yrs.	Transferred to Veteran Reserve Corps Dec.1,1863,from which mustered out Oct. 12,1864,by order of War Department.
Reeves, Charles S........	...do...	24	Oct. 5, 1861	3 yrs.	Died Feb.17,1863,at Washington, D.C.
Rex, Daniel..............	...do...	44	Oct. 5, 1861	3 yrs.	Mustered out June 27,1865,at Petersburg, Va.,by order of War Department;veteran.
Rex, Samuel W............	...do...	20	Oct. 5, 1861	3 yrs.	Mustered out Oct.5,1864,on expiration of term of service.
Rider, Alenson K.........	...do...	31	Feb. 24, 1864	3 yrs.	Mustered out June 27,1865,at Petersburg, Va.,by order of War Department.
Rose, Salman.............	...do...	23	Oct. 5, 1861	3 yrs.	Mustered out Oct. 5,1864,on expiration of term of service.
Sager, Martin W..........	...do...	21	Oct. 5, 1861	3 yrs.	Wounded June 2,1862,near Woodstock, Va.;killed July 28,1864,in action near Malvern Hill,Va.;veteran.
Saunders, Ivory B........	...do...	21	Oct. 5, 1861	3 yrs.	Died May 5,1862,at Camp Chase, O.
Shaffer, Daniel..........	...do...	20	Oct. 2, 1862	9 mos.	Drafted;mustered out July 29,1863,on expiration of term of service.

101

SIXTH REGIMENT OHIO VOLUNTEER CAVALRY.

COMPANY B.

Mustered in January 29, 1863, at Camp Cleveland, Ohio, by Captain C. O. Howard, 18th Infantry, U.S.A., Mustering Officer. Mustered out Aug. 7, 1865, at Petersburg, Va., by L. H. Bowen, 1st Lieutenant and Acting Commissary of Musters, Mustering Officer Department of Virginia.

Names.	Rank.	Age.	Date of Entering the Service	Period of Service	Remarks.
George W. Dickinson.....	Captain	24	Oct. 15, 1862	3 yrs.	Mustered as 2d Lieutenant; promoted to Captain Jan. 29, 1863; to Major July 25, 1864.
Frank C. Loveland.......	...do...	23	Oct. 26, 1861	3 yrs.	Promoted from 1st Lieutenant Co. E July 25, 1864; to Lieut.Colonel April 8, 1865.
Orlando W. Ferry........	...do...	24	Oct. 5, 1861	3 yrs.	Promoted from 1st Lieutenant Co. D May 31, 1865; mustered out with company Aug. 7, 1865; veteran.
Eusebius S. Austin......	1st Lieut.	24	Oct. 5, 1861	3 yrs.	Promoted from Sergt. Major to 2d Lieutenant Oct. 20, 1862; to 1st Lieutenant Jan. 29, 1863; to Captain Co. G May 9, 1864.
George W. Shattuck......	...do...	28	Nov. 6, 1861	3 yrs.	Promoted from 2d Lieutenant Co. H May 9, 1864; to Captain Co. H Nov. 12, 1864.
Albert W. Stiles........	...do...	34	Oct. 5, 1861	3 yrs.	Promoted from 2d Lieutenant Co. D Nov. 12, 1864; to Captain Co. E Jan. 31, 1865; veteran.
James McFarland.........	...do...	21	Oct. 21, 1861	3 yrs.	Promoted from 2d Lieutenant Co. F April 8, 1865; commissioned Captain July 30, 1865, but not mustered; mustered out with company Aug. 7, 1865; veteran.

ROSTER OF OHIO TROOPS.

Names.	Rank.	Age.	Date of Entering the Service.	Period of Service.	Remarks.
William C. St. John	2d Lieut.	44	Oct. 27, 1862	3 yrs.	Mustered as 2d Lieutenant; discharged Nov. 25, 1863, on Surgeon's certificate of disability.
Joel A. Clark	...do...	20	Oct. 21, 1862	3 yrs.	Mustered as private; appointed 1st Sergeant Dec. 10, 1862; promoted to 2d Lieutenant to date Feb. 18, 1864; to 1st Lieutenant and Regt. Quartermaster Nov. 12, 1864.
James E. Darwent	...do...	22	Jan. 2, 1864	3 yrs.	Promoted from Sergt. Major April 8, 1865; commissioned 1st Lieutenant May 31, 1865; Captain July 30, 1865, but not mustered on either commission; mustered out with company Aug. 7, 1865.
Frank D. Moran	1st Sergt.	22	Oct. 27, 1862	3 yrs.	Mustered as private; appointed Sergeant Dec. 10, 1862; 1st Sergeant April 1, 1864; promoted to 2d Lieutenant Co. M Nov. 12, 1864.
Aaron Wagoner	...do...	18	Nov. 10, 1862	3 yrs.	Appointed Corporal Dec. 10, 1862; Sergeant May 1, 1864; 1st Sergeant Jan. 1, 1865; promoted to 2d Lieutenant Co. M April 8, 1865.
David H. Sears	...do...	18	Nov. 1, 1862	3 yrs.	Mustered as private; appointed Sergeant Dec. 10, 1862; Q.M.Sergeant Feb. 1, 1865; 1st Sergeant May 1, 1865; captured Sept. 1, 1863, at Barber's Cross Roads, Va., commissioned 2d Lieutenant to date July 30, 1865, but not mustered; mustered out June 27, 1865, at Petersburg, Va., by order of War Department.

SIXTH REGIMENT OHIO VOLUNTEER CAVALRY.

Names.	Rank.	Age.	Date of Entering the Service.	Period of Service.	Remarks.
Wallace H. Bullard.......	Q.M.S.	33	Oct. 7, 1862	3 yrs.	Mustered as private; appointed Q.M.Sergeant Dec. 10, 1862; promoted to Regt. Q.M.Sergeant Nov. 10, 1864.
John G. Dobbs............	...do...	21	Nov. 3, 1862	3 yrs.	Appointed Corporal Dec. 10, 1862; wounded May 7, 1864, in battle of the Wilderness; promoted to Sergeant Feb. 1, 1865; to Q.M.Sergeant May 1, 1865; mustered out June 27, 1865, at Petersburg, Va., by order of War Department.
William A. Sawyer........	Com.Ser.	26	Nov. 1, 1862	3 yrs.	Appointed Corporal Dec. 10, 1862; Com. Sergeant June 1, 1863; mustered out June 27, 1865, at Petersburg, Va., by order of War Department.
Sir Isaac Newton.........	Sergeant	18	Nov. 9, 1862	3 yrs.	Mustered as private; appointed Sergeant Dec. 10, 1862; died Aug. 28, 1864, at Hopkinton, New York.
Thaddeus S. Pierce.......	...do...	19	Nov. 10, 1862	3 yrs.	Mustered as private; appointed Sergeant Dec. 10, 1862; mustered out June 27, 1865, at Petersburg, Va., by order of War Department.
Stephen E. Bishop........	...do...	28	Oct. 13, 1862	3 yrs.	Mustered as private; appointed Sergeant Dec. 10, 1862; wounded July 28, 1864, at Deep Bottom, Va.; discharged March 14, 1865, on Surgeon's certificate of disability.
John A. Schaffer.........	...do...	25	Nov. 2, 1862	3 yrs.	Appointed Corporal Dec. 10, 1862; Sergeant Sept. 1, 1864; mustered out June 27, 1865, at Petersburg, Va., by order of War Department.

ROSTER OF OHIO TROOPS.

Names.	Rank.	Age.	Date of Entering the Service.	Period of Service.	Remarks.
Joseph Reimer............	Sergeant	18	Nov. 27, 1862	3 yrs.	Appointed Corporal May 1, 1864; Sergeant Feb. 1, 1865; mustered out June 27, 1865, at Petersburg, Va., by order of War Department.
Daniel Lahman............	...do...	18	Nov. 5, 1862	3 yrs.	Appointed Corporal Sept. 1, 1864; Sergeant April 1, 1865; mustered out June 27, 1865, at Petersburg, Va., by order of War Department.
Austin G. Jacobs.........	...do...	28	Nov. 17, 1862	3 yrs.	Appointed Corporal Feb. 1, 1865; Sergeant May 1, 1865; mustered out June 27, 1865, at Petersburg, Va., by order of War Department.
John G. McGregor.........	Corporal	20	Nov. 1, 1862	3 yrs.	Appointed Dec. 10, 1862; mustered out June 2, 1865, at Washington, D.C., by order of War Department.
John M. Struble..........	...do...	19	Oct. 5, 1862	3 yrs.	Appointed Dec. 10, 1862; died April 9, 1864, at Brandy Station, Va.
Jacob Kinsey.............	...do...	28	Nov. 3, 1862	3 yrs.	Appointed Dec. 10, 1862; mustered out June 27, 1865, at Petersburg, Va., by order of War Department.
Carlos F. McDonald.......	...do...	18	Nov. 1, 1862	3 yrs.	Appointed July 1, 1863; promoted to Chief Bugler Feb. 1, 1864.
Richard W. Evans.........	...do...	18	Nov. 5, 1862	3 yrs.	Appointed Nov. 1, 1863; captured in action May 23, 1864; last heard of in Andersonville Prison, Ga.; no further record found.
John W. Lockhart........	...do...	24	Oct. 17, 1862	3 yrs.	Appointed March 1, 1864; mustered out July 3, 1865, at Washington, D.C., by order of War Department.

SIXTH REGIMENT OHIO VOLUNTEER CAVALRY.

Names.	Rank.	Age.	Date of Entering the Service.	Period of Service.	Remarks.
William Williams........	Corporal	18	Oct. 30, 1862	3 yrs.	Appointed March 1, 1864; mustered out June 27, 1865, at Petersburg, Va., by order of War Department.
Calvin Sowers..........	...do...	20	Feb. 29, 1862	3 yrs.	Appointed Sept. 1, 1864; mustered out June 10, 1865, at Point Lookout, Md., by order of War Department.
Albert J. Clark........	...do...	18	Jan. 13, 1863	3 yrs.	Appointed Feb. 1, 1865; mustered out with company Aug. 7, 1865.
John E. Burns..........	...do...	18	Nov. 28, 1862	3 yrs.	Appointed April 1, 1865; captured Sept. 1, 1863, at Barber's Cross Roads, Va.; mustered out June 27, 1865, at Petersburg, Va., by order of War Department.
Thomas J. Heller........	Corporal	18	Nov. 8, 1862	3 yrs.	Appointed Saddler July 1, 1863; Corporal May 1, 1865; mustered out June 27, 1865,
Homer Gridley..........	Bugler	19	Oct. 18, 1862	3 yrs.	Appointed Sept. 1, 1864; mustered out June 27, 1865, at Petersburg, Va., by order of War Department.
Joseph T. Seigfried......	...do...	18	Feb. 24, 1864	3 yrs.	Appointed Sept. 1, 1864; mustered out June 27, 1865, at Petersburg, Va., by order of War Department.
Hiram Ingalls..........	Farrier	44	Nov. 1, 1862	3 yrs.	Appointed July 1, 1863; wounded May 28, 1864, at Hawe's Shop, Va.; died June 2, 1864 at White House Landing, Va.
John C. Buchannan.......	...do...	22	Dec. 26, 1862	3 yrs.	Appointed Nov. 1, 1863;mustered out June 27, 1865, at Petersburg, Va., by order of War Department.

Names.	Rank.	Age.	Date of Entering the Service.	Period of Service.	Remarks.
Erastus R. Knowlton......	Farrier	44	Nov. 7, 1862	3 yrs.	Appointed ——; captured Nov. 21, 1863, at Fayetteville, Va..; died June 24, 1864, in Andersonville Prison, Ga.
Daniel Stetler...........	...do...	45	Nov. 10, 1862	3 yrs.	Captured July 4, 1863; transferred to Veteran Reserve Corps Dec. 5, 1863; died April 20, 1864, at Baltimore, Md.
Monroe McCollister.......	Saddler	21	Nov. 19, 1862	3 yrs.	Appointed Dec. 10, 1862; died April 17,1863, at Potomac Creek, Va.
Phillip Lambert..........	...do...	19	Nov. 3, 1862	3 yrs.	Appointed Sept. 1, 1864; mustered out with company Aug. 7, 1865.
Philip Baker.............	Wagoner	30	Nov. 19, 1862	3 yrs.	Appointed Dec. 10, 1862; died Oct. 8, 1863, at Washington,D.C.
Benjamin A. Garrett......	...do...	38	Nov. 4, 1862	3 yrs.	Appointed Dec. 10, 1862; mustered out June 27, 1865, at Petersburg,
P—— Moon.................	...do...	33	Nov. 7, 1862	3 yrs.	Appointed Dec. 10, 1862; wounded Sept. 1, 1863, at Barber's Cross Roads, Va.; died Jan. 14, 1864, at Richmond, Va.
——ridge, Oliver.........	Private	44	Nov. 21, 1862	3 yrs.	Reduced from Farrier Oct. 31, 1863; transferred to Veteran Reserve Corps Feb. 15, 1864; from which mustered out Nov. 21, 1865, at Baltimore, Md., by order of War Department.
——oid, Charles..........	...do...	38	Feb. 12, 1865	1 yr.	Mustered out June 27, 1865, at Petersburg, Va., by order of War Department.

SIXTH REGIMENT OHIO VOLUNTEER CAVALRY.

Names.	Rank.	Age.	Date of Entering the Service.	Period of Service.	Remarks.
Barrett, Robert	Private	22	Oct. 9, 1862	3 yrs.	Transferred to Co. G May 11, 1863
Beach, Lemuel	...do...	18	Feb. 26, 1864	3 yrs.	Mustered out June 27, 1865, at Petersburg, Va., by order of War Department.
Belleisle, Louis	...do...	24	Dec. 12, 1863	3 yrs.	Mustered out June 27, 1865, at Petersburg, Va., by order of War Department.
Bentz, Frederick	...do...	24	Nov. 6, 1862	3 yrs.	Mustered out June 27, 1865, at Petersburg, Va., by order of War Department.
Bissell, Collins J	...do...	19	Feb. 27, 1864	3 yrs.	Died Oct. 25, 1864, at Jefferson, O.
Bissell, Lorenzo	...do...	38	Oct. 7, 1862	3 yrs.	Mustered out June 27, 1865, at Petersburg, Va., by order of War Department.
Bloom, David	...do...	28	Oct. 7, 1862	3 yrs.	Died Feb. 20, 1864, at Washington, D.C.
Bradley, George	...do...	40	Nov. 3, 1862	3 yrs.	Mustered out June 27, 1865, at Petersburg, Va., by order of War Department.
Brink, Edward B	...do...	.....	Feb. 20, 1863	3 yrs.	Returned to 12th Regiment U.S. Infantry, where he had previously enlisted.
Brown, Buel	...do...	18	Mch. 17, 1865	1 yr.	Mustered out with company Aug. 7, 1865.
Brown, William	...do...	26	Feb. 27, 1864	3 yrs.	Mustered out June 27, 1865, at Petersburg, Va., by order of War Department.
Butler, Frederick H	...do...	19	Nov. 3, 1862	3 yrs.	Mustered out June 27, 1865, at Petersburg, Va., by order of War Department.

Names.	Rank.	Age.	Date of Entering the Service.	Period of Service.	Remarks.
Bush, Charles.............	Private	36	Feb. 24, 1863	3 yrs.	Captured Sept. 1, 1863; paroled Dec. 28, 1863, at City Point, Va.; no further record found.
Castello, Thomas.........	...do....	18	May 30, 1864	3 yrs.	Mustered out with company Aug. 7, 1865.
Chase, Osmer C...........	...do....	23	Oct. 21, 1861	3 yrs.	Transferred to Co. G May 11, 1862.
Chapman, Josiah S........	...do....	40	Nov. 17, 1862	3 yrs.	Discharged May 1, 1863, on Surgeon's certificate of disability.
Childs, William..........	...do....	18	Mch. 13, 1865	1 yr.	Mustered out with company Aug. 7, 1865.
Clark, Lester A..........	...do....	40	Mch. 17, 1865	1 yr.	Mustered out June 27, 1865, at Petersburg, Va., by order of War Department.
Culp, Samuel.............	...do....	18	Nov. 1, 1862	3 yrs.	Transferred to Veteran Reserve Corps Feb. 15, 1864; no further record found.
Culp, William R..........	...do....	18	Oct. 27, 1862	3 yrs.	Mustered out June 27, 1865, at Petersburg, Va., by order of War Department.
Darrow, Lorenzo..........	...do....	42	Oct. 9, 1861	3 yrs.	Transferred to Co. G May 11, 1862.
Darrow, Milton...........	...do....	34	Oct. 21, 1861	3 yrs.	Transferred to Co. G May 11, 1862.
Delaney, Thomas..........	...do....	22	Aug. 2, 1864	3 yrs.	Sent to General Hospital May—, 1865; no further record found.
Day, Hamilton S.E.......	...do....	18	Jan. 28, 1864	3 yrs.	Mustered out June 27, 1865, at Petersburg, Va., by order of War Department.
Dermick, William........	...do....	23	Jan. 16, 1863	3 yrs.	Wounded July 30, 1864, at Petersburg, Va.; discharged May 24, 1865, at Camp Dennison, O., on Surgeon's certificate of disability.

SIXTH REGIMENT OHIO VOLUNTEER CAVALRY.

Names.	Rank.	Age.	Date of Entering the Service.	Period of Service.	Remarks.
Earnest, Charles.........	Private	18	Dec. 26, 1862	3 yrs.	
Feidler, Charles.........	...do...	34	Oct. 6, 1864	1 yr.	Mustered out June 9, 1865, at Philadelphia, Pa., by order of War Department.
Fink, William...........	...do...	36	Oct. 6, 1862	3 yrs.	Captured July 4, 1863, at Fairfield, Pa., died Nov. 18, 1863, at Richmond, Va.
Fisher, John............	...do...	26	Aug. 5, 1864	3 yrs.	Mustered out with company Aug. 7, 1865.
Folley, Thomas..........	...do...	18	Oct. 9, 1862	3 yrs.	Died July 22, 1864, in hospital at City Point, Virginia.
Ford, Samuel J..........	...do...	18	Oct. 16, 1862	3 yrs.	Killed Sept. 1, 1863, at Barber's Cross Road (Orleans), Va.
Gallagher, William......	...do...	.....	Nov. 16, 1864	3 yrs.	Mustered out with company Aug. 7, 1865.
Garrett, George W.......	...do...	18	Jan. 5, 1863	3 yrs.	Died Dec. 27, 1864, at Brimfield, O.
Gates, Samuel...........	...do...	26	Jan. 27, 1863	3 yrs.	Discharged Aug. 17, 1863, at Philadelphia, Pa., on Surgeon's certificate of disability.
Geisinger, Samuel.......	...do...	35	Dec. 1, 1863	3 yrs.	Mustered out June 27, 1865, at Petersburg, Va., by order of War Department.
Goller, Jacob...........	...do...	25	Nov. 19, 1862	3 yrs.	Mustered out June 27, 1865, at Petersburg, Va., by order of War Department.
Gray, William P.........	...do...	18	Nov. 1, 1862	3 yrs.	Killed May 20, 1863, at Dumfries, Va., by accidental discharge of carbine.
Grubb, Simon P..........	...do...	20	Dec. 30, 1863	3 yrs.	Killed May 28, 1864, in action at Hawe's Shop, Virginia.

Names.	Rank.	Age.	Date of Entering the Service.	Period of Service.	Remarks.
Gerdley, Charles H......	Private	18	Oct. 29, 1862	3 yrs.	Mustered out June 27, 1865, at Petersburg, Va., by order of War Department.
Happert, George.........	...do...	19	Sept. 13, 1864	1 yr.	
Hawk, Michael W.........	...do...	44	Oct. 23, 1862	3 yrs.	Discharged Feb. 11, 1864, at Columbus, O., on Surgeon's certificate of disability.
Heriff, Henry..........	...do...	27	Nov. 3, 1862	3 yrs.	Transferred to Veteran Reserve Corps Dec. 2, 1864; no further record found.
Hickock, Sidney G........	...do...	18	Mch. 18, 1865	1 yr.	Mustered out June 27, 1865, at Petersburg, Va., by order of War Department.
Holcomb, Orson G.........	...do...	18	Nov. 23, 1862	3 yrs.	Discharged Feb. 9, 1864, on Surgeon's certificate of disability.
Howell, John W..........	...do...	32	Nov. 7, 1862	3 yrs.	Reduced from Com.Sergeant June 1, 1863; mustered out July 5, 1865, at Columbus, O., by order of War Department.
Hull, Harvey...........	...do...	26	Feb. 20, 1863	3 yrs.	Discharged Dec. 11, 1863, on Surgeon's certificate of disability; see battery D, 1st Regiment O.V.L.A.
Isham, Edward R..........	...do...	18	Mch. 9, 1865	1 yr.	Mustered out June 8, 1865, at Columbus, O., by order of War Department.
Kennedy, Hugh...........	...do...	21	Jan. 13, 1863	3 yrs.	
Lackey, William.........	...do...	18	Oct. 11, 1862	3 yrs.	Died Oct. 6, 1863, of wounds received Sept. 1, 1863, at Barber's Cross Roads, Va.

SIXTH REGIMENT OHIO VOLUNTEER CAVALRY.

Name.	Rank.	Age.	Date of Entering the Service.	Period of Service.	Remarks.
McCarty, Benjamin........	Private	21	Dec. 22, 1863	3 yrs.	Discharged May 24, 1865, on Surgeon's certificate of disability.
McGregor, George........	...do...	26	Jan. 5, 1864	3 yrs.	Wounded May 28, 1864, at Hawe's Shop, Va.; mustered out Aug. 22, 1865, at Philadelphia, Pa., by order of War Department.
McGregor, James P.......	...do...	18	Dec. 30, 1863	3 yrs.	Wounded June 21, 1864, mustered out June 27, 1865, at Petersburg, Va., by order of War Department.
McMahan, John............	...do...	21	Nov. 4, 1862	3 yrs.	
McNalley, John...........	...do...	30	Dec. 28, 1863	3 yrs.	
Madden, Michael..........	...do...	45	Jan. 3, 1863	3 yrs.	Discharged June 12, 1864, on Surgeon's certificate of disability.
Mantle, Samuel...........	...do...	23	Nov. 4, 1862	3 yrs.	Mustered out June 24, 1865, at Chester, Pa., by order of War Department.
Minor, Samuel............	...do...	19	Oct. 6, 1862	3 yrs.	Wounded May 7, 1864, at Todd's Tavern, Va., wounded Feb. 5, 1865, at Hatcher's Run, Va., mustered out June 22, 1865, at Philadelphia, Pa., by order of War Department.
Morton, James............	...do...	44	Oct. 7, 1862	3 yrs.	Died Dec. 7, 1863, at Bryan, O.
Morris, Thomas T.........	...do...	.....	Oct. 21, 1861	3 yrs.	Discharged July 22, 1862, on Surgeon's certificate of disability.
Muthera, Robert.........	...do...	44	Dec. 30, 1862	3 yrs.	Discharged June 19, 1864, on Surgeon's certificate of disability.

ROSTER OF OHIO TROOPS.

Names.	Rank.	Age.	Date of Entering the Service	Period of Service.	Remarks.
Olmstead, Horace........	Private	34	Feb. 18, 1865	1 yr.	Mustered out June 27, 1865, at Petersburg, Va., by order of War Department.
Orcutt, Thomas B.C......	...do...	18	Feb. 18, 1864	3 yrs.	Mustered out June 27, 1865, at Petersburg, Va., by order of War Department.
Payne, Eugene..........	...do...	19	Oct. 15, 1864	1 yr.	Sent to hospital Feb. 1, 1865; no further record found.
Priest, Peter..........	...do...	40	Nov. 1, 1862	3 yrs.	Discharged April 25, 1864, at Columbus, O., by order of War Department.
Ramalia, William........	...do...	18	Jan. 12, 1863	3 yrs.	Prisoner of war; mustered out June 27, 1865, at Petersburg, Va., by order of War Department.
Rice, Stanford.........	...do...	40	Jan. 6, 1863	3 yrs.	Sent to hospital April 30, 1863; no further record found.
Richards, Alexander.....	...do...	18	Mch. 10, 1865	1 yr.	Mustered out June 27, 1865, at Petersburg, Va., by order of War Department.
Rigal, Franklin S........	...do...	18	Nov. 7, 1862	3 yrs.	Mustered out June 27, 1865, at Petersburg, Va., by order of War Department.
Robins, Henry T.........	...do...	23	Oct. 7, 1862	3 yrs.	Mustered out June 27, 1865, at Petersburg, Va., by order of War Department.
Rutherford, Elliott......	...do...	34	Aug. 4, 1864	1 yr.	Sent to hospital from Depot ——; no further record found.
Sausaman, Frederick.....	...do...	29	Nov. 7, 1862	3 yrs.	Mustered out June 27, 1865, at Petersburg, Va., by order of War Department.

113

SIXTH REGIMENT OHIO VOLUNTEER CAVALRY.

Names.	Rank.	Age.	Date of Entering the Service.	Period of Service.	Remarks.
Schweitzer, Jacob D.	Private	36	Nov. 3, 1862	3 yrs.	Discharged Nov. 8, 1864, at Washington, D.C., on Surgeon's certificate of disability.
Seigfried, Samuel	...do...	19	Feb. 24, 1864	3 yrs.	Wounded May 28, 1864, at Hawe's Shop, Va.; mustered out June 27, 1865, at Petersburg, Va., by order of War Department.
Shaffer, Charles W.	...do...	18	Oct. 19, 1863	3 yrs.	
Shutt, Joseph	...do...	21	Nov. 5, 1862	3 yrs.	Mustered out with company Aug. 7, 1865.
Simpson, Mark	...do...	19	Dec. 19, 1863	3 yrs.	
Smart, Asa N.	...do...	21	Dec. 24, 1863	3 yrs.	Mustered out June 27, 1865, at Petersburg, Va., by order of War Department.
Smith, Moses	...do...	32	Nov. 3, 1862	3 yrs.	Discharged Dec. 13, 1864, at New York, on Surgeon's certificate of disability.
Smith, George M.	...do...	36	Oct. 17, 1862	3 yrs.	Died Aug. 26, 1863, of wounds received June 19, 1863, at Middleburg, Va.
Smith, William H.	...do...	20	Feb. 21, 1864	3 yrs.	Transferred to the Navy April 29, 1864.
Starkweather, Jerome	...do...	18	Oct. 6, 1862	3 yrs.	Died March 26, 1864, at Cleveland, O.
Steadman, Charles G.	...do...	18	Mch. 17, 1864	3 yrs.	Promoted to Regt. Hospital Steward Dec. 1, 1864.
Superment, Napoleon	...do...	19	Dec. 12, 1863	3 yrs.	Captured May 9, 1864, on Sheridan's Raid, Virginia; mustered out June 16, 1865, at Columbus, O., by order of War Department.

ROSTER OF OHIO TROOPS.

Names.	Rank.	Age.	Date of Entering the Service	Period of Service	Remarks.
Sutter, Harvey..........	Private	23	Aug. 3, 1864	3 yrs.	Sent to hospital May —, 1865; no further record found.
Taylor, Allen............	...do....	27	Jan. 23, 1863	3 yrs.	Killed Oct. 14, 1863, in action at Auburn Mills, Virginia.
Taylor, Charles.........	...do....	23	Dec. 28, 1863	3 yrs.	
Thompson, Luther J.......	...do....	29	Oct. 27, 1864	1 yr.	Mustered out June 27, 1865, at Petersburg, Va., by order of War Department.
Torrence, Corrodon......	...do....	44	Oct. 5, 1862	3 yrs.	Mustered out June 27, 1865, at Petersburg, Va., by order of War Department.
Trimble, Joseph.........	...do....	18	Feb. 21, 1864	3 yrs.	
Tyler, Stephen A........	...do....	18	Feb. 21, 1865	1 yr.	Mustered out with company Aug. 7, 1865.
Underwood, Eberly B......	...do....	24	Jan. 5, 1864	3 yrs.	Mustered out June 27, 1865, at Petersburg, Va., by order of War Department.
Webster, Samuel H.......	...do....	18	Jan. 5, 1864	3 yrs.	Wounded May 28, 1864, at Hawe's Shop, Va.; mustered out June 27, 1865, at Petersburg, Va., by order of War Department.
Wells, Joseph...........	...do....	19	Aug. 22, 1864	1 yr.	Mustered out June 27, 1865, at Petersburg, Va., by order of War Department.
Wilsey, Moses D.........	...do....	22	Oct. 17, 1862	3 yrs.	Mustered out June 27, 1865, at Petersburg, Va., by order of War Department.
Wise, Uriah J...........	...do....	20	Nov. 1, 1862	3 yrs.	Mustered out June 27, 1865, at Petersburg, Va., by order of War Department.

SIXTH REGIMENT OHIO VOLUNTEER CAVALRY.

Names.	Rank.	Age.	Date of Entering the Service.	Period of Service.	Remarks.
Wittick, Charles........	Private	44	Oct. 30, 1862	3 yrs.	Transferred to Veteran Reserve Corps Aug. 1, 1863; mustered out Aug. 10, 1865, at Washington, D.C., by order of War Department.
Young, Lorenzo..........	...do...	19	Nov. 4, 1862	3 yrs.	Died Aug. 26, 1863, at Washington, D.C.

COMPANY C.

Mustered in from October 7 to December 12, 1861, at Camp Hutchins, Warren, O., by John H. Cryer, John P. Holt, and D. Anderson, U.S. Mustering Officers. Mustered out August 7, 1865, at Petersburg, Va., by L. H. Bowen, 1st Lieutenant and Acting Commissary of Musters, Mustering Officer District of Virginia.

Names.	Rank.	Age.	Date of Entering the Service.	Period of Service.	Remarks.
John Henry Cryer........	Captain	26	Oct. 7, 1861	3 yrs.	Mustered as 2d Lieutenant; promoted to Captain Nov. 28, 1861; to Major Aug. 3, 1863.
James Henry Leeman.......	...do...	27	Oct. 7, 1861	3 yrs.	Mustered as private; promoted to 1st Lieutenant Dec. 10, 1861; to Captain Aug. 3, 1863; mustered out Oct. 6, 1864, on expiration of term of service.
Matthew H. Cryer........	...do...	23	Oct. 16, 1863	3 yrs.	Promoted from 1st Lieutenant Co. M Nov. 12, 1864; promoted to Major April 8, 1865.
Hiram G. Suiter.........	...do...	23	Dec. 11, 1861	3 yrs.	Promoted from 2d Lieutenant Co. K April 8, 1865; mustered out with company Aug. 7, 1865.
John L. Miller..........	1st Lieut.		Oct. 7, 1861	3 yrs.	Mustered as private; promoted to 2d Lieutenant Dec. 10, 1861; to 1st Lieutenant April 12, 1864; to Captain Co. I July 25, 1864.

SIXTH REGIMENT OHIO VOLUNTEER CAVALRY

Names.	Rank.	Age.	Date of Entering the Service.	Period of Service.	Remarks.
Joel A. Clark..........	R.Q.M.	20	Oct. 21, 1862	3 yrs.	Promoted from 2d Lieutenant Co. B Nov. 12, 1864; promoted to Captain Jan. 31, 1865, but declined promotion; discharged June 10, 1865.
John R. Parshal..........	...do...	26	Oct. 5, 1861	3 yrs.	Promoted to Q.M.Sergeant from Corporal Co. A Nov. 1, 1862; to 1st Lieutenant and Quartermaster Aug. 3, 1863; mustered out Oct. 12, 1864, on expiration of term of service.
Uriel H. Hutchins........	B.Q.M.	....	Oct. 28, 1861	3 yrs.	Supposed to have been discharged; no official notice received.
William H. Woodrow......	...do...	....	Nov. 5, 1861	3 yrs.	Transferred to 11th Regiment O.V.C. Sept. 20, 1862.
Charles B. Bostwick.....	...do...	....	Dec. 12, 1861	3 yrs.	Resigned May 16, 1862.
Charles C. Baker........	R.C.S.	19	Oct. 7, 1861	3 yrs.	Promoted from Sergeant Co. C Aug. 3, 1863; mustered out Nov. 27, 1864, on expiration of term of service.
Dwight H. Cory..........	...do...	21	Oct. 8, 1861	3 yrs.	Promoted to Regt. Com. Sergeant from Corporal Co. A Oct. 1, 1862; to 1st Lieutenant and Commissary of Subsistence Nov. 12, 1864; promoted to Captain May 31, 1865, but not mustered; mustered out with regiment Aug. 7, 1865; veteran.
Eusebius S. Austin.......	Ser.Maj.	21	Oct. 5, 1861	3 yrs.	Promoted from private Co. L Dec. 16, 1861; to 2d Lieutenant Co. B Oct. 20, 1862.

Names.	Rank.	Age.	Date of Entering the Service.	Period of Service.	Remarks.
William L. Thomas.......	1st Lieut.	29	Oct. 22, 1861	3 yrs.	Mustered as private; appointed 1st Sergeant Dec. 22, 1861; promoted to 2d Lieutenant Co. E April 1, 1862; to 1st Lieutenant Co. C July 25,1864; to Captain Co. F Nov. 12, 1864;vet.
David C. Ruhl...........	...do....	33	Oct. 28, 1861	3 yrs.	Mustered as private; appointed Sergeant Sept. 10, 1863; 1st Sergeant Jan. 1, 1864; promoted to 1st Lieutenant Jan. 31, 1865; resigned May 25, 1865; veteran.
Alcinus W. Fenton.......	2d Lieut.	22	Oct. 5, 1861	3 yrs.	Promoted from Sergt. Major May 9, 1864; to 1st Lieutenant and Adjutant Nov. 12, 1864; veteran.
William K. Kneal........	...do....	20	Oct. 30, 1861	3 yrs.	Promoted from Regt. Com. Sergeant April 8, 1865; promoted to 1st Lieutenant May 31, 1865, but not mustered; mustered out with company Aug. 7, 1865; veteran.
Dewayne W. Suydam.......	1st Sergt.	31	Oct. 7, 1861	3 yrs.	Mustered as private; appointed Q.M. Sergeant Dec. 10, 1861; 1st Sergeant Feb. 6, 1865; promoted to 2d Lieutenant May 31, 1865; 1st Lieutenant July 30, 1865, but not mustered on either promotion; mustered out with company Aug. 7, 1865, veteran.
Calvin H. Thomas........	Q.M.S.	18	Oct. 7, 1861	3 yrs.	Appointed Corporal ——; Sergeant Sept. 1, 1864; Q.M.Sergeant Feb. 6, 1865; wounded Dec. 9, 1864, at Hatcher's Run, Va.; mustered out with company Aug. 7,1865;veteran.

SIXTH REGIMENT OHIO VOLUNTEER CAVALRY.

Names.	Rank.	Age.	Date of Entering the Service.	Period of Service.	Remarks.
Hebron H. Dilley........	Com.Ser.	33	Oct. 7, 1861	3 yrs.	Appointed Corporal Dec. 10, 1861; Sergeant Feb. 20, 1862; Com.Sergeant —; discharged July 19, 1865, on Surgeon's certificate of disability.
Charles C. Baker........	Sergeant	19	Oct. 7, 1861	3 yrs.	Mustered as private; appointed Sergeant Dec. 10, 1861; promoted to 1st Lieutenant and Regt. Commissary of Subsistence Aug. 3, 1863.
Charles C. McCain.......	...do...	22	Oct. 7, 1861	3 yrs.	Mustered as private; appointed Sergeant Dec. 10, 1861; promoted to Regt. Q.M.Sergeant Jan. 1, 1862.
Philo Huxley............	...do...	19	Oct. 7, 1861	3 yrs.	Mustered as private; appointed Sergeant Dec. 10, 1861; discharged Dec. 12, 1862, at Washington, D.C., on Surgeon's certificate of disability.
David Trescott..........	...do...	20	Nov. 1, 1861	3 yrs.	Mustered as private; appointed Sergeant Dec. 10, 1861; transferred to 2d Regiment O.V.C. March 1, 1862.
James W. Donaldson......	...do...	24	Oct. 7, 1861	3 yrs.	Appointed Corporal Dec. 10, 1861; Sergeant June 1, 1862; wounded May 9, 1864, on Richmond Raid; mustered out April 16, 1865, by order of War Department; veteran.
Joseph L. Philman.......	...do...	28	Oct. 7, 1861	3 yrs.	Appointed Corporal Dec. 10, 1861; Sergeant Jan. 10, 1863; promoted to 2d Lieutenant July 30, 1865, but not mustered; mustered out June 27, 1865, at Petersburg, Va., by order of War Department; veteran.

ROSTER OF OHIO TROOPS.

Names.	Rank.	Age.	Date of Entering the Service.	Period of Service.	Remarks.
Charles E. Holt.........	Sergeant	18	Oct. 20, 1861	3 yrs.	Appointed Corporal Dec. 10,1861; Sergeant May 13, 1863; captured July 4, 1863, at Emmittsburgh, Md.; mustered out Nov. 11, 1864, on expiration of term of service; veteran.
Harris S. Ellett........	...do...	20	Oct. 8, 1861	3 yrs.	Appointed Corporal ——; Sergeant April 1, 1864; died July 15, 1864, at Alexandria, Va., of wounds received June 24, 1864, at St. Mary's Church, Va.; veteran.
Henry Smith.............	...do...	41	Nov. 14, 1861	3 yrs.	Appointed Corporal ——; Sergeant Sept. 1, 1864; captured Oct. 1, 1864, at Davis's Farm, Va.; died Dec. 17, 1864, in Salisbury Prison, N.C.; veteran.
William W. Reed.........	...do...	25	Dec. 12, 1861	3 yrs.	Appointed Corporal ——; Sergeant Sept. 1, 1864; mustered out to date Aug. 7, 1865; veteran.
Mark A. Nease...........	...do...	18	Nov. 28, 1861	3 yrs.	Appointed Corporal ——; Sergeant Feb. 5, 1865; mustered out June 27, 1865, at Petersburg, Va., by order of War Department; veteran
Edward Hughes..........	...do...	19	Nov. 29, 1861	3 yrs.	Appointed Corporal ——; Sergeant Feb. 6, 1865; mustered out with company Aug. 7, 1865; veteran.
Jacob Wagoner..........	...do...	18	Dec. 1, 1863	3 yrs.	Appointed Corporal Sept. 1, 1864; Sergeant April 18, 1865; mustered out with company Aug. 7, 1865;veteran.
William Haycox..........	Corporal	26	Oct. 7, 1861	3 yrs.	Appointed Dec. 10, 1861; captured July 4, 1863, at Emmittsburgh, Md.; died while a prisoner of war; date unknown.

SIXTH REGIMENT OHIO VOLUNTEER CAVALRY.

Names.	Rank.	Age.	Date of Entering the Service.	Period of Service.	Remarks.
Joseph A. Davis..........	Corporal	19	Oct. 7, 1861	3 yrs.	Appointed Dec. 10, 1861; captured Sept. 13, 1862, at Charleston, Va.; wounded June 24, 1864, at St. Mary's Church, Va.; mustered out June 27, 1865, at Petersburg, Va., by order of War Department; veteran.
Osman P. Mose...........	...do...	18	Oct. 7, 1861	3 yrs.	Appointed Dec. 10, 1861; transferred to 2d Regiment O.V.C. March 1, 1862.
Charles Wickline........	...do...	27	Oct. 7, 1861	3 yrs.	Appointed April 18, 1863; mustered out June 27, 1865, at Petersburg, Va., by order of War Department; veteran.
Levi Emmons.............	...do...	23	Dec. 11, 1861	3 yrs.	Appointed April 1, 1864; died Nov. 29, 1864 at City Point, Va.;veteran.
Doctor F. Burgess.......	...do...	30	Dec. 10, 1861	3 yrs.	Appointed Sept. 1, 1864; promoted to Regt. Q.M.Sergeant April 21, 1865; veteran.
Isaac L. Emmerson.......	...do...	19	Oct. 7, 1861	3 yrs.	Appointed Sept. 1, 1864; killed Oct. 27, 1864, in action at Boydtown Plank Road, Va.; veteran.
John Powers.............	...do...	18	Oct. 2, 1861	3 yrs.	Appointed Sept. 1, 1864; wounded and captured June 21, 1863, at Upperville, Va.; captured Oct. 1, 1864, at Davis's Farm, Va.; mustered out July 15, 1865, at Columbus, O., by order of War Department; veteran.
Hugh Derrick............	...do...	22	Dec. 10, 1861	3 yrs.	Appointed Dec. 17, 1864; wounded and captured June 21, 1863, at Upperville, Va.; wounded May 29,1864, at New Castle, Va.; mustered out June 27, 1865, at Petersburg, Va., by order of War Department; veteran.

Names.	Rank.	Age.	Date of Entering the Service.	Period of Service.	Remarks.
Joseph Reed............	Corporal	18	Nov. 12, 1861	3 yrs.	Appointed ——; killed June 24, 1864 at St. Mary's Church, Va.; veteran.
Noah Montgomery.........	...do...	25	Oct. 7, 1861	3 yrs.	Appointed ——; mustered out with company Aug. 7, 1865; veteran.
Ephraim T. Hays.........	...do...	22	Oct. 8, 1861	3 yrs.	Appointed ——; absent since March ——, 1865; no further record; veteran.
Levi M. Votaw..........	...do...	27	Oct. 27, 1861	3 yrs.	Appointed ——; mustered out with company Aug. 7, 1865; veteran.
Jerome O. Woods.........	...do...	18	Oct. 18, 1861	3 yrs.	Appointed Jan. 1, 1865; mustered out with company Aug. 7, 1865; veteran.
Hugh Watson............	Bugler	18	Oct. 7, 1861	3 yrs.	Appointed Dec. 10, 1861; transferred to 2d Regiment O.V.C. Jan. 14, 1862.
William Porter..........	...do...	16	Oct. 28, 1861	3 yrs.	Appointed Dec. 10, 1861; discharged Nov. 18, 1862, at Bealeton Station, Va., on Surgeon's certificate of disability.
William K. Miller.......	...do...	....	Oct. 31, 1861	3 yrs.	Appointed ——; discharged Sept. 20, 1862, at Baltimore, Md., on Surgeon's certificate of disability.
Joseph J. Street........	...do...	19	Mch. 21, 1864	3 yrs.	Appointed ——; captured June 7, 1864, near Ayletts, Va.; no further record found.
Nicholas Selkirk........	Farrier	27	Oct. 18, 1861	3 yrs.	Appointed Dec. 10, 1861; discharged Sept. 18, 1862, at Washington, D.C., on Surgeon's certificate of disability.
George Carruthers.......	...do...	43	Oct. 12, 1861	3 yrs.	Appointed Dec. 10, 1861; discharged April 18, 1862, at Washington, D.C., on Surgeon's certificate of disability.

SIXTH REGIMENT OHIO VOLUNTEER CAVALRY.

Names.	Rank.	Age.	Date of Entering the Service.	Period of Service.	Remarks.
Isaac M. Votaw..........	Farrier	23	Oct. 27, 1861	3 yrs.	Appointed ——; captured Nov. 15, 1863, at Fayetteville, Va.; died Aug. 5, 1864, in Andersonville Prison,Ga.
Charles E. Roberts.......	...do...	18	Mch. 21, 1864	3 yrs.	Appointed ——; mustered out with company Aug. 7, 1865.
Joseph Young............	Saddler	22	Nov. 28, 1861	3 yrs.	Appointed Dec. 10, 1861; promoted to Regt. Saddler Sergeant May 1, 1863.
Alphinus H. Tullis.......	...do...	28	 1861	3 yrs.	Mustered out with company Aug. 7, 1865, veteran.
John M. Moore..........	Wagoner	50	Oct. 7, 1861	3 yrs.	Appointed Dec. 10, 1861; mustered out Feb. 2, 1865, at Alexandria, Va., on expiration of term of service.
Agnew, Abraham..........	Private	23	Oct. 2, 1862	9 mos.	Drafted; mustered out July 29, 1863, on expiration of term of service.
Altaffer, John...........	...do...	19	Feb. 22, 1864	3 yrs.	Mustered out June 27, 1865, at Petersburg, Va., by order of War Department.
Altaffer, William........	...do...	19	Mch. 7, 1864	3 yrs.	Mustered out July 14, 1865, at Columbus, O., by order of War Department.
Beaumont, George F......	...do...	25	Mch. 7, 1864	3 yrs.	Died Jan. 28, 1865, at Salina, O.
Beckwith, Edwin.........	...do...	35	Mch. 1, 1865	1 yr.	Mustered out June 27, 1865, at Petersburg, Va., by order of War Department.
Beckwith, Orlando F.....	...do...	17	Feb. 16, 1865	1 yr.	Mustered out June 27, 1865, at Petersburg, Va., by order of War Department.
Bishop, Howell S........	...do...	42	Oct. 7, 1861	3 yrs.	Discharged March 7, 1862, at Columbus, O., on Surgeon's certificate of disability.

Names.	Rank.	Age.	Date of Entering the Service.	Period of Service.	Remarks.
Bishop, Philip..........	Private	24	Mch. 11, 1865	1 yr.	Mustered out June 27, 1865, at Petersburg, Va., by order of War Department.
Bohn, Christopher......	...do...	18	Nov. 20, 1861	3 yrs.	Wounded and captured June 21, 1863, at Upperville, Va.; mustered out Nov. 21, 1864, on expiration of term of service.
Boone, William H.......	...do...	20	Oct. 11, 1862	3 yrs.	Mustered out May 30, 1865, at Petersburg, Va., by order of War Department.
Boswell, Joel..........	...do...	36	Oct. 2, 1862	9 mos.	Drafted; mustered out July 29, 1863, on expiration of term of service.
Braden, Robert G.......	...do...	18	Feb. 16, 1865	1 yr.	Mustered out June 27, 1865, at Petersburg, Va., by order of War Department.
Bull, Albert..........	...do...	39	Oct. 7, 1861	3 yrs.	Discharged Dec. 23, 1862, on Surgeon's certificate of disability.
Burnett, Calvin.......	...do...	26	Dec. 11, 1861	3 yrs.	Mustered out Dec. 2, 1864, on expiration of term of service.
Button, Alfred........	...do...	18	Oct. 28, 1861	3 yrs.	Captured July 4, 1863, at Emmittsburg, Md.; died Dec. 31, 1863, in prison at Richmond, Virginia.
Calihan, John T.......	...do...	21	Oct. 7, 1861	3 yrs.	
Calaway, Wilson.......	...do...	21	Feb. 16, 1865	1 yr.	Mustered out June 27, 1865, at Petersburg, Va., by order of War Department.
Campbell, Calvin N....	...do...	21	Feb. 17, 1865	1 yr.	Mustered out June 27, 1865, at Petersburg, Va., by order of War Department.
Campbell, Edward P....	...do...	18	Mch. 21, 1864	3 yrs.	Mustered out June 27, 1865, at Petersburg, Va., by order of War Department.
Carriher, Albert E....	...do...	21	Nov. 6, 1861	3 yrs.	Mustered out June 27, 1865, at Petersburg, Va., by order of War Department; veteran.

SIXTH REGIMENT OHIO VOLUNTEER CAVALRY.

Names.	Rank.	Age.	Date of Entering the Service.	Period of Service.	Remarks.
Carriher, Frederick F...	Private	18	Nov. 6, 1861	3 yrs.	Killed Nov. 27,1863, at Mine Run, Va.
Carriher, Henry..........	...do...	27	Nov. 6, 1861	3 yrs.	Mustered out with company Aug. 7,1865.
Champlin, Elihah.........	...do...	41	Dec. 9, 1861	3 yrs.	Died Dec. 30, 1863, at Richmond, Va.
Coiley, Charles..........	...do...	39	Dec. 2, 1861	3 yrs.	Transferred to Veteran Reserve Corps Nov. 15, 1863; mustered out Dec. 2, 1864, on expiration of term of service.
Colby, Joseph............	...do...	29	Nov. 5, 1861	3 yrs.	Discharged on Surgeon's certificate of disability; date and place unknown.
Cook, Love D.............	...do...	21	Oct. 14, 1861	3 yrs.	
Cook, James.............	...do...	22	April 5, 1864	3 yrs.	Never reported for duty.
Conley, David...........	...do...	30	Dec. 11, 1861	3 yrs.	
Corbit, Patrick.........	...do...	21	April 1, 1864	3 yrs.	
Corlers, Aaron A........	...do...	19	Oct. 17, 1861	3 yrs.	Mustered out Oct. 16, 1864, on expiration of term of service.
Cory, Lewis D...........	...do...	18	Feb. 18, 1864	3 yrs.	Mustered out with company Aug. 7,1865.
Cowgil, Milton H........	...do...	26	Feb. 4, 1861	3 yrs.	Wounded (date and place unknown); died June 30, 1864, at Washington, D.C.
Crowder, John J.........	...do...	16	Feb. 15, 1865	1 yr.	Mustered out June 27, 1865, at Petersburg, Va., by order of War Department.
Dilly, Archibald........	...do...	30	Sept. 6, 1861	3 yrs.	Discharged March 6, 1862, at Columbus, O., on Surgeon's certificate of disability.
Dunn, Harry.............	...do...	18	Mch. 14, 1864	3 yrs.	Mustered out with company Aug. 7,1865.
Emmurn, Jesse...........	...do...	34	Oct. 7, 1861	3 yrs.	Died Nov. 16, 1862, at Fairfax Court House, Va.
Emmerson, Walter........	...do...	18	Feb. 6, 1864	3 yrs.	Captured Oct. 1, 1864; mustered out June 16, 1865, at Camp Chase, O., by order of War Department.

125

Names.	Rank.	Age.	Date of Entering the Service.	Period of Service.	Remarks.
Entrikin, Emmon E........	Private	21	Oct. 28, 1861	3 yrs.	Discharged Dec. 12, 1862, at Washington, D.C., on Surgeon's certificate of disability.
Farmer, Jacob F..........	...do...	20	Mch. 11, 1864	3 yrs.	Mustered out with company Aug.7,1865.
Fenton, Arthur E.........	...do...	21	Feb. 9, 1865	1 yr.	Mustered out June 27, 1865, at Petersburg, Va., by order of War Department.
Fenton, Collins W........	...do...	20	Feb. 11, 1865	1 yr.	Mustered out June 27, 1865, at Petersburg, Va., by order of War Department.
Gibbons, Samuel H........	...do...	20	Oct. 7, 1861	3 yrs.	Mustered out with company Aug. 7, 1865; veteran.
Goliver, William.........	...do...	21	Oct. 14, 1862	3 yrs.	Mustered out July 14, 1865, at Columbus, O., by order of War Department.
Graney, David............	...do...	20	Feb. 8, 1865	1 yr.	Mustered out June 27, 1865, at Petersburg, Va., by order of War Department.
Greer, Robert J..........	...do...	20	Oct. 12, 1861	3 yrs.	Captured July 4, 1863, at Emmittsburg, Md.; died May 29, 1864, in Andersonville Prison, Georgia.
Griswold, Wesley W.......	...do...	18	Dec. 12, 1861	3 yrs.	Died Oct. 8, 1862, at Washington, D.C.
Harper, Elisha K.........	...do...	21	Nov. 9, 1861	3 yrs.	Transferred to 58th Co., 2d Battalion Veteran Reserve Corps, Nov. 15, 1863, from which mustered out Nov. 11, 1864, on expiration of term of service.
Herring, Philip..........	...do...	26	Oct. 2, 1862	9 mos.	Drafted; mustered out July 29, 1863, at Warrenton, Va., on expiration of term of service.
Hess, William M..........	...do...	23	Oct. 7, 1861	3 yrs.	Discharged May 4, 1863, on Surgeon's certificate of disability.

SIXTH REGIMENT OHIO VOLUNTEER CAVALRY.

Names.	Rank.	Age.	Date of Entering the Service	Period of Service.	Remarks.
Howser, Sabastian........	Private	41	Oct. 17, 1861	3 yrs.	Discharged April 13, 1863, at Washington, D.C., on Surgeon's certificate of disability.
Hovey, Orrin N..........	...do...	26	Oct. 2, 1862	9 mos.	Drafted; mustered out July 29, 1863, at Warrenton, Va., on expiration of term of service.
Jennings, William H.....	...do...	18	Jan. 18, 1864	3 yrs.	Discharged Dec. 4, 1864, on Surgeon's certificate of disability.
Jobes, Charles A.........	...do...	18	Mch. 2, 1864	3 yrs.	Mustered out with company Aug.7,1865.
Keeler, James...........	...do...	24	Oct. 27, 1861	3 yrs.	
Kelly, Moses M..........	...do...	24	Oct. 8, 1861	3 yrs.	Killed July 21, 1864, in action at Poolsville, Md.
Kelly, William J........	...do...	28	Oct. 7, 1861	3 yrs.	Mustered out Oct. 7, 1864, at Ft. Delaware, Md., on expiration of term of service.
Kent, William E.........	...do...	19	Oct. 8, 1861	3 yrs.	Captured Oct. 10, 1862, at Haymarket, Va.; wounded Oct. 1, 1864, at Davis's Farm, Va.; mustered out with Co. Aug. 7, 1865; veteran.
King, Albert...........	...do...	19	Feb. 26, 1864	3 yrs.	Mustered out with company Aug. 7,1865.
King, Cyrns............	...do...	18	Feb. 29, 1864	3 yrs.	Killed Oct. 1, 1864, at Davis's Farm, Va.
Knowles, Archibald A....	...do...	22	Mch. 21, 1861	3 yrs.	Transferred to Veteran Reserve Corps Sept. 20, 1864; mustered out Aug. 7, 1865, at Washington, D.C., by order of War Department.
Knowles, Jackson........	...do...	19	Mch. 21, 1864	3 yrs.	Captured Oct. 1, 1864; died Feb. 8, 1865, in Salisbury Prison, N.C.

127

ROSTER OF OHIO TROOPS.

Names.	Rank.	Age.	Date of Entering the Service	Period of Service.	Remarks.
Lape, Augustus............	Private	19	Oct. 12, 1861	3 yrs.	Died Nov. 18, 1862, at Haymarket, Va., of wounds received Oct. 26, 1862, at Thoroughfare Gap, Va.
Laughlin, Parmenas P....	...do...	25	Oct. 19, 1861	3 yrs.	Captured July 4, 1863, at Emmittsburg, Md.; discharged June 16, 1864, at Annapolis, Md., on Surgeon's certificate of disability.
Lewis, Boynton...........	...do...	23	Feb. 11, 1865	1 yr.	Mustered out June 27, 1865, at Petersburg, Va., by order of War Department.
Lewis, Wiley.............	...do...	28	Feb. 11, 1865	1 yr.	Mustered out June 27, 1865, at Petersburg, Va., by order of War Department.
Livingston, Alpheus P...	...do...	20	Oct. 9, 1861	3 yrs.	Transferred to Co. F, 14th Regt. Veteran Reserve Corps, Sept. 1, 1863.
McCartney, John..........	...do...	23	Oct. 27, 1861	3 yrs.	
McCracken, Andrew........	...do...	21	Feb. 13, 1865	1 yr.	Mustered out June 27, 1865, at Petersburg, Va., by order of War Department.
McElhaney, Henry.........	...do...	22	Mch. 21, 1864	3 yrs.	Mustered out June 27, 1865, at Petersburg, Va., by order of War Department.
Mahaney, Thomas M........	...do...	19	Feb. 21, 1865	1 yr.	Mustered out June 27, 1865, at Petersburg, Va., by order of War Department.
Markham, Ozro............	...do...	39	Mch. 1, 1865	1 yr.	Mustered out June 27, 1865, at Petersburg, Va., by order of War Department.
Markham, Orlando.........	...do...	32	Mch. 1, 1865	yr.	Mustered out June 27, 1865, at Petersburg, Va., by order of War Department.
Mason, Robert............	...do...	18	Feb. 15, 1865	1 yr.	Mustered out June 27, 1865, at Petersburg, Va., by order of War Department.
Meek, John B.............	...do...	32	Oct. 9, 1862	9 mos.	Drafted; mustered out July 29, 1863, at Warrenton, Va., on expiration of term of service.

SIXTH REGIMENT OHIO VOLUNTEER CAVALRY.

Names.	Rank.	Age.	Date of Entering the Service.	Period of Service.	Remarks.
Miller, Allen..........	Private	27	Oct. 7, 1861	3 yrs.	Captured July 4, 1863, at Emmittsburg, Md.; died Feb. 5, 1864, in prison at Richmond, Virginia.
Moore, James M..........	...do...	23	Oct. 15, 1861	3 yrs.	Discharged Feb. 11, 1862, at Alexandria, Va., on Surgeon's certificate of disability.
Morrell, Benjamin F......	...do...	30	Oct. 8, 1861	3 yrs.	Died June 29, 1862, at Strasburg, Va.
Morris, Jesse...........	...do...	21	Oct. 8, 1861	3 yrs.	Died July 29, 1862, at Luray, Va.
Morrison, Adelbert.......	...do...	18	Nov. 12, 1861	3 yrs.	Captured July 11, 1862, at Luray Va.; died in Rebel Prison; date and place unknown.
Nelson, Thomas..........	...do...	26	Oct. 7, 1861	3 yrs.	Captured Nov. 16, 1863, at White Sulphur Springs, Va.; died Aug. 25, 1864, in Andersonville Prison, Ga.
O'Bryan, John...........	...do...	33	Oct. 12, 1861	3 yrs.	Mustered out with company Aug. 7, 1865; veteran.
Packer, Hugh M..........	...do...	....	Nov. 12, 1861	3 yrs.	Wounded June 24, 1864, at St. Mary's Church, Va.; mustered out June 27, 1865, at Petersburg, Va., by order of War Department; veteran.
Parmelee, William H......	...do...	25	Feb. 15, 1865	1 yr.	Mustered out June 27, 1865, at Petersburg, Va., by order of War Department.
Payton, Hamilton........	...do...	35	Nov. 18, 1861	3 yrs.	Wounded June 24, 1864, at St. Mary's Church, Va.; discharged June 8, 1865, on Surgeon's certificate of disability; veteran.
Perrine, George W.......	...do...	20	Oct. 7, 1861	3 yrs.	Reduced from 1st Sergeant at his own request; mustered out June 27, 1865, at Petersburg, Va., by order of War Department; veteran.

Names.	Rank.	Age.	Date of Entering the Service.	Period of Service.	Remarks.
Porter, James H.........	Private	19	Oct. 29, 1861	3 yrs.	Discharged June 12, 1862, by order of War Department.
Pyle, Joseph............	...do...	32	Oct. 7, 1861	3 yrs.	Transferred to 21st Battery Ind. Artillery ——, from which mustered out June 21, 1865, with battery.
Randall, Bradford W.....	...do...	20	Oct. 2, 1862	9 mos.	Drafted; mustered out July 29, 1863, at Warrenton, Va., on expiration of term of service.
Reed, Albert D..........	...do...	19	Mch. 5, 1864	3 yrs.	Wounded June 24, 1864, at St. Mary's Church, Va.; mustered out June 27, 1865, at Petersburg, Va., by order of War Department.
Ritter, William........	...do...	34	Feb. 23, 1864	3 yrs.	Mustered out June 22, 1865, at Philadelphia, Pa., by order of War Department.
Rodig, Herman..........	...do...	19	Mch. 10, 1865	1 yr.	Mustered out June 27, 1865, at Petersburg, Va., by order of War Department.
Rose, Oscar A..........	...do...	20	Oct. 14, 1861	3 yrs.	Discharged July 8, 1862, by order of War Department.
Roxbery, Corsin........	...do...	21	Oct. 29, 1861	3 yrs.	Transferred from Co. B, 2d O.V.C., ——; discharged Sept. 23, 1862, on Surgeon's certificate of disability.
Rudd, John.............	...do...	21	Feb. 27, 1865	1 yr.	Mustered out June 27, 1865, at Petersburg, Va., by order of War Department.
Rundlett, John.........	...do...	29	Nov. 11, 1861	3 yrs.	Discharged March 11, 1862, on Surgeon's certificate of disability.
Rupart, Adam...........	...do...	37	Oct. 7, 1861	3 yrs.	
Ryan, Edward...........	...do...	19	Dec. 21, 1863	3 yrs.	
Ryan, John.............	...do...	24	Feb. 28, 1864	3 yrs.	Died Oct. 19,1862, at Washington, D.C.

SIXTH REGIMENT OHIO VOLUNTEER CAVALRY.

Names.	Rank.	Age.	Date of Entering the Service.	Period of Service.	Remarks.
Sailors, David..........	Private	27	Feb. 15, 1864	3 yrs.	Captured Oct. 1, 1864, at Davis' Farm, Va.; died Dec. 23, 1864, in Salisbury Prison, N.C.
Sandford, Benjamin F....	...do...	38	Dec. 28, 1863	3 yrs.	
Smith, Jacob A...........	...do...	25	Oct. 7, 1861	3 yrs.	Discharged Dec. 22, 1862, at Washington, D.C., on Surgeon's certificate of disability.
Smith, Simon E...........	...do...	18	Mch. 21, 1864	3 yrs.	Captured Oct. 1, 1864, at Davis' Farm, Va.; died Feb. 8, 1865, in Salisbury Prison, N.C.
Stanley, Gideon..........	...do...	18	Mch. 21, 1864	3 yrs.	Mustered out June 10, 1865, at Point Lookout, Md., by order of War Department.
State, John..............	...do...	19	Dec. 19, 1863	3 yrs.	
Stannard, John...........	...do...	26	Nov. 16, 1861	3 yrs.	Died Oct. 9, 1862, at Washington, D.C.
Steible, Charles A.......	...do...	18	Feb. 17, 1865	1 yr.	Mustered out June 27, 1865, at Petersburg, Va., by order of War Department.
Stevens, Ray.............	...do...	18	Dec. 7, 1861	3 yrs.	Died Jan. 20, 1862, at Columbus, O.
Strawn, William B.......	...do...	18	Jan. 18, 1864	3 yrs.	Mustered out with company Aug.7,1865.
Strong, Horace..........	...do...	28	Feb. 22, 1865	1 yr.	Mustered out June 27,1865,at Petersburg, Va., by order of War Department.
Spicer, George W........	...do...	18	Mch. 14, 1864	3 yrs.	Mustered out with company Aug.7,1865.
Summerlin, Wilson.......	...do...	47	Nov. 12, 1861	3 yrs.	Discharged Sept. 18, 1862, at Washington, D.C., on Surgeon's certificate of disability.
Sweney, Patrick.........	...do...	18	Feb. 22, 1863	3 yrs.	
Thomas, George W........	...do...	23	Jan. 25, 1865	1 yr.	Mustered out June 27,1865,at Petersburg, Va., by order of War Department.

Names.	Rank.	Age.	Date of Entering the Service.	Period of Service.	Remarks.
Tobin, Morris..........	Private	20	Oct. 7, 1861	3 yrs.	Wounded July —, 1863, in battle of Gettysburg, Pa.; discharged Jan. 5, 1864, at Philadelphia Pa.; on Surgeon's certificate of disability.
Tullis, Charles E.......	...do...	25	Oct. 7, 1861	3 yrs.	Mustered out June 27, 1865, at Petersburg, Va., by order of War Department; veteran.
Tullis, Seth C..........	...do...	22	Oct. 25, 1861	3 yrs.	Mustered out with company Aug.7, 1865; veteran.
Turner, John B..........	...do...	31	Feb. 28, 1865	1 yr.	Mustered out June 27,1865,at Petersburg, Va., by order of War Department.
Watters, Lewis..........	...do...	20	Oct. 28, 1862	3 yrs.	Mustered out June 6,1865,at Petersburg, Va., by order of War Department.
Webster, Alfred.........	...do...	44	Feb. 16, 1865	1 yr.	Mustered out June 27,1865,at Petersburg, Va., by order of War Department.
—elpley, George........	...do...	18	Mch. 1, 1865	1 yr.	Mustered out June 27,1865,at Petersburg, Va., by order of War Department.
Whitehead, John W.......	...do...	18	Feb. 25, 1864	3 yrs.	Mustered out with company Aug.7,1865.
Wilcox, Travilla A......	...do...	18	Nov. 18, 1861	3 yrs.	Mustered out Nov. 19, 1864, on expiration of term of service.
Wilkey, Henry..........	...do...	36	Dec. 28, 1861	3 yrs.	Mustered out Oct. 31,1864,at Columbus, O., on expiration of term of service.
Williams, Jonas A.......	...do...	18	Mch. 14, 1864	3 yrs.	Mustered out with company Aug.7,1865.
Wilson, Frank..........	...do...	18	Feb. 16, 1865	1 yr.	Mustered out June 27,1865,at Petersburg, Va., by order of War Department.
Wilson, William G.......	...do...	20	Jan. 14, 1864	3 yrs.	Died June 18, 1864,at Washington, D.C.
Wilson, William E.......	...do...	34	Feb. 15, 1865	1 yr.	Mustered out June 19,1865,at Washington,D.C.,by order of War Department.
Young, John...........	...do...	23	Oct. 2, 1862	9 mos.	Drafted;mustered out July 29,1863,at Warrenton,Va., on expiration of term of service.

Names.	Rank.	Age.	Date of Entering the Service.	Period of Service.	Remarks.
Henry Wilcox	...do....	22	June 3, 1863	3 yrs.	Promoted from private Co. E July 1, 1865;promoted to 1st Lieutenant July 30,1865, but not mustered; mustered out with regiment Aug. 7, 1865.
George M. St. John......	Q.M.S.	27	Oct. 24, 1861	3 yrs.	Promoted from Q.M.Sergeant Co.K Dec. 31,1861; discharged July 14,1862, on Surgeon's certificate of disability.
Charles C. McCain.......	...do....	22	Oct. 7, 1861	3 yrs.	Promoted from Sergeant Co. C Jan.1, 1862;transferred to 2d Regiment O.V.C. March 1, 1862.
Wallace H. Bullard......	...do....	33	Oct. 7, 1862	3 yrs.	Promoted from Q.M.Sergeant Co. B Nov. 10,1864;to 1st Lieutenant Co. K April 8, 1865.
Doctor F. Burgess.......	...do....	30	Dec. 10, 1861	3 yrs.	Promoted from Corporal Co. C April 21,1865;promoted to 2d Lieutenant May 31,1865;to 1st Lieutenant July 30, 1865, but not mustered on either commission;mustered out June 27,1865, at Petersburg,Va.,by order of War Department; veteran.
John G. Carson..........	...do....	27	Nov. 6, 1861	3 yrs.	Promoted from Saddler Co. L Sept. 1, 1862;mustered out Nov.8,1864,on expiration of term of service.
Frank Trunkey...........	...do....	29	Oct. 7, 1861	3 yrs.	Discharged Sept. 17,1862, by order of War Department.
Samuel W. Castle........	...do....	26	Oct. 18, 1861	3 yrs.	Promoted from Sergeant Co. I Aug. 1, 1862;discharged Oct.15,1862,by order of War Department.
Madison R. Headley......	Com.Ser.	22	Oct. 21, 1861	3 yrs.	Transferred to Co. D, 2d Regiment O.V.C., March 1, 1862.

COMPANY D

Mustered in December 4, 1861, at Camp Hutchins, Warren, Ohio, by B. C. Stanhope, and others, U. S. Mustering Officers. Mustered out August 7, 1865, at Petersburg, Va., by L. H. Bowen, 1st Lieutenant and Acting Commissary of Musters, Mustering Officer Department of Virginia.

Names.	Rank.	Age.	Date of Entering the Service.	Period of Service.	Remarks.
Norman A. Barrett........	Captain	29	Oct. 11, 1861	3 yrs.	Mustered as 2d Lieutenant; promoted to Captain Dec. 9, 1861; to Major Aug. 3, 1864.
John N. Roberts..........	...do....	23	Oct. 9, 1861	3 yrs.	Promoted from 1st Lieutenant Co. G Aug. 3, 1863; to Major Nov. 12,1864, but not mustered; mustered out Nov. 16, 1864, on expiration of term of service.
Alcinus W. Fenton........	...do....	22	Oct. 5, 1861	3 yrs.	Promoted from 1st Lieutenant and Adjutant Jan. 31, 1865; detailed as Acting Inspector General on staff of Major General Crook May 8, 1865; relieved and returned to duty with company July 29, 1865; mustered out Aug. 17, 1865, at Cleveland, O., by order of War Department; veteran.
Lewis R. Prior..........	1st Lieut.	40	Oct. 15, 1861	3 yrs.	Mustered as private; promoted to 1st Lieutenant Dec. 9, 1861; resigned July 16, 1862; recommissioned as Captain Co. F April 12, 1863.
Robert E. Hedden........	...do....	23	Oct. 15, 1861	3 yrs.	Mustered as private; promoted to 2d Lieutenant Dec. 9, 1861; to 1st Lieutenant July 16, 1862; mustered out Dec. 29, 1864, on expiration of term of service.

Names.	Rank.	Age.	Date of Entering the Service.	Period of Service.	Remarks.
Caleb A. Rising.........	Hos.St'd.	26	Oct. 31, 1861	3 yrs.	Promoted from private Co. D Jan.1, 1862;mustered out Nov.12, 1864, on expiration of term of service.
Hiram A. Walling.........	...do...	21	Oct. 5, 1861	3 yrs.	Promoted from private Co. A Dec. 1, 1864;commissioned 2d Lieutenant April 8,1865;1st Lieutenant May 31, 1865, but not mustered on either commission;mustered out with regiment Aug. 7,1865; veteran.
Charles G. Steadman......	...do...	18	Mch. 17, 1864	3 yrs.	Promoted from private Co. B Dec. 1, 1864;commissioned 2d Lieutenant April 8,1865;1st Lieutenant May 31, 1865, but not mustered on either commission; mustered out with regiment Aug.7,1865.
Winthrope Pelton........	Vet.Surg.	40	Dec. 11, 1861	3 yrs.	Promoted to Veterinary Surgeon from Capt.Stanhope's Company, Dec.31,1861; discharged Oct.16,1862,by order of War Department.
Thomas Kinghorn..........	...do...	32	Oct. 18, 1861	3 yrs.	Promoted from Farrier Co. A Dec. 31, 1861; discharged Oct. 16, 1862, by order of War Department.
Robert Kinghorn.........	...do...	28	Oct. 14, 1861	3 yrs.	Promoted from Farrier Co. A May 1, 1863;mustered out Oct. 14,1864, by order of War Department; veteran.
Ira H. Morey............	Ch'f Bug.	28	Oct. 21, 1861	3 yrs.	Promoted from Bugler Co. I;discharged Nov.6,1862,by order of War Department.
John Morey..............	...do...	32	Oct. 21, 1861	3 yrs.	Promoted from Bugler Co. I Dec. 31, 1861; discharged Oct.12,1862, by order of War Department.
Carlos F. McDonald......	...do...	18	Nov. 1, 1862	3 yrs.	Promoted from Corporal Co.B Feb.1,1864; mustered out with regiment Aug.7,1865.

SIXTH REGIMENT OHIO VOLUNTEER CAVALRY.

Names.	Rank.	Age.	Date of Entering the Service.	Period of Service.	Remarks.
John G. Carson............	Q.M.S.	27	Nov. 6, 1861	3 yrs.	Promoted from Saddler Co. L Sept. 1, 1862; mustered out Nov. 8, 1864 on expiration of term of service.
Frank Trunkey............	...do...	29	Oct. 7, 1861	3 yrs.	Discharged Sept. 17, 1862, by order of War Department.
Samuel W. Castle.........	...do...	26	Oct. 18, 1861	3 yrs.	Promoted from Sergeant Co. I Aug. 1, 1862; discharged Oct. 15, 1862, by order of War Department.
Madison R. Headley......	Com.Ser.	22	Oct. 21, 1861	3 yrs.	Transferred to Co. D, 2d Regiment O.V.C., March 1, 1862.
Daniel E. Hedden.........	...do...	18	Oct. 15, 1861	3 yrs.	Promoted from private Co. D Jan. 1, 1862; discharged Oct. 16, 1862, by order of War Department.
William K. Kneal.........	...do...	20	Oct. 30, 1861	3 yrs.	Promoted from Q.M.Sergeant Co. I Dec. 1, 1864; to 2d Lieutenant Co. C April 8, 1865; veteran.
George T. Keller.........	...do...	19	Dec. 8, 1861	3 yrs.	Promoted to Sergt. Major from Corporal Co. G Dec. 31, 1861; transferred to Regt. Com. Sergeant June 1, 1862; reduced to ranks and assigned to Co. G July 25, 1862.
William H. Bazell........	...do...	29	Dec. 2, 1861	3 yrs.	Promoted from Sergeant Co. H Aug. 1, 1862, but declined promotion.
Charles Wolcutt..........	...do...	20	Oct. 16, 1861	3 yrs.	Promoted from Sergeant Co. D April 9, 1865; commissioned 2d Lieutenant May 31, 1865; 1st Lieutenant July 30, 1865, but not mustered on either commission; mustered out with regiment Aug. 7, 1865; veteran.

SIXTH REGIMENT OHIO VOLUNTEER CAVALRY.

Names.	Rank.	Age.	Date of Entering the Service.	Period of Service.	Remarks.
Daniel E. Hedden........	Com.Ser.	18	Oct. 15, 1861	3 yrs.	Promoted from private Co. D Jan.1,1862; discharged Oct.16,1862,by order of War Department.
William K. Kneal........	...do...	20	Oct. 30, 1861	3 yrs.	Promoted from Q.M.Sergeant Co. I Dec. 1,1864; to 2d Lieutenant Co. C April 8,1865;veteran.
George T. Keller........	...do...	19	Dec. 8, 1861	3 yrs.	Promoted to Sergt.Major from Corporal Co. G Dec.31,1861;transferred to Regt. Com.Sergeant June 1,1862;reduced to ranks and assigned to Co. G July 25, 1862.
William H. Bazell.......	...do...	29	Dec. 2, 1861	3 yrs.	Promoted from Sergeant Co. H Aug. 1, 1862, but declined promotion.
Charles Wolcutt.........	...do...	20	Oct. 16, 1861	3 yrs.	Promoted from Sergeant Co. D April 9, 1865;commissioned 2d Lieutenant May 31,1865; 1st Lieutenant July 30,1865, but not mustered on either commission; mustered out with regiment Aug. 7, 1865; veteran.
William W. Steadman.....	Hos.St'd.	21	Aug. 21, 1861	3 yrs.	Transferred from Cotter's Battery and promoted to Hospital Steward Dec. 17, 1861;discharged Oct. 16,1862,by order of War Department.
Samuel A. Dryden........	...do...	24	Dec. 4, 1861	3 yrs.	Transferred to 2d Battalion Sept.20, 1862.
Frank E. Crosby.........	...do...	25	Oct. 5, 1861	3 yrs.	Promoted from Corporal Co. A Oct.1, 1862; discharged Oct. 16,1862,by order of War Department.
Orlando W. Ferry........	...do...	24	Oct. 5, 1861	3 yrs.	Promoted from Corporal Co. A Jan. 1, 1863;to 2d Lieutenant Co. F Nov. 12, 1864; veteran.

Names.	Rank.	Age.	Date of Entering the Service.	Period of Service.	Remarks.
Orlando W. Ferry.........	1st Lieut.	24	Oct. 5, 1861	3 yrs.	Promoted from 2d Lieutenant Co. F Jan. 31, 1865; to Captain Co. B May 31, 1865; veteran.
Josiah E. Wood..........	2d Lieut.	24	Oct. 14, 1861	3 yrs.	Mustered as private; appointed 1st Sergeant Dec. 14, 1861; promoted to 2d Lieutenant July 16, 1862; wounded March 17, 1863, at Kelly's Ford, Va.; promoted to 1st Lieutenant Co. G to date May 9, 1864.
Albert W. Stiles.........	...do...	34	Oct. 5, 1861	3 yrs.	Promoted from 1st Sergeant Co. A May 9, 1864; to 1st Lieutenant Co. B Nov. 12, 1864; veteran.
Joseph Brown.............	1st Sergt.	43	Nov. 2, 1861	3 yrs.	Mustered as private; appointed Sergeant Dec. 14, 1861; 1st Sergeant Sept. 1, 1862; died May 19, 1864 at Portsmouth Grove, Va.
George W. Prior..........	...do...	28	Oct. 23, 1861	3 yrs.	Mustered as private; appointed Sergeant Dec. 14, 1861; captured Aug. 1—, 1862; appointed 1st Sergeant April 1, 1864; killed May 9, 1864, near Childsbury, Va.
James McFarland..........	...do...	21	Oct. 21, 1861	3 yrs.	Appointed Corporal Dec. 14, 1861; Sergeant Dec. 1, 1862; 1st Sergeant Nov. 1, 1864; promoted to 2d Lieutenant Co. F Jan. 31, 1865; veteran.
Hill D. Mercer...........	...do...	22	Oct. 15, 1861	3 yrs.	Appointed Corporal April 1, 1862; Sergeant Jan. 1, 1863; 1st Sergeant Jan. 1, 1865; promoted to 2d Lieutenant July 30, 1865, but not mustered; mustered out with company Aug. 7, 1865; veteran.

SIXTH REGIMENT OHIO VOLUNTEER CAVALRY.

Names.	Rank.	Age.	Date of Entering the Service.	Period of Service.	Remarks.
William B. Brisbine.......	Q.M.S.	19	Dec. 10, 1861	3 yrs.	Appointed Corporal July 1, 1862; Sergeant April 1, 1863; wounded May 8, 1864, at Todd's Tavern, Va.; appointed Q.M.Sergeant June 1, 1865; promoted to 2d Lieutenant July 30, 1865, but not mustered; mustered out with company Aug. 7, 1865; veteran.
Horace Pardee............	Com.Ser.	29	Oct. 18, 1861	3 yrs.	Appointed Corporal April 1, 1862; Com. Sergeant Sept. 1, 1863; mustered out Oct. 20, 1864, on expiration of term of service.
Wilson Kincaid...........	...do...	18	Dec. 9, 1861	3 yrs.	Appointed Corporal Sept. 21, 1863; Com.Sergeant June 1, 1865; mustered out with company Aug. 7, 1865;veteran.
Frank C. Loveland........	Sergeant	23	Oct. 26, 1861	3 yrs.	Mustered as private; appointed Sergeant Dec. 14, 1861; promoted to Regt. Q.M.Sergeant March 1, 1862.
Benjamin Robbins.........	...do...	43	Oct. 12, 1861	3 yrs.	Mustered as private; appointed Sergeant Dec. 14, 1861; discharged Aug. 22, 1863, on Surgeon's certificate of disability.
John B. Clark............	...do...	23	Oct. 12, 1861	3 yrs.	Appointed Corporal Dec. 14, 1861; Sergeant March 1, 1862; mustered out June 27, 1865, at Petersburg, Va.; veteran.
Alonson A. Grant.........	...do...	26	Nov. 5, 1861	3 yrs.	Appointed Corporal April 1, 1862; Sergeant Sept. 1, 1862; died May 30, 1863, at Potomac Creek, Va.
Sylvianus Pennell........	...do...	20	Oct. 12, 1861	3 yrs.	Appointed Corporal Dec. 14, 1861; Sergeant Sept. 1, 1862; discharged Dec. 17, 1862, at Washington, D.C., on Surgeon's certificate of disability.

Names.	Rank.	Age.	Date of Entering the Service.	Period of Service.	Remarks.
Albinus R. Fell.........	Sergeant	22	Dec. 9, 1861	3 yrs.	Appointed Corporal April 1, 1862; Sergeant Dec. 1, 1862; wounded May 9, 1864, on Sheridan's Raid, Va.; mustered out Dec. 11, 1864, on expiration of term of service.
Charles Wolcutt..........	...do...	20	Oct. 16, 1861	3 yrs.	Appointed Corporal April 1, 1862; Sergeant June 1, 1864; promoted to Regt. Com.Sergeant April 9, 1865; veteran.
William M. Sheffleton....	...do...	27	Dec. 7, 1861	3 yrs.	Appointed Corporal Sept. 1, 1862; Sergeant Dec. 1, 1864; mustered out June 27, 1865, at Petersburg, Va., by order of War Department; veteran.
William J. Hickok........	...do...	20	Oct. 16, 1861	3 yrs.	Appointed Corporal April 1, 1863; Sergeant Dec. 1, 1864; mustered out June 27, 1865, at Petersburg, Va., by order of War Department.
William A. Burbank.......	...do...	18	Oct. 12, 1861	3 yrs.	Appointed Corporal April 1, 1865; Sergeant June 1, 1865; mustered out with company Aug. 7, 1865; veteran.
Eldin G. Dixon...........	Corporal	24	Oct. 2, 1862	9 mos.	Drafted; appointed Jan. 1, 1863; mustered out July 29, 1863, on expiration of term of service.
Alferd H. Pierce.........	...do...	18	Nov. 22, 1861	3 yrs.	Captured June —, 1862; appointed June 1, 1864; wounded June 24, 1864, at St. Mary's Church, Va.; mustered out June 27, 1865, at Petersburg, Va., by order of War Department; veteran.
William Galloway.........	...do...	19	Dec. 10, 1861	3 yrs.	Appointed Sept. 1, 1862; mustered out June 27, 1865, at Petersburg, Va., by order of War Department; veteran.

SIXTH REGIMENT OHIO VOLUNTEER CAVALRY.

Names.	Rank.	Age.	Date of Entering the Service.	Period of Service.	Remarks.
Oliver B. Hall............	Corporal	24	Oct. 31, 1861	3 yrs.	Appointed Jan. 1, 1863; discharged Sept. 22, 1863, at Columbus, O., on Surgeon's certificate of disability.
Robert W. McCartney......	...do...	20	Oct. 16, 1861	3 yrs.	Appointed Sept. 1, 1862; wounded July —, 1863, at Gettysburg, Pa.; mustered out Oct. 16, 1864, on expiration of term of service.
Henry C. Bortel..........	...do...	20	Feb. 13, 1864	3 yrs.	Wounded Dec. 9, 1864, at Hatcher's Run, Va.; appointed Corporal June 1, 1865; mustered out with company on Aug. 7, 1865.
Charles W. Patterson.....	...do...	21	Oct. 12, 1861	3 yrs.	Appointed ——; mustered out Oct. 12, 1864, on expiration of term of service.
Amos Wills...............	...do...	24	Oct. 5, 1861	3 yrs.	Appointed ——; mustered out June 27, 1865, at Petersburg, Va., by order of War Department; veteran.
Dudley Hall..............	...do...	20	Oct. 31, 1861	3 yrs.	Appointed Dec. 14, 1861, killed May 18, 1863, near Dumfries, Va.
Henry F. Burns...........	...do...	43	Nov. 4, 1861	3 yrs.	Appointed Dec. 14, 1861; discharged July 18, 1862, on Surgeon's certificate of disability.
David E. Meeker..........	...do...	18	Oct. 30, 1861	3 yrs.	Appointed Dec. 1, 1864; wounded Dec. 9, 1864; at Hatcher's Run, Va.; mustered out with company Aug. 7, 1865; veteran.
Anson A. Judd............	...do...	18	Nov. 12, 1861	3 yrs.	Appointed Dec. 1, 1864; mustered out June 27, 1865, at Petersburg, Va., by order of War Department; veteran.
Mathew W. King...........	...do...	18	Nov. 25, 1861	3 yrs.	Appointed Dec. 1, 1864; mustered out June 27, 1865, at Petersburg, Va., by order of War Department; veteran.

Names.	Rank.	Age.	Date of Entering the Service.	Period of Service.	Remarks.
James Nichols............	Corporal	18	Oct. 12, 1861	3 yrs.	Appointed March 1, 1865; mustered out with company Aug. 7, 1865; veteran.
William Lucas............	...do...	18	Feb. 18, 1864	3 yrs.	Appointed June 1, 1865; mustered out with company Aug. 7, 1865.
Charles Hamlin...........	...do...	22	Oct. 18, 1861	3 yrs.	Appointed Dec. 14, 1861; captured June 16, 1862; transferred to Veteran Reserve Corps Oct. 9, 1863.
James B. Ormsby..........	...do...	20	Nov. 7, 1861	3 yrs.	Appointed Dec. 14, 1861.
Harrison A. Lee..........	Bugler	24	Dec. 8, 1861	3 yrs.	Appointed Dec. 14, 1861; discharged April 24, 1862, at Washington, D.C., by order of War Department.
Horace A. Prior..........	...do...	17	Dec. 3, 1861	3 yrs.	Appointed Dec. 14, 1861; died Nov. 9, 1862, at Alexandria, Va.
George Hopkinson.........	Farrier	20	Oct. 16, 1861	3 yrs.	Appointed Dec. 14, 1861; discharged Aug. 14, 1862, at Baltimore, Md., on Surgeon's certificate of disability.
George W. Gilbert........	...do...	21	Dec. 9, 1861	3 yrs.	Appointed Dec. 14, 1861; captured Nov. 15, 1863, at Fayetteville, Va., died July 26, 1864, in Andersonville Prison, Ga.
Andrew C. Meeker.........	...do...	33	Nov. 2, 1861	3 yrs.	Appointed Feb. 1, 1865; mustered out with company Aug. 7, 1865; veteran.
Aaron Hudson.............	Saddler	38	Nov. 18, 1861	3 yrs.	Appointed Dec. 14, 1861; mustered out Nov. 17, 1864, on expiration of term of service.
Horace Blattenberg.......	...do...	24	Nov. 19, 1861	3 yrs.	Appointed ——; promoted to Regt. Saddler Sergeant Dec. 31, 1861.
Plemon Cook..............	...do...	32	Nov. 2, 1861	3 yrs.	Appointed Sept. 1, 1862; mustered out June 27, 1865, at Petersburg, Va., by order of War Department; veteran.

SIXTH REGIMENT OHIO VOLUNTEER CAVALRY.

Names.	Rank.	Age.	Date of Entering the Service.	Period of Service.	Remarks.
Abbey, Arthur A.	Private	20	Oct. 2, 1862	9 mos.	Drafted; mustered out July 29, 1863, on expiration of term of service.
Aldrich, Edward	...do...	19	Oct. 2, 1862	9 mos.	Drafted; mustered out July 29, 1863, on expiration of term of service.
Alfred, Samuel N.	...do...	21	Feb. 18, 1864	3 yrs.	Discharged April 4, 1865, at West Philadelphia, Pa., on Surgeon's certificate of disability.
Allen, Joel	...do...	19	Feb. 23, 1864	3 yrs.	Mustered out June 10, 1865, at Point Lookout, Md., by order of War Department.
Allen, Wallace	...do...	18	Feb. 20, 1864	3 yrs.	Mustered out June 14, 1865, by order of War Department.
Barker, William F.	...do...	18	Mch. 4, 1865	1 yr.	Mustered out with company Aug. 7, 1865.
Barney, Goodrich	...do...	28	Oct. 2, 1862	9 mos.	Drafted; mustered out July 29, 1863, on expiration of term of service.
Barr, Allen N.	...do...	20	Feb. 24, 1864	3 yrs.	Mustered out with company Aug.7,1865.
Bell, Joseph S.	...do...	20	Feb. 11, 1864	3 yrs.	Died July 6, 1864, at Alexandria,Va.
Bennett, Franklin	...do...	18	Jan. 4, 1864	3 yrs.	Captured May 9, 1864, on Sheridan's Raid, Va.; died in prison, date and place unknown.
Black, Benjamin H.	...do...	26	Feb. 24, 1864	3 yrs.	Mustered out June 27, 1865, at Petersburg, Va., by order of War Department.
Blear, Daniel	...do...	23	Oct. 2, 1862	9 mos.	Drafted; mustered out July 29, 1863, on expiration of term of service.
Bonesteel, Levi	...do...	18	Nov. 5, 1861	3 yrs.	Discharged Jan. 8, 1864, on Surgeon's certificate of disability.
Bridges, Isaac	...do...	44	Nov. 4, 1861	3 yrs.	Mustered out Nov. 3, 1864, on expiration of term of service.

ROSTER OF OHIO TROOPS.

Names.	Rank.	Age.	Date of Entering the Service	Period of Service.	Remarks.
Brobst, Daniel.........	Private	33	Dec. 9, 1861	3 yrs.	Discharged July 21, 1862, at Columbus, O., by order of War Department.
Brown, Norman.........	...do...	38	Nov. 2, 1861	3 yrs.	Captured Sept. 1, 1863, at Barber's Cross Roads, Va.; died Feb. 8, 1864, at Richmond, Va.
Caldwell, David........	...do...	18	Feb. 13, 1864	3 yrs.	Mustered out with company Aug.7,1865.
Carpenter, Oliver P......	...do...	18	Dec. 2, 1861	3 yrs.	Died March 18, 1862, at Chardon, O.
Chapman, George.........	...do...	28	Jan. 30, 1865	1 yr.	Mustered out with company Aug.7,1865.
Clark, Matthew D........	...do...	19	Feb. 9, 1865	1 yr.	Discharged July 18, 1865, at Washington, D.C., on Surgeon's certificate of disability.
Clark, Richard.........	...do...	45	Nov. 5, 1861	3 yrs.	Discharged Dec. 18, 1862, at Washington, D.C., on Surgeon's certificate of disability.
Clark, Thomas S.........	...do...	19	Feb. 13, 1864	3 yrs.	Captured June 24, 1864, at St. Mary's Church, Va.; mustered out June 27, 1865, at Petersburg, Va., by order of War Department.
Colbridge, George........	...do...	34	Oct. 22, 1861	3 yrs.	Discharged Oct. 18, 1862, at Washington, D.C., on Surgeon's certificate of disability.
Cowdray, Linas A..........	...do...	18	Feb. 18, 1864	3 yrs.	Killed April 5, 1865, at Jettersville Station, Virginia.
Cox, Patrick............	...do...	26	Nov. 29, 1861	3 yrs.	Captured Sept. 1, 1863, at Barber's Cross Roads, Va.; mustered out Dec. 23, 1864, on expiration of term of service.
Dabney, Robert..........	...do...	18	Oct. 28, 1861	3 yrs.	Transferred to Veteran Reserve Corps Sept. 1, 1863, from which mustered out Dec. 14, 1865, by order of War Department; re-enlisted in Veteran Reserve Corps.

144

SIXTH REGIMENT OHIO VOLUNTEER CAVALRY.

Names.	Rank.	Age.	Date of Entering the Service.	Period of Service.	Remarks.
Dalton, Patrick..........	Private	26	Jan. 29, 1864	3 yrs.	Mustered out with company Aug.7,1865.
Davidson, William R......	...do...	18	Dec. 5, 1861	3 yrs.	Captured Sept. 1, 1863, at Barber's Cross Roads, Va.; mustered out April 8, 1865, at Columbus, O., on expiration of term of service.
Downes, Frank............	...do...	23	Dec. 8, 1861	3 yrs.	Died Sept.15,1862,at Georgetown, D.C.
Ely, Caleb...............	...do...	23	Oct. 15, 1861	3 yrs.	Discharged May 17, 1863, at Washington, D.C., on Surgeon's certificate of disability.
Ferguson, John H.........	...do...	22	Oct. 21, 1863	3 yrs.	Mustered out with company Aug.7,1865.
Fickel, Henry H..........	...do...	32	Feb. 26, 1864	3 yrs.	Mustered out June 22, 1865, at Philadelphia, Pa., by order of War Department.
Force, Robert............	...do...	42	Oct. 14, 1861	3 yrs.	Mustered out June 27, 1865, at Petersburg, Va., by order of War Department; veteran.
Force, Royal.............	...do...	20	April 1, 1862	3 yrs.	Mustered out April 2, 1865, on expiration of term of service.
Forley, Thomas...........	...do...	30	Nov. 14, 1861	3 yrs.	Discharged July 31, 1862, at Columbus, O., on Surgeon's certificate of disability.
Goff, Dwight C...........	...do...	25	Nov. 4, 1861	3 yrs.	Mustered out Nov. 4, 1864, on expiration of term of service.
Grate, Gibbs.............	...do...	21	Oct. 4, 1863	3 yrs.	Died Feb. 15,1865, at Baltimore, Md.
Grim, James.............	...do...	18	Feb. 12, 1864	3 yrs.	Mustered out with company Aug.7,1865.
Hall, Riley.............	...do...	40	Nov. 18, 1861	3 yrs.	Discharged July 22, 1862, at Columbus, O., on Surgeon's certificate of disability.
Hall, Thomas............	...do...	19	Oct. 15, 1861	3 yrs.	Died May 10, 1862, at Farmington, O.

145

ROSTER OF OHIO TROOPS.

Names.	Rank.	Age.	Date of Entering the Service.	Period of Service.	Remarks.
Hall, Wesley M..........	Private	21	Feb. 26, 1864	3 yrs.	Mustered out with company Aug. 7, 1865.
Harbaker, Francis.........	...do...	18	Oct. 31, 1861	3 yrs.	Mustered out June 17, 1865, at Petersburg, Va., by order of War Department; veteran.
Harris, Hiram C..........	...do...	19	Oct. 2, 1862	9 mos.	Drafted; mustered out July 29, 1863, on expiration of term of service.
Hartsom, Fordyce..........	...do...	43	Oct. 12, 1861	3 yrs.	Discharged July 22, 1862, at Columbus, O., on Surgeon's certificate of disability.
Harshorn, Samuel B........	...do...	28	Oct. 17, 1861	3 yrs.	Discharged May 20, 1862, at Wheeling, W.Va., on Surgeon's certificate of disability.
Hays, Picton...........	...do...	19	Dec. 9, 1861	3 yrs.	Transferred to Veteran Reserve Corps Nov. 1, 1863; from which mustered out Dec. 8, 1864, on expiration of term of service.
Hastings, James P.........	...do...	23	Oct. 2, 1862	9 mos.	Drafted; died Jan. 30, 1863, at Washington, District of Columbia.
Hays, George..........	...do...	21	Dec. 3, 1861	3 yrs.	Captured Sept. 1, 1863, at Barber's Cross Roads, Va.; mustered out Jan. 13, 1865, at Columbus, O., on expiration of term of service.
Hedden, Daniel E..........	...do...	18	Oct. 15, 1861	3 yrs.	Promoted to Regt. Commissary Sergeant Jan. 1, 1862.
Hickok, James S..........	...do...	44	Nov. 22, 1863	3 yrs.	Mustered out June 27, 1865, at Petersburg, Va., by order of War Department.
Hoover, Jacob C..........	...do...	30	Nov. 2, 1861	3 yrs.	Discharged May 1, 1862, at Columbus, O., on Surgeon's certificate of disability.
Hudson, Augstin H........	...do...	26	Jan. 30, 1865	1 yr.	Mustered out with company Aug. 7, 1865.

SIXTH REGIMENT OHIO VOLUNTEER CAVALRY.

Names.	Rank.	Age.	Date of Entering the Service.	Period of Service.	Remarks.
Hudson, Cleveland..........	Private	21	Oct. 22, 1861	3 yrs.	Discharged Nov. 22, 1862, on Surgeon's certificate of disability.
Jacobs, William M..........	...do...	19	Feb. 22, 1864	3 yrs.	Captured May 9, 1864, on Sheridan's Raid, Va.; died in Andersonville Prison; date unknown.
Jennings, Charles H.......	...do...	24	Oct. 2, 1862	9 mos.	Drafted; mustered out July 29, 1863, on expiration of term of service.
Johnson, James...........	...do...	18	Oct. 31, 1861	3 yrs.	Discharged July 18, 1862, at Warrenton, Va., on Surgeon's certificate of disability.
Johnston, James..........	...do...	18	Feb. 29, 1864	3 yrs.	Mustered out June 27, 1865, at Petersburg, Va.,by order of War Department.
Johnson, William.........	...do...	19	Feb. 24, 1864	3 yrs.	Captured May 9, 1864, on Sheridan's Raid, Va.; discharged July 8, 1865, at New York City, on Surgeon's certificate of disability.
Joyce, Daniel B..........	...do...	39	Jan. 5, 1864	3 yrs.	Mustered out June 6, 1865, at Philadelphia, Pa., by order of War Department.
Kincaid, Irwin...........	...do...	18	Dec. 9, 1861	3 yrs.	Discharged July 21, 1862, at Columbus, O., on Surgeon's certificate of disability.
King, George T...........	...do...	24	Oct. 12, 1864	3 yrs.	Died Feb. 14, 1865, in hospital near Petersburg, Va.
King, Miles..............	...do...	21	Oct. 31, 1861	3 yrs.	Discharged Sept. 26, 1862, at Columbus, O., on Surgeon's certificate of disability.
Kyle, Joseph.............	...do...	36	Nov. 1, 1861	3 yrs.	
Kiyear, Jacob............	...do...	18	Dec. 23, 1863	3 yrs.	Mustered out with company Aug.7,1865.

Names.	Rank.	Age.	Date of Entering the Service.	Period of Service.	Remarks.
Long, Charles............	Private	29	Oct. 31, 1861	3 yrs.	Captured Nov. 5, 1863, near Sulphur Springs, Va.; mustered out Nov. 3, 1864, on expiration of term of service.
Loveless, George.........	...do...	19	Oct. 31, 1861	3 yrs.	Mustered out June 27, 1865, at Petersburg, Va., by order of War Department; veteran.
Lowry, Robert W..........	...do...	18	Dec. 3, 1861	3 yrs.	Captured Sept. 1, 1863, at Barber's Cross Roads, Va.; died April 1, 1864, in Libby Prison, Va.
McCormick, John..........	...do...	21	April 1, 1864	3 yrs.	
McDonald, Perry..........	...do...	22	Oct. 7, 1861	3 yrs.	
McLean, Charles..........	...do...	40	Dec. 4, 1863	3 yrs.	Transferred to Veteran Reserve Corps ——; from which mustered out Aug. 24, 1865, at Washington, D.C., by order of War Department.
Maher, William..........	...do...	30	Dec. 31, 1863	3 yrs.	
Maloney, James..........	...do...	22	Feb. 11, 1864	3 yrs.	
Minard, John............	...do...	22	April 1, 1864	3 yrs.	
Nolan, James............	...do...	44	Dec. 16, 1863	3 yrs.	Captured Feb. 26, 1865; mustered out June 16, 1865, at Camp Chase, O., by order of War Department.
Older, Silas S..........	...do...	20	Feb. 14, 1864	3 yrs.	Mustered out with company Aug.7,1865.
Osborn, Harmon B........	...do...	22	Oct. 18, 1861	3 yrs.	Discharged Aug. 29, 1862, at Baltimore, Md., on Surgeon's certificate of disability.
Oviatt, Homer...........	...do...	24	Oct. 18, 1861	3 yrs.	Mustered out Nov. 3, 1864, on expiration of term of service.
Packard, Joseph O.......	...do...	28	Jan. 8, 1864	3 yrs.	Mustered out to date Aug.7,1865, at Columbus, O.,by order of War Department.
Pardee, Arba...........	...do...	26	July 1, 1862	3 yrs.	

148

SIXTH REGIMENT OHIO VOLUNTEER CAVALRY.

Names.	Rank.	Age.	Date of Entering the Service.	Period of Service.	Remarks.
Paroult, Joseph............	Private	21	Dec. 21, 1863	3 yrs.	
Patterson, Myron S........	...do...	18	Oct. 14, 1861	3 yrs.	Mustered out Oct. 15, 1864, on expiration of term of service.
Peterman, William........	...do...	26	Nov. 3, 1861	3 yrs.	Discharged Dec. 22, 1862, at Washington, D.C., on Surgeon's certificate of disability.
Powers, William..........	...do...	40	Jan. 9, 1864	3 yrs.	
Ramalia, Amos.............	...do...	21	Nov. 12, 1861	3 yrs.	Wounded July 28, 1864, at Deep Bottom, Va.; died Nov. 3, 1864, at Newton Falls, O.
Ramalia, Joshua..........	...do...	23	Nov. 18, 1861	3 yrs.	Discharged May 1, 1862, at Columbus, O., on Surgeon's certificate of disability.
Rankin, William..........	...do...	21	April 1, 1864	3 yrs.	
Rising, Caleb A..........	...do...	26	Oct. 31, 1861	3 yrs.	Promoted to Hospital Steward Jan.1, 1862.
Rinear, Demming..........	...do...	18	Dec. 9, 1861	3 yrs.	Died July 12,1862,at New Creek, Va.
Sanders, James............	...do...	35	Dec. 10, 1861	3 yrs.	Mustered out Dec. 11, 1864, on expiration of term of service.
Simpson, James............	...do...	22	April 1, 1864	3 yrs.	
Skinner, Reuben...........	...do...	24	Oct. 2, 1862	9 mos.	Drafted; mustered out July 29, 1863, on expiration of term of service.
Smith, Ira...............	...do...	18	Oct. 18, 1861	3 yrs.	Discharged July 18, 1862, on Surgeon's certificate of disability.
Smith, Simon E...........	...do...	19	April 4, 1864	3 yrs.	Killed May 28, 1864, in action at Hawe's Shop, Virginia.
Sutliffe, Joseph J........	...do...	25	Nov. 26, 1861	3 yrs.	Discharged Feb. 5, 1863, at Newark, N.J., on Surgeon's certificate of disability.

149

ROSTER OF OHIO TROOPS.

Names.	Rank.	Age.	Date of Entering the Service.	Period of Service.	Remarks.
Sweezy, John............	Private	18	Nov. 18, 1861	3 yrs.	Discharged June 30, 1862, at Columbus, O., on Surgeon's certificate of disability.
Thompson, Cassius O.......	...do...	18	Feb. 24, 1864	3 yrs.	Died Aug.10,1864, at City Point, Va.
Tressel, Leonard..........	...do...	18	Oct. 22, 1863	3 yrs.	Mustered out June 27, 1865, at Petersburg, Va., by order of War Department.
Tucker, Charles..........	...do...	18	Dec. 7, 1861	3 yrs.	Captured Sept. 1, 1863, at Barber's Cross Roads, Va.; died Jan. 18,1864, at Richmond, Virginia.
Wade, Charles...........	...do...	21	Nov. 5, 1861	3 yrs.	Discharged June 16, 1862, on Surgeon's certificate of disability.
Waterman, Richard.........	...do...	37	Dec. 5, 1861	3 yrs.	Discharged May 11, 1862, at Columbus, O., on Surgeon's certificate of disability.
Wickham, James T..........	...do...	18	Feb. 14, 1864	3 yrs.	Mustered out June 27, 1865, at Petersburg, Va.,by order of War Department.
Wight, Lewis P...........	...do...	24	Nov. 5, 1861	3 yrs.	Captured Sept. 1, 1863, at Barber's Cross Roads, Va.; mustered out Nov. 5, 1864, on expiration of term of service.
Williams, John...........	...do...	23	April 6, 1864	3 yrs.	Drafted;mustered out Nov.27,1863, on expiration of term of service.
Willoughby, Lycurgus......	...do...	18	Nov. 2, 1862	9 mos.	
Wilson, Alexander B.F.....	...do...	18	Jan. 1, 1864	3 yrs.	Wounded Oct.27,1864,at battle of South Side Railroad,Va.;discharged June 20, 1865, on Surgeon's certificate of disability.
Wilson, Robert L.........	...do...	18	Dec. 28, 1863	3 yrs.	Mustered out with company Aug.7,1865.
Wolcutt, Theodore S.......	...do...	38	Nov. 4, 1861	3 yrs.	Reduced from Q.M.Sergeant at his own request Dec.1,1862;mustered out Nov. 2,1864,on expiration of term of service.

SIXTH REGIMENT OHIO VOLUNTEER CAVALRY.

COMPANY E.

Mustered in February 6, 1863, at Camp Cleveland, Ohio, by C. O. Howard, Captain 18th Infantry, U.S.A., Mustering Officer. Mustered out August 7, 1865, at Petersburg, Va., by L. H. Bowen, 1st Lieutenant and Acting Commissary of Muster, Mustering Officer, Department of Virginia.

Names.	Rank.	Age.	Date of Entering the Service.	Period of Service.	Remarks.
William J. Gray.........	Captain	38	Oct. 5, 1861	3 yrs.	Promoted from Sergeant Co. A to 2d Lieutenant Dec. 22, 1862; to Captain Feb. 6, 1863; commissioned Major Nov. 12, 1864, but not mustered. Mustered out Feb. 17, 1865, on expiration of term of service.
Albert W. Stiles.........	...do...	34	Oct. 5, 1861	3 yrs.	Promoted from 1st Lieutenant Co. B Jan. 31, 1865; resigned June 17, 1865; veteran.
Frank C. Loveland........	1st Lieut.	23	Oct. 26, 1861	3 yrs.	Promoted to 2d Lieutenant from Sergt. Major Oct. 28, 1862; to 1st Lieutenant Feb. 6, 1963; promoted to Captain Co. B July 26, 1864.
Wells A. Bushnell........	...do...	22	Oct. 5, 1861	3 yrs.	Promoted from 1st Sergeant Co. A Jan. 31, 1865; commissioned Captain May 31, 1865, but not mustered; resigned May 27, 1865; veteran.
William L. Thomas........	2d Lieut.	29	Oct. 22, 1861	3 yrs.	Promoted from 1st Sergeant Co. C to date April 1, 1862; wounded May 28, 1864, at Aenon Church, Va.; promoted to 1st Lieutenant Co. C July 25, 1864; veteran.
Benjamin Bingham.........	...do...	44	Oct. 6, 1861	3 yrs.	Promoted from Wagoner Co. A Feb. 10, 1863; wounded Oct. 14,1863, near Warrenton Station, Va.; commissioned 1st Lieutenant July 13, 1864, but not mustered;discharged Feb. 9,1864, on Surgeon's certificate of disability.

ROSTER OF OHIO TROOPS.

Names.	Rank.	Age.	Date of Entering the Service.	Period of Service.	Remarks.
William A. Knowlton......	2d Lieut.	23	Oct. 12, 1862	3 yrs.	Mustered out Aug. 26, 1865, at Camp Dennison, O., by order of War Department.
David W. McIntosh........	1st Sergt.	28	Oct. 15, 1862	3 yrs.	Mustered as private; appointed Sergeant Sept. 1, 1863; 1st Sergeant Oct. 12, 1864; promoted to Sergt. Major May 5, 1865.
Alonzo D. Squires........	Q.M.S.	18	Oct. 21, 1862	3 yrs.	Appointed Corporal Nov. 1, 1864;Q.M. Sergeant May 1, 1865; mustered out June 27, 1865, at Petersburg, Va., by order of War Department.
Charles W. DeWitt........	Com.Ser.	21	April 4, 1863	3 yrs.	Appointed Corporal May 1, 1863;Com. Sergeant July 1, 1864; mustered out with company Aug. 7, 1865.
William W. Fenton........	...do...	26	Oct. 9, 1862	3 yrs.	Mustered as private; appointed Com. Sergeant Jan. 1, 1863; discharged Dec. 22, 1863, on Surgeon's certificate of disability.
Chancey B. Timmerman.....	...do...	35	Oct. 28, 1862	3 yrs.	Mustered as private; appointed Com. Sergeant Jan. 1, 1863; mustered out June 27, 1865, at Petersburg, Va., by order of War Department.
Loton Warner.............	Sergeant	28	Nov. 11, 1862	3 yrs.	Mustered as private; appointed Sergeant Nov. 1, 1863; mustered out June 27, 1865, at Petersburg, Va., by order of War Department.
Newell Blackford........	...do...	22	Oct. 22, 1862	3 yrs.	Appointed Corporal Jan. 1, 1863; Sergeant Jan. 1, 1864; mustered out June 27, 1865, at Petersburg, Va., by order of War Department.

SIXTH REGIMENT OHIO VOLUNTEER CAVALRY.

Names.	Rank.	Age.	Date of Entering the Service.	Period of Service.	Remarks.
George Stone............	Sergeant	22	Oct. 22, 1862	3 yrs.	Appointed Corporal Jan. 1, 1863; Sergeant May 1, 1863; wounded June 17, 1863, at Aldie Va.; discharged Sept. 18, 1863, on Surgeon's certificate of disability.
Daniel Jacobs..........	...do...	37	Nov. 19, 1862	3 yrs.	Appointed Corporal Jan. 1, 1863; Sergeant July 1, 1864; captured Feb. 6, 1865, at Hatcher's Run, Va.; discharged June 12, 1865, on Surgeon's certificate of disability.
Sanford J. Peters........	...do...	22	Oct. 29, 1862	3 yrs.	Wounded July 6, 1863, near Williamsport, Md.; appointed Sergeant from private May 5, 1865; mustered out June 27, 1865, at Petersburg, Va., by order of War Department.
James Butler...........	Corporal	22	Dec. 12, 1862	3 yrs.	Appointed Jan. 1, 1863.
Henry Kellogg..........	...do...	19	Oct. 17, 1862	3 yrs.	Appointed Jan. 1, 1863; mustered out June 27, 1865, at Petersburg, Va., by order of War Department.
Alfred J. Dodge.........	...do...	21	Oct. 27, 1862	3 yrs.	Appointed Jan. 1, 1863; mustered out June 27, 1865, at Petersburg, Va., by order of War Department.
Gotlieb Popp..........	...do...	42	Dec. 20, 1862	3 yrs.	Appointed March 1, 1863; transferred Veteran Reserve Corps March 15, 1864, from which discharged Aug. 16, 1865, on Surgeon's certificate of disability.
Decatur Stephenson.......	...do...	42	Nov. 4, 1862	3 yrs.	Appointed Jan. 1, 1864; mustered out June 29, 1865, at Petersburg, Va., by order of War Department.
Augustus F. Chapell.......	...do...	18	Nov. 23, 1862	3 yrs.	Appointed Nov. 1, 1864; mustered out June 27, 1865, at Petersburg, Va., by order of War Department.

153

Names.	Rank.	Age.	Date of Entering the Service.	Period of Service.	Remarks.
John Hood...............	Corporal	38	Nov. 17, 1862	3 yrs.	Captured July 4, 1863, at Emmittsburg, Md.; appointed Nov. 1, 1864; mustered out June 27, 1865, at Petersburg, Va., by order of War Department.
Milo Plumley............	...do...	18	Jan. 1, 1863	3 yrs.	Appointed May 1, 1865; mustered out June 27, 1865, at Petersburg, Va., by order of War Department.
Frederick Crist.........	...do...	19	Mch. 2, 1864	3 yrs.	Mustered out with company Aug.7,1865.
Andrew Meed.............	...do...	22	Nov. 19, 1862	3 yrs.	Transferred to Veteran Reserve Corps Nov. 6,1863; mustered out July 31, 1865, at Washington, D.C., by order of War Department.
Orrin N. Woodworth.......	...do...	25	Oct. 29, 1862	3 yrs.	Wounded May 28, 1864, at Hawe's Shop Va.; died Sept. 1, 1864, at ——.
Francis Kelsey..........	Bugler	21	Oct. 21, 1862	3 yrs.	Appointed Jan. 1, 1863; transferred to Veteran Reserve Corps June 16, 1865; from which mustered out July 24, 1865, at Washington, D.C., by order of War Department.
Dilon Harkelrode.......	...do...	19	Oct. 22, 1862	3 yrs.	Appointed Jan. 1, 1863; transferred to Veteran Reserve Corps Feb. 15, 1864, from which mustered out Aug. 11, 1865, at Washington, D.C., by order of War Department.
Pearl E. Frayer.........	...do...	18	Feb. 29, 1864	3 yrs.	Mustered out with company Aug.7,1865.
Walter E. Hopkins.......	...do...	20	Dec. 29, 1862	3 yrs.	Died March 6, 1863, at Ashtabula,O.
Dolphin E. Gardner......	Farrier	32	Nov. 4, 1862	3 yrs.	Appointed Jan.1, 1863; mustered out June 27, 1865, at Petersburg, Va., by order of War Department.

SIXTH REGIMENT OHIO VOLUNTEER CAVALRY.

Names.	Rank.	Age.	Date of Entering the Service.	Period of Service.	Remarks.
Benjaman F. Howe..........	Farrier	30	Nov. 5, 1862	3 yrs.	Appointed Jan. 1, 1863; mustered out June 27, 1865, at Petersburg, Va., by order of War Department.
John L. Wager.............	Saddler	36	Sept.20, 1862	3 yrs.	Appointed Jan. 1, 1863; transferred to Veteran Reserve Corps Nov. 1, 1863; discharged from same Nov. 9, 1863, on Surgeon's certificate of disability.
James Rich................	Wagoner	44	Oct. 8, 1862	3 yrs.	Appointed Jan. 1, 1863; mustered out June 27,1865, at Petersburg, Va., by order of War Department.
William Marlow............	...do...	31	Oct. 6, 1862	3 yrs.	Appointed Jan. 1, 1863; mustered out June 27, 1865, at Petersburg, Va., by order of War Department.
Benjamin F. Whiston.......	...do...	37	Oct. 14, 1862	3 yrs.	Appointed Jan. 1, 1863; mustered out June 27, 1865, at Petersburg, Va., by order of War Department.
Alger, George M...........	Private	18	Dec. 20, 1862	3 yrs.	Died Feb.13,1864,at Washington,D.C.
Applegate, Benjamin F.....	...do...	36	Jan. 5, 1863	3 yrs.	
Barry, Patrick............	...do...	20	Dec. 15, 1863	3 yrs.	Transferred to Veteran Reserve Corps Sept. 30, 1864;from which mustered out Sept. 5, 1865, at Columbus, O., by order of War Department.
Beardsley, Henry..........	...do...	18	Feb. 17, 1864	3 yrs.	Mustered out with company Aug.7,1865.
Bishop, Addison J.........	...do...	18	Oct. 31, 1862	3 yrs.	Discharged March 28,1863,at Columbus, O., on Surgeon's certificate of disability.
Bryant, John D............	...do...	18	Mch. 7, 1864	3 yrs.	Mustered out March 23, 1865, at Washington, D.C., by order of War Department.
Campbell, George..........	...do...	28	Dec. 25, 1862	3 yrs.	Died Aug.14,1864, at City Point, Va.

155

Names.	Rank.	Age.	Date of Entering the Service.	Period of Service.	Remarks.
Canfield, Justin E.......	Private	18	Nov. 1, 1862	3 yrs.	Died Feb. 22, 1863, at Cleveland, O.
Canfield, William A.......	...do...	19	Nov. 1, 1862	3 yrs.	Died Aug.23,1863,at Washington,D.C.
Carpenter, Washington I..	...do...	18	Dec. 20, 1862	3 yrs.	Wounded June 17, 1863, at Aldie, Va.; transferred to Veteran Reserve Corps ——; discharged from same April 25, 1864, on Surgeon's certificate of disability.
Case, George C.B..........	...do...	18	Jan. 3, 1863	3 yrs.	
Cathfield, Jerome.........	...do...	32	Oct. 29, 1862	3 yrs.	Wounded June 21, 1863, at Upperville, Va.; died July 14, 1863, at Washington, D.C.
Clark, Henry.............	...do...	22	Nov. 25, 1862	3 yrs.	Reduced from Corporal April 8,1863; died Feb.21,1865,at Annapolis, Md.
Clark, John Q.............	...do...	18	Dec. 12, 1863	3 yrs.	Died Aug.29,1864,at Alexandria, Va.
Cox, William.............	...do...	22	Nov. 3, 1862	3 yrs.	
Crist, Jonathan E........	...do...	18	Mch. 2, 1864	3 yrs.	Captured Oct. 1, 1864, at Yellow Tavern, Va.; no further record found.
Cronin, Cornelius........	...do...	25	Nov. 15, 1862	3 yrs.	
Cummings, Archibald......	...do...	40	Nov. 7, 1862	3 yrs.	Captured May 9, 1864, on Sheridan's Raid, Va.; died Sept. 25, 1864, in Andersonville Prison, Ga.
Dillabaugh, Albert.......	...do...	19	Dec. 18, 1862	3 yrs.	Mustered out June 27,1865, at Petersburg, Va., by order of War Department.
Dunham, Allison..........	...do...	18	Nov. 8, 1862	3 yrs.	
Ellis, Clark.............	...do...	18	Oct. 23, 1862	3 yrs.	Killed Sept.16,1864,at Hawkinsville, Va.
Feilon, Joseph...........	...do...	20	Feb. 20, 1863	3 yrs.	Mustered out June 27, 1865, at Petersburg, Va., by order of War Department.

SIXTH REGIMENT OHIO VOLUNTEER CAVALRY.

Names.	Rank.	Age.	Date of Entering the Service.	Period of Service.	Remarks.
Ferrell, John............	Private	36	Feb. 17, 1863	3 yrs.	Mustered out June 27, 1865, at Petersburg, Va., by order of War Department.
Fobes, Frances...........	...do...	18	Oct. 10, 1862	3 yrs.	Captured Oct. 1, 1864, at Yellow Tavern, Va.; mustered out May 18, 1865, at Baltimore, Md., by order of War Department.
Green, Thomas...........	...do...	25	Nov. 7, 1862	3 yrs.	
Grist, John D...........	...do...	19	Dec. 17, 1863	3 yrs.	Prisoner of War; mustered out with company Aug. 7, 1865.
Gunn, Christopher C......	...do...	18	Jan. 16, 1864	3 yrs.	Mustered out with company Aug.7,1865.
Hannum, Miflin..........	...do...	36	Oct. 31, 1862	3 yrs.	Reduced from Corporal at his own request June 1,1865;mustered out June 27, 1865, at Petersburg, Va., by order of War Department.
Harmon, John F..........	...do...	28	Oct. 22, 1862	3 yrs.	Transferred to Co. H March 15, 1863.
Harrison, William H......	...do...	22	Dec. 21, 1863	3 yrs.	Mustered out with company Aug.7,1865.
Higgins, Henry..........	...do...	20	Feb. 16, 1863	3 yrs.	Mustered out June 27,1865, at Petersburg, Va., by order of War Department.
Huntley, Lay G..........	...do...	20	Nov. 3, 1862	3 yrs.	Transferred to Veteran Reserve Corps Sept. 30,1863, from which mustered out Sept. 1, 1865, at Washington,D.C., by order of War Department.
James, Samuel H.........	...do...	24	Nov. 21, 1862	3 yrs.	
Jentz, John.............	...do...	19	Oct. 29, 1862	3 yrs.	Wounded June 21, 1863, at Upperville, Va.; captured Oct. 1, 1864, at Yellow Tavern, Va.; mustered out June 16, 1865, at Camp Chase, O., by order of War Department.

Names.	Rand.	Age.	Date of Entering the Service.	Period of Service.	Remarks.
Jewitt, Joseph E.........	Private	21	Oct. 25, 1862	3 yrs.	Captured May 9, 1864, on Sheridan's Raid, Va.; died in prison at Milten, Ga., date unknown.
Keck, Sherman...........	...do...	19	Feb. 15, 1864	3 yrs.	Mustered out with company Aug.7,1865.
Knapp, Lewis............	...do...	20	Nov. 24, 1862	3 yrs.	Mustered out June 27,1865,at Petersburg, Va., by order of War Department.
Knowles, Ranson J.......	...do...	18	Jan. 5, 1864	3 yrs.	Mustered out June 14,1865, at Chester, Pa., by order of War Department.
Lampson, Nathan.........	...do...	20	Oct. 7, 1862	3 yrs.	Also borne on rolls an "Lamphier"; wounded May 28, 1864, at Hawe's Shop, Va.; died Sept.1,1864,at Washington, D.C.
Lane, Oliver G..........	...do...	25	Oct. 13, 1862	3 yrs.	Reduced from Sergeant July —,1864; mustered out June 17, 1865, at Washington,D.C.,by order of War Department.
Lawson, John C..........	...do...	21	April 15, 1863	3 yrs.	Died Oct.18,1864,at Washington,D.C.
Logan, James H..........	...do...	18	Nov. 23, 1862	3 yrs.	Captured Dec. 18,1863, near Warrenton Junction, Va.; died June 4, 1864, in Andersonville Prison, Ga.
Loomis, Andrew J........	...do...	26	Nov. 14, 1862	3 yrs.	Mustered out June 27,1865,at Petersburg,Va.,by order of War Department.
McBride, James..........	...do...	19	Dec. 14, 1863	3 yrs.	Discharged July 7,1865, at Baltimore, Md.,on Surgeon's certificate of disability.
McCoy, Thompson P.......	...do...	17	July 17, 1863	3 yrs.	Transferred to Veteran Reserve Corps Sept. 15, 1864.
McDermott, Peter........	...do...	35	Feb. 9, 1864	3 yrs.	
McDugal, Angus..........	...do...	35	Jan. 1, 1863	3 yrs.	Transferred to Veteran Reserve Corps Feb.15,1864;from which discharged June 9,1865,at Alexandria,Va.,on Surgeon's certificate of disability.

SIXTH REGIMENT OHIO VOLUNTEER CAVALRY.

Names.	Rank.	Age.	Date of Entering the Service.	Period of Service.	Remarks.
McGill, John..............	Private	35	Feb. 3, 1863	3 yrs.	Discharged Aug. 6, 1863, on Surgeon's certificate of disability.
McMillen, Richard.........	...do...	20	Dec. 19, 1863	3 yrs.	
Mason, Charles E..........	...do...	19	Dec. 15, 1862	3 yrs.	Reduced from Corporal ——; mustered out June 27, 1865, at Petersburg, Va.,by order of War Department.
May, Alexander............	...do...	41	Oct. 21, 1862	3 yrs.	Transferred to Veteran Reserve Corps ——; mustered out Aug. 8, 1865 at Washington, D.C., by order of War Department.
Meed, Sherman II..........	...do...	21	Nov. 8, 1862	3 yrs.	Captured July 4, 1863, near Emmittsburg, Md.; mustered out June 16, 1865, at Columbus, O., by order of War Department.
Mier, John................	...do...	20	Oct. 2, 1862	3 yrs.	Mustered out June 27,1865,at Petersburg,Va.,by order of War Department.
Miller, Jacob.............	...do...	39	July 10, 1863	3 yrs.	Discharged March 24, 1864, at Warrenton, Va., on Surgeon's certificate of disability.
Miller, Henry J...........	...do...	17	Feb. 1, 1864	3 yrs.	Captured May 28,1864,at Aenon Church, Va.; no further record found.
Millikin, John............	...do...	21	Oct. 21, 1863	3 yrs.	
Montgomery, Thomas........	...do...	27	Dec. 15, 1863	3 yrs.	
Mosgrove, Jerry...........	...do...	18	Dec. 21, 1863	3 yrs.	
Mulloy, Charles...........	...do...	22	Jan. 27, 1863	3 yrs.	Transferred to Veteran Reserve Corps April 12,1865;from which mustered out Aug.25,1865,at Washington, D.C., by order of War Department.
Neiswanger, Henry.........	...do...	18	Feb. 2, 1864	3 yrs.	Transferred to Veteran Reserve Corps Jan.15,1865,from which discharged Feb.7,1865,on Surgeon's certificate of disability.

ROSTER OF OHIO TROOPS.

Names.	Rank.	Age.	Date of Entering the Service.	Period of Service.	Remarks.
Nicholson, Rufus........	Private	18	Jan. 30, 1863	3 yrs.	
Northrope, James........	...do...	18	Oct. 7, 1862	3 yrs.	Transferred to Veteran Reserve Corps Jan.1,1864;from which mustered out Aug.18,1865,at Washington,D.C., by order of War Department.
Pelton, Augustus........	...do...	46	Oct. 29, 1862	3 yrs.	Transferred to Veteran Reserve Corps Jan.—,1864,from which discharged May 6,1865,on Surgeon's certificate of disability.
Perry, Justin..........	...do...	37	Oct. 22, 1862	3 yrs.	Transferred to Veteran Reserve Corps June 16,1864,from which discharged Jan. 15, 1865, on Surgeon's certificate of disability.
Rolph, Daniel..........	...do...	29	Oct. 14, 1862	3 yrs.	Discharged April 20,1863,at Columbus, O.,on Surgeon's certificate of disability.
Shores, William........	...do...	18	Nov. 16, 1862	3 yrs.	
Sim, Ely F.............	...do...	18	Dec. 12, 1862	3 yrs.	Mustered out June 27,1865,at Peters-burg, Va.,by order of War Department.
Simmonds, George.......	...do...	25	Feb. 17, 1863	3 yrs.	Discharged July 3,1863,at Washington, D.C.,on Surgeon's certificate of disability.
Sloat, Charles.........	...do...	17	Nov. 15, 1862	3 yrs.	
Spencer, Allen H.......	...do...	40	Oct. 31, 1862	3 yrs.	Discharged May 29,1863,at Columbus, O.,on Surgeon's certificate of disability.
St. Clair, James B.....	...do...	18	Dec. 18, 1862	3 yrs.	Wounded Oct.27,1864,at Boydton Plank Road,Va.;mustered out June 27,1865, at Petersburg, Va., by order of War Department.
Stellewell, William G...	...do...	44	Feb. 4, 1864	3 yrs.	Mustered out with company Aug.7,1865.

SIXTH REGIMENT OHIO VOLUNTEER CAVALRY.

Names.	Rank.	Age.	Date of Entering the Service.	Period of Service.	Remarks.
Stewart, John A...........	Private	42	Feb. 12, 1863	3 yrs.	Transferred to Veteran Reserve Corps Nov. 15,1864;from which mustered out Aug.7,1865,at Washington,D.C., by order of War Department.
Stewart, Stephen R........	...do...	36	Oct. 16, 1862	3 yrs.	Reduced from 1st Sergeant July 1,1863; discharged Jan.14,1865,on Surgeon's certificate of disability.
Stone, Elias P............	...do...	22	Oct. 8, 1862	3 yrs.	Killed April 5,1865,at Jettersville, Va.
Torney, William..........	...do...	21	Dec. 17, 1862	3 yrs.	
Tracy, Leroy H............	...do...	18	Nov. 1, 1862	3 yrs.	Wounded Oct.1,1864,at Yellow Tavern, Va.;killed Dec.9,1864, at Hatcher's Run, Va.
Tyler, Avery B............	...do...	21	Nov. 13, 1862	3 yrs.	Reduced from Q.M.Sergeant May 1,1865; mustered out June 27,1865,at Peters- burg,Va., by order of War Department.
Van Orman, George P.......	...do...	26	Nov. 7, 1862	3 yrs.	Reduced from Q.M.Sergeant Oct.28,1863; transferred to Veteran Reserve Corps June 6,1865;from which mustered out June 26,1865,by order of War Dept.
Waldron, Charles E........	...do...	19	Feb. 15, 1864	3 yrs.	Wounded May 9,1864,on Sheridan's Raid, Va.;died May 20,1864,near Harrison's Landing, Va.
Wilcox, George...........	...do...	31	June 30, 1863	3 yrs.	Mustered out May 25,1865,at Peters- burg, Va.,by order of War Department.
Wilcox, Henry............	...do...	22	June 3, 1863	3 yrs.	Promoted to Sergt.Major July 1,1865.
Wiseman, Hugh............	...do...	22	Feb. 20, 1863	3 yrs.	Mustered out June 27,1865,at Peters- burg,Va., by order of War Department.
Woffle, Josiah J..........	...do...	20	Feb. 13, 1864	3 yrs.	Mustered out with company Aug.7,1865.
Wood, William H..........	...do...	33	Jan. 28, 1863	3 yrs.	

SIXTH REGIMENT OHIO VOLUNTEER CAVALRY.

COMPANY F.

Mustered in December 25, 1863, at Camp Cleveland, O., by H. Douglas, Captain 18th Infantry, U. S. A., Mustering Officer. Mustered out August 7, 1865, at Petersburg, Va., by L. H. Bowen, 1st Lieutenant and Acting Commissary of Musters, Mustering Officer Department of Virginia.

Names.	Rank.	Age.	Date of Entering the Service.	Period of Service.	Remarks.
Lewis R. Prior............	Captain	42	Aug. 12, 1863	3 yrs.	Discharged July 31,1864, on Surgeon's certificate of disability.
William L. Thomas.........	...do...	29	Oct. 22, 1861	3 yrs.	Promoted from 1st Lieutenant Co. C Nov. 12, 1864; to Major July 30,1865, but not mustered; mustered out with company Aug. 7, 1865, veteran.
Isaac N. Wilcox...........	1st Lieut.	30	Aug. 25, 1863	3 yrs.	Mustered as 2d Lieutenant; promoted to 1st Lieutenant Dec. 25, 1863; commissioned Captain Nov. 12, 1864, but not mustered; discharged Dec. 1, 1864, on Surgeon's certificate of disability.
Frank D. Moran...........	...do...	22	Oct. 27, 1862	3 yrs.	Promoted from 2d Lieutenant Co. M Jan. 31, 1865; commissioned Captain July 30, 1865, but not mustered; mustered out with company Aug. 7,1865.
George W. Milliken.......	2d Lieut.	23	Aug. 21, 1863	3 yrs.	Died Feb. 28, 1864, at Cleveland, O.; commissioned 1st Lieutenant Aug. 11, 1864.
John Marshall............	...do...	....	Nov. 16, 1863	3 yrs.	Mustered as private; promoted to 2d Lieutenant Feb. 28, 1864; discharged Oct.29,1864,by order of War Dept.
Orlando W. Ferry.........	...do...	24	Oct. 5, 1861	3 yrs.	Promoted from Hospital Steward Nov. 12,1864;to 1st Lieutenant Co.D Jan. 31,1865; veteran.

ROSTER OF OHIO TROOPS.

Names.	Rank.	Age.	Date of Entering the Service.	Period of Service.	Remarks
Oliver H. Simmons........	Ser.Maj.	20	Nov. 4, 1863	3 yrs.	Promoted from 1st Sergeant Co. F Aug. 15, 1864; to 1st Lieutenant Co. M Nov. 12, 1864.
James E. Darwent.........	...do...	22	Jan. 2, 1864	3 yrs.	Promoted from 1st Sergeant Co. M Dec. 1, 1864; to 1st Lieutenant Co. B April 8, 1865.
David W. McIntosh........	...do...	28	Oct. 15, 1862	3 yrs.	Promoted from 1st Sergeant Co. E May 5, 1865; promoted to 1st Lieutenant May 31, 1865, but not mustered; mustered out June 27, 1865, at Petersburg, Va., by order of War Department.
Henry Wilcox.............	...do...	22	June 3, 1863	3 yrs.	Promoted from private Co. E July 1, 1865; promoted to 1st Lieutenant July 30, 1865, but not mustered; mustered out with regiment Aug. 7, 1865.
George M. St. John.......	Q.M.S.	27	Oct. 24, 1861	3 yrs.	Promoted from Q.M.Sergeant Co. K Dec. 31, 1861; discharged July 14, 1862, on Surgeon's certificate of disability.
Charles C. McCain........	...do...	22	Oct. 7, 1861	3 yrs.	Promoted from Sergeant Co. C Jan. 1, 1862; transferred to 2d Regiment O.V.C. March 1, 1862.
Wallace H. Bullard.......	...do...	33	Oct. 7, 1862	3 yrs.	Promoted from Q.M.Sergeant Co. B Nov. 10, 1864; to 1st Lieutenant Co. K April 8, 1865.
Doctor F. Burgess........	...do...	30	Dec. 10, 1861	3 yrs.	Promoted from Corporal Co.C April 21, 1865; promoted to 2d Lieutenant May 31, 1865; to 1st Lieutenant July 30, 1865, but not mustered on either commission; mustered out June 27, 1865, at Petersburg Va., by order of War Department.

ROSTER OF OHIO TROOPS.

Name.	Rank.	Age.	Date of Entering the Service.	Period of Service.	Remarks.
James McFarland..........	2d Lieut.	21	Oct. 21, 1861	3 yrs.	Promoted from 1st Sergeant Co.D Jan. 31, 1865; to 1st Lieutenant Co. B April 8, 1865; veteran.
Charles P. McElligott....	...do...	24	Nov. 1, 1861	3 yrs.	Promoted from 1st Sergeant Co. A April 8, 1865; commissioned 1st Lieutenant May 31, 1865, but not mustered; mustered out with company Aug.7, 1865; veteran.
Oliver H. Simmons........	1st Sergt.	20	Nov. 4, 1863	3 yrs.	Mustered as private; appointed 1st Sergeant Dec. 25,1863; promoted to Sergt. Major Aug. 15, 1864.
George W. Anderson.......	...do...	22	Dec. 22, 1863	3 yrs.	Mustered as private; appointed Sergeant Dec. 25, 1863; 1st Sergeant Sept. 1, 1864; captured Oct. 1,1864, at Yellow Tavern, Va.; died Nov. 13, 1864, in Salisbury Prison, N.C.; commissioned 1st Lieutenant April 8, 1865.
John P. Frank............	...do...	24	Oct. 15, 1863	3 yrs.	Appointed Corporal Dec. 25,1863; Sergeant Dec. 1, 1864; 1st Sergeant March 1, 1865; mustered out June 27, 1865,at Petersburg, Va.,by order of War Department.
Erastus F. Merwin........	Q.M.S.	34	Sept.16,1863	3 yrs.	Mustered as private; appointed Q.M. Sergeant Dec. 25,1863;captured Oct. 1,1864, at Yellow Tavern, Va.;died Nov.20,1864,in Salisbury Prison,N.C.
George E. Davis..........	...do...	25	Oct. 4, 1863	3 yrs.	Appointed Corporal Dec. 25,1863; Sergeant March 1,1865;Q.M.Sergeant June 1,1865;mustered out with company Aug. 7, 1865.

SIXTH REGIMENT OHIO VOLUNTEER CAVALRY.

Names.	Rank.	Age.	Date of Entering the Service.	Period of Service.	Remarks.
William H. Baldwin........	Com.Ser.	38	Nov. 5, 1863	3 yrs.	Mustered as private;appointed Com. Sergeant Dec.26,1863;mustered out June 27,1865,at Petersburg, Va., by order of War Department.
Peter Bailey..............	Sergeant	22	Oct. 15, 1863	3 yrs.	Mustered as private; appointed Sergeant Dec.25,1863;captured Oct.1,1864, at Yellow Tavern,Va., died March 31, 1865, at his home in Ohio.
Alanson Kennedy..........	...do...	44	Nov. 10, 1863	3 yrs.	Mustered as private; appointed Sergeant Dec.25,1863;mustered out June 27,1865,at Petersburg,Va.,by order of War Department.
Andrew A. Birrell........	...do...	24	Jan. 4, 1864	3 yrs.	Mustered as private; appointed Sergeant Jan. 5,1864; died Aug. 16,1864, of wounds received June 24, 1864, at St. Mary's Church, Va.
Henry C. De Wolf.........	...do...	20	Nov. 19, 1863	3 yrs.	Appointed Corporal Dec. 25, 1863; Sergeant March 1, 1865; commissioned 2d Lieutenant July 30, 1865, but not mustered; mustered out June 27,1865, at Petersburg, Va., by order of War Department.
Charles S. Gorman........	...do...	22	Dec. 14, 1863	3 yrs.	Appointed Corporal Feb. 9, 1864; Sergeant June 1, 1865; mustered out with company Aug. 7, 1865.
Lyman W. Dickerson.......	...do...	18	Sept.16, 1863	3 yrs.	Appointed Bugler Dec. 25,1863;Corporal March 1, 1865; Sergeant June 1, 1865; mustered out with company Aug. 7, 1865.
George W. Paine..........	...do...	23	Dec. 21, 1863	3 yrs.	Appointed Corporal March 1, 1865;Sergeant June 1,1865;mustered out with company Aug. 7, 1865.

Names.	Rank.	Age.	Date of Entering the Service.	Period of Service.	Remarks.
Frederick M. Cascel......	Corporal	22	Dec. 19, 1863	3 yrs.	Appointed Dec. 25, 1863; mustered out June 22,1865, at Philadelphia, Pa., by order of War Department.
George H. Bonesteel......	...do...	23	Oct. 3, 1863	3 yrs.	Appointed Dec. 25, 1863;captured Oct. 1,1864, at Yellow Tavern, Va.;died Dec. 19,1864,in Salisbury Prison,N.C.
George W. Grim...........	...do...	29	Jan. 2, 1864	3 yrs.	Appointed Dec.1,1864;wounded Feb.5, 1865,at Hatcher's Run,Va.;discharged Aug.16,1865,on Surgeon's certificate of disability.
David Lewis.............	...do...	20	Oct. 15, 1863	3 yrs.	Appointed March 1,1865; mustered out June 27,1865,at Petersburg, Va., by order of War Department.
Lewis Sharp.............	...do...	19	Dec. 28, 1863	3 yrs.	Appointed March 1,1865;mustered out with company Aug. 7, 1865.
Amos B. Case...........	...do...	26	Dec. 12, 1863	3 yrs.	Appointed June 1,1865;mustered out with company Aug. 7, 1865.
William Ford...........	...do...	21	Dec. 17, 1863	3 yrs.	Appointed June 1,1865; mustered out with company Aug. 7, 1865.
George W. Mowen........	...do...	18	Oct. 24, 1863	3 yrs.	Appointed June 1,1865; mustered out with company Aug. 7, 1865.
James Mee.............	...do...	21	Dec. 15, 1863	3 yrs.	Appointed June 1,1865; mustered out with company Aug. 7, 1865.
Daniel W. Harrington.....	...do...	21	Jan. 1, 1864	3 yrs.	Appointed ——; mustered out June 27, 1865, at Petersburg, Va., by order of War Department.
Allen B. Wheeler.........	Bugler	28	Nov. 28, 1863	3 yrs.	Appointed Dec. 25, 1863; died May 22,1865, at home in Ohio.
David S. Morris.........	...do...	19	Dec. 19, 1863	3 yrs.	Appointed ——; captured June 20,1864; mustered out to date Aug. 7,1865,by order of War Department.

166

SIXTH REGIMENT OHIO VOLUNTEER CAVALRY.

Names.	Rank.	Age.	Date of Entering the Service.	Period of Service.	Remarks.
Josiah Linton............	Farrier	32	Oct. 28, 1863	3 yrs.	Appointed Dec. 25, 1863; died Jan. 28, 1864, at Cleveland, O.
Oscar F. Haskins.........	...do....	36	Dec. 12, 1863	3 yrs.	Appointed Dec. 25,1863; mustered out June 27,1865, at Petersburg, Va., by order of War Department.
Jacob Hartman............	...do....	23	Sept.24, 1863	3 yrs.	Appointed ——;mustered out June 27, 1865,at Petersburg, Va., by order of War Department.
George W. Chamberlin.....	Saddler	21	Dec. 22, 1863	3 yrs.	Appointed Dec. 25,1863;discharged June 15,1864,at Washington,D.C., on Surgeon's certificate of disability.
Solon L. Darling.........	Wagoner	23	Dec. 12, 1863	3 yrs.	Appointed Dec. 25,1863:mustered out June 27,1865,at Petersburg, Va., by order of War Department.
Ball, Fayette E..........	Private	25	Dec. 18, 1863	3 yrs.	Mustered out June 19,1865,at Columbus, O., by order of War Department.
Beckley, Edwin...........	...do....	33	Dec. 19, 1863	3 yrs.	Reduced from Corporal March 1,1865; mustered out June 15,1865,at Chester, Pa., by order of War Department.
Bennett, Charles.........	...do....	20	Dec. 26, 1863	3 yrs.	Mustered out June 27,1865,at Petersburg, Va., by order of War Department.
Bonesteel, Ezra..........	...do....	18	Dec. 21, 1863	3 yrs.	Mustered out June 27,1865,at Petersburg,Va.,by order of War Department.
Bugbee, William H. H......	...do....	24	Feb. 15, 1865	1 yr.	Mustered out June 27,1865,at Petersburg,Va.,by order of War Department.
Campbell, Charles........	...do....	18	Dec. 18, 1863	3 yrs.	Mustered out June 27,1865,at Petersburg,Va.,by order of War Department.
Card, Simeon.............	...do....	22	Oct. 24, 1863	3 yrs.	Reduced from Corporal March 1,1865; mustered out May 24,1865,at Philadelphia, Pa.,by order of War Dept.

167

ROSTER OF OHIO TROOPS.

Names.	Rank.	Age.	Date of Entering the Service.	Period of Service.	Remarks.
Carr, Joel................	Private	19	Oct. 20, 1863	3 yrs.	Transferred to Co.L Sept.30,1864.
Chamberlain, Jacob F.....	...do...	18	Jan. 23, 1864	3 yrs.	Mustered out with company Aug.7,1865.
Cox, Silas...............	...do...	25	Nov. 9, 1863	3 yrs.	Mustered out with company Aug.7,1865.
Creamer, Alonzo..........	...do...	18	Oct. 20, 1863	3 yrs.	Mustered out June 27,1865,at Petersburg,Va.,by order of War Department.
Croft, Dwight............	...do...	44	Dec. 19, 1863	3 yrs.	Mustered out July 24,1865,at Washington,D.C., by order of War Department.
Daniels, Philemon........	...do...	17	Sept.25, 1863	3 yrs.	Mustered out with company Aug.7,1865.
Daniels, Andrew..........	...do...	16	Sept.24, 1863	3 yrs.	Wounded Sept.30,1864,at Davis' Farm, Va.; died Oct. 7, 1864.
Dunnings, John...........	...do...	18	Oct. 9, 1863	3 yrs.	Mustered out June 24,1865,at Chester, Pa.,by order of War Department.
Ellenwood, Harrison......	...do...	19	Nov. 20, 1863	3 yrs.	Captured April 4,1865,at Jettersville, Va.:mustered out June 16,1865,at Columbus, O., by order of War Dept.
Folk, David..............	...do...	21	Oct. 31, 1863	3 yrs.	Captured July 12,1864,at Lee's Mills, Va.; mustered out June 27,1865, at Petersburg,Va.,by order of War Dept.
Frasier, John............	...do...	28	Dec. 20, 1863	3 yrs.	Mustered out June 17,1865,at Petersburg,Va.,by order of War Department.
Fullwiler, Eli...........	...do...	21	Dec. 19, 1863	3 yrs.	Mustered out with company Aug.7,1865.
Gibbons, Isaac C.........	...do...	18	Dec. 11, 1863	3 yrs.	Transferred to Veteran Reserve Corps Nov.20,1864;from which mustered out Aug.8,1865,at Washington,D.C., by order of War Department.
Gilbert, William A.......	...do...	18	Oct. 1, 1863	3 yrs.	Mustered out June 27,1865,at Petersburg,Va.,by order of War Department.
Gordon, George F.........	...do...	23	Oct. 3, 1863	3 yrs.	
Grate, John H...........	...do...	18	Oct. 4, 1863	3 yrs.	

SIXTH REGIMENT OHIO VOLUNTEER CAVALRY.

Names.	Rank.	Age.	Date of Entering the Service.	Period of Service.	Remarks.
Grinnells, Nathaniel......	Private	18	Jan. 2, 1864	3 yrs.	Captured Oct.1,1864,at Davis' Farm, Va.; mustered out June 27, 1865,at Petersburg,Va.,by order of War Dept.
Harmon, William..........	...do....	24	Dec. 17, 1863	3 yrs.	Captured Dec.8.1864,at Hatcher's Run, Va.;mustered out June 16,1865, at Columbus, O., by order of War Dept.
Hardesty, Thomas.........	...do....	18	Dec. 29, 1863	3 yrs.	Mustered out with company Aug.7,1865.
Herrick, Erwin..........	...do....	18	Dec. 28, 1863	3 yrs.	Mustered out June 27,1865,at Petersburg,Va.,by order of War Department.
Herst, Edward............	...do....	19	Dec. 28, 1863	3 yrs.	Mustered out June 27,1865,at Petersburg,Va.,by order of War Department.
Holcomb, Orin, Jr........	...do....	18	Dec. 23, 1863	3 yrs.	Captured Oct.1,1864,at Davis'Farm, Va.;died Dec.6,1864,in Salisbury Prison, N.C.
Hunt, William............	...do....	28	Dec. 23, 1863	3 yrs.	Transferred to Northwestern Department Sept. 25, 1864.
Jackson, Bruce H.........	...do....	18	Sept.24, 1863	3 yrs.	Captured Oct.1,1864,at Davis' Farm, Va.;mustered out July 31,1865,at Camp Chase,O., by order of War Dept.
Jenkins, Thomas.........	...do....	30	Dec. 9, 1863	3 yrs.	Captured Oct.1,1864,at Yellow Tavern, Va.;died Nov.25,1864,in Salisbury Prison, North Carolina.
Johnson, Calvin W........	...do....	24	Dec. 22, 1863	3 yrs.	Transferred to Veteran Reserve Corps; from which mustered out Nov.21,1865, at Washington,D.C.,by order of War Department.
Johnson, Hamilton........	...do....	29	Feb. 15, 1865	1 yr.	Mustered out June 27,1865,at Petersburg,Va.,by order of War Department.
Keep, Asa H..............	...do....	29	Dec. 17, 1863	3 yrs.	Mustered out with company Aug.7,1865.

Names.	Rank.	Age.	Date of Entering the Service.	Period of Service.	Remarks.
King, Miles.............	Private	25	Sept. 26, 1863	3 yrs.	Mustered out June 10, 1865, at Point Lookout, Md., by order of War Dept.
Larne, Cryness...........	...do...	18	Dec. 21, 1863	3 yrs.	Mustered out with company Aug. 7, 1865.
Law, Oliver.............	...do...	23	Jan. 2, 1864	3 yrs.	Discharged March 16, 1864, at Cleveland, O., on Surgeon's certificate of disability.
Lawrence, William........	...do...	22	Oct. 21, 1863	3 yrs.	Mustered out with company Aug. 7, 1865.
Lawyer, George A...........	...do...	17	Jan. 4, 1864	3 yrs.	Mustered out with company Aug. 7, 1865.
Long, John G..............	...do...	21	Dec. 17, 1863	3 yrs.	Transferred to Veteran Reserve Corps Nov. 20, 1864; from which mustered out Aug. 7, 1865, at Washington, D.C., by order of War Department.
Lyons, Leroy.............	...do...	18	Oct. 1, 1863	3 yrs.	Mustered out June 19, 1865, at Columbus, O., by order of War Department.
McCarty, Timothy..........	...do...	20	Dec. 28, 1863	3 yrs.	
Merwin, Tod.............	...do...	18	Dec. 19, 1863	3 yrs.	Mustered out June 27, 1865, at Petersburg, Va., by order of War Department.
Mowen, Hosea.............	...do...	23	Oct. 15, 1863	3 yrs.	Mustered out June 27, 1865, at Petersburg, Va., by order of War Department.
Mowen, Tobias.............	...do...	19	Dec. 19, 1863	3 yrs.	Killed Sept. 30, 1864, at Davis'Farm, Va.
Osterhant, Abram...........	...do...	23	Dec. 26, 1863	3 yrs.	Discharged June 24, 1864, at Cleveland, O., on Surgeon's certificate of disability.
Oviatt, Joseph.............	...do...	19	Dec. 14, 1863	3 yrs.	Mustered out June 27, 1865, at Petersburg, Va., by order of War Department.
Pardee, Elijah K...........	...do...	26	Oct. 3, 1863	3 yrs.	Mustered out with company Aug. 7, 1865.
Pardee, Henry C...........	...do...	18	Oct. 3, 1863	3 yrs.	Mustered out June 27, 1865, at Petersburg, Va., by order of War Department.

SIXTH REGIMENT OHIO VOLUNTEER CAVALRY.

Names.	Rank.	Age.	Date of Entering the Service.	Period of Service.	Remarks.
Peck, John L.............	Private	23	Jan. 13, 1864	3 yrs.	Mustered out June 27,1865,at Petersburg,Va.,by order of War Department.
Pletscher, John..........	...do...	18	Dec. 3, 1863	3 yrs.	Mustered out June 27,1865,at Petersburg,Va.,by order of War Department.
Price, William...........	...do...	18	Sept.16, 1863	3 yrs.	Accidentally wounded Feb.5,1865; mustered out with company Aug.7,1865.
Pummell, William H.......	...do...	19	Oct. 3, 1863	3 yrs.	Died Jan.20,1864,at Cleveland, O.
Robbe, James H...........	...do...	18	Dec. 11, 1863	3 yrs.	Mustered out June 27,1865,at Petersburg,Va.,by order of War Department.
Robbins, Leavitt W.......	...do...	18	Sept.15, 1863	3 yrs.	Mustered out June 27,1865,at Petersburg,Va.,by order of War Department.
Roberts, Lucas, O........	...do...	27	Oct. 25, 1863	3 yrs.	Captured Oct.1,1864,at Yellow Tavern, Va.;died March 9,1865,in Salisbury Prison, North Carolina.
Rudd, Benjamin M.........	...do...	21	Jan. 2, 1864	3 yrs.	Mustered out June 27,1865,at Petersburg,Va.,by order of War Department.
Scott, Absalom...........	...do...	30	Dec. 20, 1863	3 yrs.	Captured Oct.1,1864,at Yellow Tavern, Va.;died Nov.23,1864,in Salisbury Prison, North Carolina.
Seamans, Dwight..........	...do...	22	Feb. 15, 1865	1 yr.	Mustered out June 27,1865,at Petersburg,Va.,by order of War Department.
Sharp, Andrew J..........	...do...	18	Nov. 9, 1863	3 yrs.	Mustered out with company Aug.7,1865.
Sharp, Daniel J..........	...do...	20	Dec. 22, 1863	3 yrs.	Died Nov.5,1864,at his home in Ohio.
Sharp, Lewis.............	...do...	19	Dec. 28, 1863	3 yrs.	Mustered out with company Aug.7,1865.
Simmons, Henry B.........	...do...	18	Jan. 5, 1864	3 yrs.	Mustered out June 27,1865,at Petersburg,Va.,by order of War Department.
Smith, Stephen A.........	...do...	26	Dec. 29, 1863	3 yrs.	Died Nov.26,1864,at Cleveland, O.
Thomson, Albert J........	...do...	18	Dec. 21, 1863	3 yrs.	Mustered out June 27,1865,at Petersburg,Va.,by order of War Department.

171

ROSTER OF OHIO TROOPS.

Names.	Rank.	Age.	Date of Entering the Service.	Period of Service.	Remarks.
Tracy, Seneca............	Private	34	Nov. 4, 1863	3 yrs.	Mustered out June 27,1865,at Petersburg,Va.,by order of War Department.
Wallace, Charles..........	...do...	32	Dec. 17, 1863	3 yrs.	Mustered out June 27,1865,at Petersburg, Va.,by order of War Department.
Wallace, John.............	...do...	18	Dec. 18, 1863	3 yrs.	
Warren, Walter L..........	...do...	28	Dec. 30, 1863	3 yrs.	Mustered out to date June 16,1865, by order of War Department.
Washburn, Guy H...........	...do...	21	Feb. 15, 1865	1 yr.	Mustered out May 23,1865,at Columbus, O., by order of War Department.
Watkins, John.............	...do...	26	Dec. 15, 1863	3 yrs.	Transferred to Veteran Reserve Corps Nov.20,1864;from which mustered out July 24,1865,at Washington,D.C.,by order of War Department.
Wheeler, William J........	...do...	18	Dec. 15, 1863	3 yrs.	Mustered out June 27,1865,at Petersburg,Va.,by order of War Department.
Wheeler, William H. H.....	...do...	26	Nov. 20, 1863	3 yrs.	Mustered out June 27,1865,at Petersburg,Va.,by order of War Department.
Williams, Lafayette.......	...do...	18	Oct. 1, 1863	3 yrs.	Mustered out June 27,1865,at Petersburg,Va.,by order of War Department.
Williams, Wallace.........	...do...	19	Oct. 30, 1863	3 yrs.	Mustered out June 27,1865,at Petersburg,Va.,by order of War Department.
Woodard, John W...........	...do...	29	Mch. 14, 1865	1 yr.	Mustered out June 27,1865,at Petersburg,Va.,by order of War Department.
Wyatt, Joel W.............	...do...	27	Jan. 2, 1864	3 yrs.	Mustered out June 27,1865,at Petersburg,Va.,by order of War Department.
Young, Henry..............	...do...	32	Dec. 16, 1863	3 yrs.	Mustered out June 27,1865,at Petersburg,Va.,by order of War Department.

SIXTH REGIMENT OHIO VOLUNTEER CAVALRY.

COMPANY G.

Mustered in from October 9 to December 10, 1861, at Camp Hutchins, Warren, O., by B. C. Stanhope, and others, U.S.Mustering Officers. Mustered out August 7, 1865, at Petersburg, Va., by L. H. Bowen, 1st Lieutenant and Acting Commissary of Musters, Mustering Officer, Department of Virginia.

Names.	Rank.	Age.	Date of Entering the Service.	Period of Service.	Remarks.
James C. Richart.........	Captain	32	Nov. 6, 1861	3 yrs.	Mustered as 2d Lieutenant; promoted to Captain Dec.14,1861;wounded Oct.14,1863, at Bristoe Station, Va.; promoted to Major Jan. 1, 1864.
Eusebius S. Austin.......	...do....	24	Oct. 5, 1861	3 yrs.	Promoted from 1st Lieutenant Co. B May 9,1864; killed Oct.27,1864, near Boydtown Plank Road, Va.
William K. Miller........	...do....	23	Dec. 27, 1863	3 yrs.	Promoted from 2d Lieutenant Co. M Nov. 12,1864; promoted to Major July 30,1865, but not mustered; mustered out with company Aug. 7, 1865.
John N. Roberts..........	1st Lieut.	23	Oct. 9, 1861	3 yrs.	Mustered as private; promoted to 1st Lieutenant Dec.14,1861; wounded June 21,1863,at Upperville, Va.;promoted to Captain Co. D Aug. 7,1863.
Josiah E. Wood...........	...do....	24	Oct. 14, 1861	3 yrs.	Promoted from 2d Lieutenant Co. D May 9,1864;wounded July 28,1864, at Deep Bottom,Va.;discharged Dec. 10, 1864, on Surgeon's certificate of disability.
Ezra A. Faunce...........	...do....	23	Oct. 12, 1861	3 yrs.	Promoted from 1st Sergeant Co. I Jan. 31,1865;mustered out June 16,1865, at Camp Chase, O.,by order of War Department, veteran.

Names.	Rank.	Age.	Date of Entering the Service.	Period of Service.	Remarks.
George L. Wilson.........	2d Lieut.	24	Oct. 9, 1861	3 yrs.	Mustered as private;promoted to 2d Lieutenant Dec.14,1861;wounded March 17,1863,at Kelly's Ford, Va.;wounded June 21,1863,at Upperville,Va.; promoted to 1st Lieutenant May 9, 1864,but not mustered; mustered out Oct.11,1864,on expiration of term of service.
Henry M. Baldwin.........	1st Sergt.	26	Oct. 28, 1861	3 yrs.	Mustered as private; appointed 1st Sergeant Dec.14,1861;promoted to Sergt.Major Nov.1,1862.
John W. Dunlap...........	...do...	20	Oct. 15, 1861	3 yrs.	Mustered as private; appointed Sergeant Dec.14,1861;1st Sergeant Nov. 1,1862; died June 19,1863, at Washington,D.C.,of wounds received June 9,1863,in battle of Stevensburg,Va.
Charles G. Miller........	...do...	23	Nov. 6, 1861	3 yrs.	Mustered as private; appointed Q.M. Sergeant Dec.14,1861;1st Sergeant June 2,1863;promoted to 2d Lieutenant Co. A May 9,1864;veteran.
William M. Davis.........	...do...	22	Nov. 6, 1861	3 yrs.	Mustered as private;appointed Sergeant Dec.14,1861;Q.M.Sergeant June 20,1863;1st Sergeant July 15, 1864;promoted to 1st Lieutenant and Adjutant Jan.31,1865;veteran.
William G. Stigleman.....	...do...	18	Oct. 22, 1861	3 yrs.	Appointed Corporal Oct. 15,1862; Sergeant July 15,1864;1st Sergeant Feb.6,1865;promoted to 2d Lieutenant May 31,1865;1st Lieutenant July 30,1865,but not mustered on either promotion;mustered out with company Aug.7,1865; veteran.

SIXTH REGIMENT OHIO VOLUNTEER CAVALRY.

Names.	Rank.	Age.	Date of Entering the Service.	Period of Service.	Remarks.
Isaac N. Crooks............	Q.M.S.	23	Dec. 7, 1861	3 yrs.	Appointed Corporal Aug.10,1862;Q.M. Sergeant July 15,1864;promoted to 2d Lieutenant July 30,1865,but not mustered out with company Aug.7,1865; veteran.
Truman Reeves.............	Com.Ser.	21	Oct. 5, 1861	3 yrs.	Appointed Corporal Dec.14,1861;Com. Sergeant Oct.15,1862;wounded May 28, 1864,at Hawe's Shop,Va.;discharged Jan.5,1865,on Surgeon's certificate of disability; veteran.
William T. Barrett........	Sergeant	22	Nov. 8, 1861	3 yrs.	Mustered as private;appointed Sergeant Dec.14,1861;wounded Sept.1, 1863,at Barber's Cross Roads,Va.; discharged May 5,1864,at Columbus, O.,on Surgeon's certificate of disability.
Miles G. Butler...........	...do...	24	Oct. 14, 1861	3 yrs.	Mustered as private; appointed Sergeant Dec.14,1861;discharged April 12,1862,on Surgeon's certificate of disability.
Frank L. Shafer...........	...do...	21	Nov. 5, 1861	3 yrs.	Appointed Corporal Dec.14,1861;Sergeant April 23,1862;wounded June 21,1863,at Upperville, Va.;died Sept.2,1863,at Orlean,Va.,of wounds received Sept.1,1863,at Barber's Cross Roads, Va.
Ralph Fowler..............	...do...	18	Oct. 25, 1861	3 yrs.	Appointed Corporal Dec.14,1861;Sergeant Oct.15,1862;captured Sept.1, 1863,at Barber's Cross Roads,Va.; mustered out Nov.3,1864,on expiration of term of service.

175

ROSTER OF OHIO TROOPS.

Names.	Rank.	Age.	Date of Entering the Service.	Period of Service.	Remarks.
George W. Gillis.........	Sergeant	28	Nov. 6, 1861	3 yrs.	Appointed Corporal Dec. 14, 1861; Sergeant Nov.11,1862;mustered out Feb.3,1865,on expiration of term of service.
Edwin D. McKee............	...do...	21	Oct. 25, 1861	3 yrs.	Appointed Corporal Dec.14,1861; Sergeant —;mustered out June 27, 1865,at Petersburg,Va., by order of War Department.
Miron H. Barber..........	...do...	31	Dec. 10, 1861	3 yrs.	Appointed Corporal April 23,1862; Sergeant July 1,1863;wounded Nov. 27,1863,near Mine Run,Va.;transferred to Co. I,14th Regiment Veteran Reserve Corps,May 19,1864, from which mustered out Dec.9,1864, on expiration of term of service.
Clarence L. Anderson.....	...do...	18	Dec. 6, 1861	3 yrs.	Appointed Corporal July 1,1863;Sergeant Sept.1,1864; died Oct.3,1864, at Washington D.C.; veteran.
Gilbert L. Medley........	...do...	20	Nov. 30, 1861	3 yrs.	Appointed Corporal Sept.1,1864;Sergeant Dec.1,1864;wounded March 31, 1865,at Dinwiddie Court House,Va.; discharged June 21,1865,on Surgeon's certificate of disability; veteran.
James H. Miller..........	...do...	22	Nov. 8, 1861	3 yrs.	Appointed Corporal Sept.1,1864;Sergeant Feb.6,1865;mustered out with company Aug.7,1865; veteran.
John F. Smith............	...do...	19	Dec. 10, 1861	3 yrs.	Appointed Corporal Sept.1,1864;Sergeant March 8,1865;mustered out with company Aug.7,1865;veteran.
William Phillips.........	...do...	23	Nov. 26, 1861	3 yrs.	Mustered as private;appointed Sergeant May 1,1865;mustered out June 27,1865,at Petersburg,Va.,by order of War Department; veteran.

SIXTH REGIMENT OHIO VOLUNTEER CAVALRY.

Names.	Rank.	Age.	Date of Entering the Service.	Period of Service.	Remarks.
Luther B. Shurtleff......	Sergeant	18	Oct. 22, 1861	3 yrs.	Appointed Corporal Dec.1,1864;Sergeant May 1,1865;mustered out with company Aug.7,1865; veteran.
George Williams..........	Corporal	26	Nov. 30, 1861	3 yrs.	Appointed Feb. 26,1862;captured Sept.1,1863,at Barber's Cross Roads, Va.;died Dec. 17,1863,at Annapolis, Md.
Julius Hill..............	...do...	21	Dec. 10, 1861	3 yrs.	Appointed June 23,1862;transferred to Veteran Reserve Corps July 1, 1863.
John L. Keen.............	...do...	18	Oct. 18, 1861	3 yrs.	Appointed Sept.1,1862;killed Oct. 27,1864,at Boydtown Plank Road, Va.; veteran.
Stewart Groscost.........	...do...	19	Oct. 18, 1861	3 yrs.	Appointed Oct. 15,1862;captured July 4,1863,at South Mt.Gap, Md.; mustered out Feb.3,1865,on expiration of term of service.
William H. McClure.......	...do...	18	Oct. 31, 1861	3 yrs.	Appointed Dec.31,1862;discharged Sept.25,1863,on Surgeon's certificate of disability.
Lemuel Granger...........	...do...	18	Nov. .., 1861	3 yrs.	Appointed July 1,1863;captured Sept.1,1863,at Barber's Cross Roads, Va.;discharged Nov.8,1864,on expiration of term of service.
David M. Musser..........	...do...	19	Oct. 18, 1861	3 yrs.	Appointed——;wounded May 6,1864,in the Wilderness; mustered out June 27,1865,at Petersburg,Va.,by order of War Department; veteran.
Hiram Hull...............	...do...	18	Dec. 8, 1861	3 yrs.	Wounded June 24,1864,at St.Mary's Church,Va.;appointed Corporal Dec. 1,1864;wounded March 31,1865, at Dinwiddie Court House,Va.;discharged Sept.6,1865,on Surgeon's certificate of disability; veteran.

ROSTER OF OHIO TROOPS.

Names.	Rank.	Age.	Date of Entering the Service.	Period of Service.	Remarks.
John Lafferty............	Corporal	24	Nov. 30, 1861	3 yrs.	Appointed March 8,1865;mustered out with company Aug.5,1865; veteran.
Samuel Treep.............	...do...	22	Nov. 26, 1861	3 yrs.	Appointed May 1,1865;mustered out June 27,1865,at Petersburg,Va.,by order of War Department.
Bernard Derring.........	...do...	18	Nov. 15, 1861	3 yrs.	Appointed May 1,1865;mustered out with company Aug.7,1865; veteran.
John W. McKibin.........	...do...	18	Feb. 13, 1864	3 yrs.	Appointed May 1,1865;mustered out June 27,1865,at Petersburg,Va.,by order of War Department.
Edwin W. Tanner.........	Bugler	20	Nov. 6, 1861	3 yrs.	Appointed Dec.14,1861;discharged Nov.28,1862,at Washington,D.C.,by order of War Department.
Alfred Wheier...........	...do...	18	Oct. 18, 1861	3 yrs.	Appointed Dec.14,1861;discharged Nov.30,1862,by order of War Dept.
Henry F. Kinnaman.......	...do...	18	Dec. 4, 1861	3 yrs.	Appointed ———;captured Sept.1,1863, at Barber's Cross Roads,Va.;mustered out Dec.4,1864,on expiration of term of service.
John Gilmore...........	Farrier	20	Nov. 6, 1861	3 yrs.	Appointed Dec.14,1861;mustered out Nov.26,1864,at Columbus,O.,on expiration of term of service.
Henry Van Hout.........	...do...	36	Nov. 6, 1861	3 yrs.	Appointed Dec.6,1861;mustered out Nov.8,1864,on expiration of term of service.
Silas H. Warring.......	...do...	38	Feb. 14, 1865	1 yr.	Mustered out with company Aug.7,1865.
Robert T. McClain......	Saddler	22	Oct. 14, 1861	3 yrs.	Appointed Dec.14,1861;captured Sept. 1,1863,at Barber's Cross Roads,Va.; died April 15,1864,in Richmond Prison,Va.

SIXTH REGIMENT OHIO VOLUNTEER CAVALRY.

Names.	Rank.	Age.	Date of Entering the Service	Period of Service.	Remarks.
John O. Conner..........	Wagoner	38	Oct. 25, 1861	3 yrs.	Appointed Dec. 14, 1861.
Nathan C. Tyler..........	...do...	27	Oct. 6, 1861	3 yrs.	Mustered out June 27,1865,at Petersburg,Va.,by order of War Department; veteran.
Ague, Freeman..........	Private	23	Mch. 1, 1865	1 yr.	Mustered out June 27,1865,at Petersburg,Va.,by order of War Department.
Austin, Horace..........	...do...	19	Jan. 24, 1865	1 yr.	Mustered out June 27,1865,at Petersburg,Va.,by order of War Department.
Barrett, Robert..........	...do...	22	Oct. 9, 1862	3 yrs.	Transferred from Co. B May 11,1863; captured Sept.1,1863,at Barber's Cross Roads,Va.;died Jan.24,1864,in Richmond Prison, Va.
Bates, Howard..........	...do...	35	Dec. 14, 1863	3 yrs.	Mustered out May 30,1865,by order of War Department.
Battenfield, Joseph H....	...do...	18	Mch. 13, 1865	1 yr.	Mustered out with company Aug.7,1865.
Beasey, Wilson..........	...do...	18	Dec. 9, 1861	3 yrs.	Discharged Oct.21,1862,by order of War Department.
Berry, Lemuel..........	...do...	34	Feb. 27, 1865	1 yr.	Mustered out June 27,1865,at Petersburg,Va.,by order of War Department.
Black, John..........	...do...	20	Dec. 6, 1861	3 yrs.	Prisoner of war;no further record found.
Black, John..........	...do...	23	Mch. 1,1865	1 yr.	Mustered out June 6,1865,at Mower General Hospital,Philadelphia,Pa., by order of War Department.
Boden, William..........	...do...	19	Feb. 15, 1864	3 yrs.	Prisoner of war;mustered out June 27, 1865,at Petersburg,Va.,by order of War Department.
Borts, William..........	...do...	19	Nov. 11, 1861	3 yrs.	Killed May 28,1864,at Hawe's Shop, Va.; veteran.

179

Names.	Rank.	Age.	Date of Entering the Service.	Period of Service.	Remarks.
Brister, John.............	Private	21	Oct. 31, 1861	3 yrs.	Discharged May 22,1862,by order of War Department.
Brister, Isaac...........	...do...	22	Dec. 10, 1861	3 yrs.	Wounded Nov.9,1863,at Bealeton Station,Va.;mustered out Dec.20,1864, at Columbus,O.,on expiration of term of service.
Brown, William...........	...do...	26	Oct. 1, 1862	9 mos.	Drafted;mustered out July 29,1863,on expiration of term of service.
Burdick, Lorenzo.........	...do...	18	Jan. 24, 1865	1 yr.	Mustered out July 5,1865,at Peters-burg,Va.,by order of War Department.
Cameron, John............	...do...	18	Oct. 14, 1861	3 yrs.	Captured Sept.1,1863,at Barber's Cross Roads,Va.;mustered out Oct.14, 1864,on expiration of term of service.
Carew, George...........	...do...	36	Nov. 6, 1861	3 yrs.	Mustered out June 26,1865,at Peters-burg,Va.,by order of War Dept.;veteran.
Chappell, Melvin D.......	...do...	18	Dec. 10, 1861	3 yrs.	Mustered out Dec. 10,1864,on expira-tion of term of service.
Chase, Osmer C...........	...do...	23	Oct. 21, 1861	3 yrs.	Transferred from Co.B May 11,1862; discharged Sept.27,1864,at Columbus, O.,by order of War Department.
Cooley, Richard S........	...do...	19	Nov. 6, 1861	3 yrs.	Captured Sept.1,1863,at Barber's Cross Roads,Va.;mustered out Nov.8, 1864,on expiration of term of service.
Criss, Albert J..........	...do...	18	Nov. 15, 1861	3 yrs.	Transferred to Co.K May 20, 1862.
Darrow, Henry............	...do...	18	Jan. 4, 1864	3 yrs.	Captured Oct.1,1864,at Yellow Tavern, Va.;mustered out June 27,1865,at Petersburg,Va.,by order of War Dept.
Darrow, Lorenzo..........	...do...	42	Oct. 9, 1861	3 yrs.	Transferred from Co.B May 11,1862; discharged Dec.20,1862,by order of War Department.
Darrow, Milton...........	...do...	34	Oct. 21, 1861	3 yrs.	Transferred from Co.B May 11,1862; discharged Nov.17,1864,on Surgeon's certificate of disability.

180

SIXTH REGIMENT OHIO VOLUNTEER CAVALRY.

Names.	Rank.	Age.	Date of Entering the Service.	Period of Service.	Remarks.
Devease, Isaac..........	Private	20	Oct. 2, 1862	9 mos.	Drafted;mustered out July 29,1863,on expiration of term of service.
Diaziogene, Christian....	...do...	30	Dec. 9, 1861	3 yrs.	
Eagle, William..........	...do...	42	Mch. 23, 1863	3 yrs.	
Elliott, Edwin..........	...do...	20	Dec. 6, 1861	3 yrs.	Died May 31,1862,at Columbus, O.
Evans, John L...........	...do...	21	Dec. 7, 1861	3 yrs.	Captured Nov.13,1863,near Fayette-ville,Va.;mustered out June 3,1865, at Columbus,O.,by order of War Department; veteran.
Fendon, James...........	...do...	21	April 1, 1864	3 yrs.	
Foster, Frederick.......	...do...	21	Jan. 24, 1865	1 yr.	Mustered out June 27,1865,at Peters-burg,Va.,by order of War Department.
Fowler, George R........	...do...	21	Mch. 27, 1865	1 yr.	Mustered out June 27,1865,at Peters-burg,Va.,by order of War Department.
Francen, Peter..........	...do...	34	Mch. 13, 1865	1 yr.	Mustered out with company Aug.7,1865.
Grames, George A........	...do...	18	Feb. 13, 1864	3 yrs.	Mustered out with company Aug.7,1865.
Granan, James...........	...do...	35	Oct. 12, 1861	3 yrs.	Discharged March 9,1863,at Washington, D.C.,on Surgeon's certificate of disa-bility.
Hake, Enos H............	...do...	18	Nov. 30, 1861	3 yrs.	Wounded Oct. 14,1863,near Bristoe Station,Va.;discharged Feb.28,1864, on Surgeon's certificate of disability.
Harmon, Shannon.........	...do...	18	Oct. 22, 1861	3 yrs.	Captured Sept.1,1863,at Barber's Cross Roads,Va.;mustered out Oct.22, 1864,on expiration of term of service.
Harrison, Bernard.......	...do...	18	Nov. 11, 1861	3 yrs.	Mustered out Nov.11,1864,on expira-tion of term of service.
Harshman, Curtis O......	...do...	18	Dec. 9, 1861	3 yrs.	
Hastings, William H.....	...do...	26	Mch. 24, 1864	3 yrs.	Died Feb.21,1862,at Camp Dennison,O.

181

ROSTER OF OHIO TROOPS.

Names.	Rank.	Age.	Date of Entering the Service.	Period of Service.	Remarks.
Hauk, Thomas M...........	Private	24	Nov. 15, 1861	3 yrs.	Prisoner of war; mustered out Nov. 16,1864,on expiration of term of service.
Herst, Erwin.............	...do...	18	Jan. 30, 1865	1 yr.	Mustered out with company Aug.7,1865.
Hickey, John.............	...do...	26	Nov. 9, 1861	3 yrs.	Transferred to Veteran Reserve Corps, from which mustered out Dec.10,1864, on expiration of term of service.
Holder, Joseph H.........	...do...	20	Dec. 6, 1861	3 yrs.	Captured Oct.1,1864,at Yellow Tavern, Va.;mustered out June 5,1865, at Columbus, O., on Surgeon's certificate of disability.
Holstead, Gideon V.......	...do...	43	Oct. 28, 1861	3 yrs.	Discharged April 28,1862,at Columbus, O.,on Surgeon's certificate of disability.
Jack, John..............	...do...	32	Nov. 6, 1861	3 yrs.	Died Oct.1,1864,at City Point, Va.; veteran.
Jack, William...........	...do...	31	Feb. 20, 1864	3 yrs.	Mustered out June 14, 1865, at Chester, Pa.,by order of War Department.
Jarvis, John............	...do...	22	April 1, 1864	3 yrs.	
Jones, Charles B........	...do...	40	Nov. 6, 1861	3 yrs.	Discharged Jan.22,1863,at Washington, D.C.,on Surgeon's certificate of disability.
Kay, John..............	...do...	18	Dec. 10, 1861	3 yrs.	Mustered out Dec.12,1864,on expiration of term of service.
Keeler, Charles H.......	...do...	20	Nov. 28, 1861	3 yrs.	
Keller, George T.......	...do...	19	Dec. 8, 1861	3 yrs.	Discharged Dec.5,1862,by order of War Dept.
Keeler, John...........	...do...	26	Nov. 28, 1861	3 yrs.	
Kellogg, George A......	...do...	22	Oct. 2, 1862	9 mos.	Drafted;mustered out July 29,1863,on expiration of term of service.

SIXTH REGIMENT OHIO VOLUNTEER CAVALRY.

Names.	Rank.	Age.	Date of Entering the Service.	Period of Service.	Remarks.
Kincade, Thomas.........	Private	42	Nov. 30, 1861	3 yrs.	Died Sept.26,1862,at Newport, Va.
Kinsman, William H........	...do....	28	April 6, 1864	3 yrs.	
Kline, Benjamin T........	...do....	19	Nov. 5, 1861	3 yrs.	Died June 28,1863,at Washington, D.C.,of wounds received June 21,1863, at Upperville, Virginia.
Knox, Thomas S...........	...do....	23	Nov. 8, 1861	3 yrs.	Discharged March 19,1862,at Columbus, O., on Surgeon's certificate of disability.
Lalley, Patrick..........	...do....	21	Jan. 4, 1864	3 yrs.	
Landers, Andrew..........	...do....	18	Feb. 23, 1864	3 yrs.	Captured Oct.1,1864,at Yellow Tavern, Va.;mustered out July 18,1865,at Columbus, O.,by order of War Dept.
Lawless, Matthew.........	...do....	19	Feb. 16, 1864	3 yrs.	
Leonard, Hugh............	...do....	19	Mch. 21, 1865	1 yr.	Mustered out June 27,1865,at Peters-burg,Va.,by order of War Department.
Libus, Lucas.............	...do....	19	Oct. 2, 1862	9 mos.	Drafted; wounded March 17,1863,at Kelly's Ford,Va.;mustered out July 29,1863,on expiration of term of service.
Lynch, David.............	...do....	21	Dec. 28, 1863	3 yrs.	
McCanna, Patrick.........	...do....	29	Feb. 22, 1864	3 yrs.	Captured Oct.1,1864,at Yellow Tavern, Va.;furlough had May 15,1865;no further record found.
McCormick, William S.....	...do....	22	Oct. 2, 1862	9 mos.	Drafted;mustered out July 29,1863,on expiration of term of service.
McGilligan, Barney.......	...do....	32	Oct. 12, 1861	3 yrs.	
McKerchan, John..........	...do....	18	Dec. 21, 1863	3 yrs.	
McNalley, Patrick........	...do....	21	Jan. 4, 1864	3 yrs.	

SIXTH REGIMENT OHIO VOLUNTEER CAVALRY.

Names.	Rank.	Age.	Date of Entering the Service.	Period of Service.	Remarks.
Mauby, Joseph..........	Private	24	Oct. 28, 1861	3 yrs.	Reduced from Corporal at own request June 24,1862;captured July 4,1862, at South Mountain Gap,Md.;mustered out Oct.28,1864,on expiration of term of service.
Miller, Joseph B........	...do...	....	Dec. 7, 1861	3 yrs.	Wounded May 28,1864,at Hawe's Shop, Va.;mustered out March 25,1865,on Surgeon's certificate of disability; veteran.
Mills, Samuel..........	...do...	26	Oct. 14, 1861	3 yrs.	Discharged Aut.22,1862,on Surgeon's certificate of disability.
Moore, William..........	...do...	18	Dec. 10, 1861	3 yrs.	Captured Oct.1,1864,at Yellow Tavern, Va.;mustered out with company Aug. 7,1865; veteran.
Morris, David..........	...do...	32	Dec. 21, 1863	3 yrs.	
Morris, James L..........	...do...	34	Jan. 4, 1864	3 yrs.	Mustered out June 3,1865,by order of War Department.
Morris, Thomas..........	...do...	29	Nov. 6, 1861	3 yrs.	Mustered out June 27,1865,at Peters-burg,Va.,by order of War Department.
Nelligan, Michael......	...do...	28	Feb. 19, 1864	3 yrs.	Died Sept.3,1864,at Cleveland,O.
Nolan, James..........	...do...	19	Dec. 16, 1863	3 yrs.	Mustered out June 27,1865,at Peters-burg,Va.,by order of War Department.
O'Donnell, Hugh..........	...do...	25	Dec. 9, 1861	3 yrs.	Discharged Nov.9,1862,at Washington, D.C.,on Surgeon's certificate of disability.
Osborn, Emory..........	...do...	19	Oct. 2, 1862	9 mos.	Drafted;wounded June 17,1863,at Aldie, Va.;mustered out July 29,1863, on expiration of term of service.
Parks, Samuel W..........	...do...	18	Dec. 9, 1861	3 yrs.	Captured July 4,1863,at Gettysburg, Pa.;discharged Jan.5,1865,on expira-tion of term of service.

Names.	Rank.	Age.	Date of Entering the Service	Period of Service.	Remarks.
Patterson, Allen..........	Private	20	Oct. 18, 1861	3 yrs.	Discharged Aug.28,1862,on Surgeon's certificate of disability.
Pettibone, Albert A.......	...do...	18	Jan. 4, 1864	3 yrs.	Wounded Feb.6,1865,at Hathcer's Run, Va.;discharged May 3,1865,on Surgeon's certificate of disability.
Porter, Charles A.........	...do...	18	April 3, 1865	1 yr.	Mustered out June 27,1865,at Petersburg,Va.,by order of War Department.
Pratt, Orlando M..........	...do...	24	Nov. 11, 1861	3 yrs.	Discharged April 9,1862,at Columbus, O.,on Surgeon's certificate of disability.
Rader, John..............	...do...	19	Dec. 4, 1861	3 yrs.	Discharged Jan.31,1863,on Surgeon's certificate of disability.
Ratliff, Samuel E........	...do...	27	Mch. 9, 1865	1 yr.	Mustered out June 27,1865,at Petersburg,Va.,by order of War Department.
Reichard, William........	...do...	20	Jan. 27, 1864	3 yrs.	Mustered out June 27,1865,at Petersburg,Va.,by order of War Department.
Rice, David.............	...do...	19	Mch. 1, 1865	1 yr.	Mustered out June 27,1865,at Petersburg,Va.,by order of War Department.
Roark, James............	...do...	30	Dec. 5, 1861	3 yrs.	Captured Sept.1,1863,at Barber's Cross Roads,Va.;died Aug.6,1864,in Andersonville Prison, Ga.
Rudisel, Sylvanus.......	...do...	18	Dec. 9, 1861	3 yrs.	Discharged by civil authority Jan. 16,1862.
Sands, George..........	...do...	18	Feb. 12, 1864	3 yrs.	Mustered out with company Aug.7,1865.
Sears, David S.........	...do...	25	Oct. 31, 1861	3 yrs.	Captured Sept.1,1863,at Barber's Cross Roads,Va.;mustered out Nov.8, 1864,on expiration of term of service.
Sheehan, Dennis........	...do...	43	Feb. 16, 1864	3 yrs.	Missing in action March 31,1865,at Dinwiddie Court House, Va.;no further record found.

SIXTH REGIMENT OHIO VOLUNTEER CAVALRY.

Names.	Rank.	Age.	Date of Entering the Service.	Period of Service.	Remarks.
Sheible, William..........	Private	24	Dec. 9, 1861	3 yrs.	Missing in Action Sept.1,1863,at Barber's Cross Roads,Va.;no further record found.
Shirer, Benjamin F........	...do...	18	Feb. 18, 1864	3 yrs.	Captured Oct.1,1864,at Yellow Tavern, Va.;died Jan.16,1865,in Salisbury Prison, North Carolina.
Smith, Hiram..............	...do...	24	Feb. 24, 1864	3 yrs.	Mustered out June 27,1865,at Peters- burg,Va.,by order of War Department.
Snow, Calvin..............	...do...	24	April 5, 1865	3 yrs.	Mustered out June 27,1865,at Peters- burg,Va.,by order of War Department.
Swartz, Jonathan..........	...do...	18	Feb. 29, 1864	3 yrs.	Mustered out June 27,1865,at Peters- burg,Va.,by order of War Department.
Taylor, Charles...........	...do...	36	Nov. 8, 1861	3 yrs.	Discharged Sept.14,1864,at Washington, D.C.,on Surgeon's certificate of disability.
Thorp, George S...........	...do...	21	Oct. 10, 1861	3 yrs.	Captured Sept.1,1863,at Barber's Cross Roads,Va.;died Nov.22,1863 in prison at Richmond, Va.
Thorp, John S.............	...do...	44	Oct. 29, 1861	3 yrs.	Discharged Feb.12,1863,at New York, on Surgeon's certificate of disability.
Thornton, Benjamin........	...do...	43	Nov. 6, 1861	3 yrs.	Discharged Sept.23,1863,by order of War Department.
Tracy, David D............	...do...	25	Nov. 6, 1861	3 yrs.	Discharged Aug.21,1862,on Surgeon's certificate of disability.
Tribfilner, Joseph........	...do...	38	Mch. 2, 1864	3 yrs.	Wounded June 24,1864,at St.Mary's Church, Virginia.
Traxler, Joseph...........	...do...	24	Oct. 2, 1862	9 mos.	Drafted;mustered out July 29,1863, on expiration of term of service.
Truesdale, John H.........	...do...	18	Dec. 10, 1861	3 yrs.	Discharged by civil authority Dec. 18, 1861.

Name.	Rank.	Age.	Date of Entering the Service.	Period of Service.	Remarks.
Whittey, Patrick........	Private	34	Nov. 6, 1861	3 yrs.	Transferred to Veteran Reserve Corps June 1,1864.
Williams, Roger.........	...do...	18	Feb. 14, 1864	3 yrs.	Mustered out June 27,1865,at Petersburg,Va.,by order of War Department.
Wright, John............	...do...	27	April 12,1865	1 yr.	Mustered out June 27,1865,at Petersburg,Va., by order of War Department.
Zimmerman, Josiah.......	...do...	18	Feb. 24, 1864	3 yrs.	Wounded and captured June 24,1864, at St.Mary's Church,Va.;no further record found.

COMPANY H.

Mustered in from October 16 to December 30, 1861, at Ironton, Ohio by Joseph L. Barber, U. S. Mustering Officer. Mustered out August 7, 1865, at Petersburg, Va., by L. H. Bowen, 1st Lieutenant and Acting Commissary of Musters, Mustering Officer, Department of Virginia.

Name.	Rank.	Age.	Date of Entering the Service.	Period of Service.	Remarks.
Joseph L. Barber........	Captain	48	Oct. 16, 1861	3 yrs.	Mustered as 2d Lieutenant;promoted to Captain Dec.15,1861;discharged April 14,1864,on Surgeon's certificate of disability.
Dyas C. Ellis...........	...do...	28	Oct. 28, 1861	3 yrs.	Mustered as private; promoted to 1st Lieutenant Dec.15,1861;to Captain April 13,1864;mustered out Nov.15,1864,on expiration of term of service.
George W. Shattuck......	...do...	28	Nov. 6, 1861	3 yrs.	Mustered as private;promoted to 2d Lieutenant Dec.15,1861;to 1st Lieutenant Co.B May 9,1864;to Captain Co.H Nov.12,1864;promoted to Major April 8,1865,to Lieut.Colonel July 30,1865,but not mustered on either promotion;mustered out with company Aug.7,1865.

SIXTH REGIMENT OHIO VOLUNTEER CAVALRY

Names.	Rank.	Age.	Date of Entering the Service.	Period of Service.	Remarks.
Simon D. Young..........	2d Leiut.	23	Oct. 28, 1861	3 yrs.	Promoted from 1st Sergeant Co. K May 9,1864;promoted to 1st Lieutenant Nov.12,1864,but not mustered; mustered out Feb.25,1865,on expiration of term of service.
Augustus S. Reckard......	1st Sergt.	20	Oct. 23, 1861	3 yrs.	Appointed Corporal Dec.30,1861;1st Sergeant Feb.11,1862;killed June 17, 1863,at Aldie Va.
Hiram G. Suiter..........	...do....	23	Dec. 11, 1861	3 yrs.	Mustered as private;appointed Sergeant Dec.30,1861;1st Sergeant Sept. 1,1863; promoted to 2d Lieutenant Co.K July 25,1864.
Francis M. Pritchard.....	...do....	25	Oct. 23, 1861	3 yrs.	Appointed Corporal Feb.11,1862;Sergeant July 1,1863;1st Sergeant Sept. 1,1864;missing in action and supposed to be killed Sept.29,1864,at Hatcher's Run, Va.
William H. Bazell........	...do....	29	Dec. 2, 1861	3 yrs.	Mustered as private;appointed Sergeant Dec.30,1861;reduced to ranks at his own request June 22,1862;promoted to Regt.Com.Sergeant,Aug.1,1862,but declined promotion; appointed Com.Sergeant Oct.15,1862;1st Sergeant,Oct. 11,1864;mustered out Dec.2,1864, on expiration of term of service.
Fletcher Golden..........	...do....	37	Dec. 29, 1863	3 yrs.	Mustered as private; appointed 1st Sergeant Oct.1,1864;wounded Feb.5, 1865,at Hatcher's Run,Va.;promoted to 2d Lieutenant May 31,1865,but not mustered;mustered out June 27,1865, at Petersburg,Va.,by order of War Dept.

ROSTER OF OHIO TROOPS.

Names.	Rank.	Age.	Date of Entering the Service.	Period of Service.	Remarks.
Joel Stover	Q.M.S.	45	Oct. 25, 1861	3 yrs.	Mustered as private; appointed Q.M. Sergeant Dec.20,1861;mustered out Nov.3,1864,on expiration of term of service.
Israel P. Cross	...do...	21	Dec. 31, 1861	3 yrs.	Appointed Corporal Jan.1,1863;wounded May 9,1864,on Sheridan's Raid,Va.; appointed Q.M.Sergeant March 1,1865; mustered out June 27,1865,at Petersburg,Va.,by order of War Dept.;veteran.
Asher Sperry	Com.Ser.	19	Dec. 4, 1861	3 yrs.	Appointed Corporal Sept.1,1863;Com. Sergeant March 1,1865;mustered out June 27,1865,at Petersburg,Va.;veteran.
James M. Noble	Sergeant	29	Dec. 12, 1861	3 yrs.	Mustered as private;appointed Ser- geant Dec.30,1861;mustered out Dec. 4,1864,on expiration of term of service.
Thomas Lambert	...do...	23	Oct. 18, 1861	3 yrs.	Appointed Corporal Dec.30,1861;Ser- geant July 1,1862;died June 30,1863, at Washington, D.C.
William M. Smith	...do...	30	Nov. 10, 1861	3 yrs.	Mustered as private;appointed Ser- geant Oct.15,1862;mustered out June 27,1865,at Petersburg,Va.,by order of War Department; veteran.
Richard Butler	...do...	33	Dec. 4, 1861	3 yrs.	Appointed Corporal Jan.1,1863;Sergeant Sept.1,1863;mustered out Dec.2,1864, on expiration of term of service.
William G. Lambert	...do...	19	Dec. 23, 1861	3 yrs.	Mustered as private;appointed Sergeant Jan.1,1864;promoted to 2d Lieutenant July 30,1865,but not mustered; mus- tered out with company Aug.7,1865; veteran.

189

SIXTH REGIMENT OHIO VOLUNTEER CAVALRY

Names.	Rank.	Age.	Date of Entering the Service.	Period of Service.	Remarks.
Andrew Primm............	Sergeant	19	Dec. 2, 1861	3 yrs.	Appointed Corporal Sept.1,1863;Sergeant March 1,1865;mustered out with company Aug.7,1865; veteran.
William Porter............	...do...	23	Nov. 2, 1861	3 yrs.	Appointed Corporal Sept.1,1863;Sergeant March 1,1865;mustered out with company Aug. 7,1865; veteran.
Henry C. Gillett..........	Corporal	....	Oct. 23, 1861	3 yrs.	Appointed Jan.1,1863;discharged Dec. 9,1863,on Surgeon's certificate of disability.
John E. Hunter...........	...do...	18	Oct. 28, 1861	3 yrs.	Appointed Jan.1,1863;captured Jan. 13,1863,near Garrisonville,Va.; wounded Oct.14,1863, in action at Auburn Mills,Va.;mustered out Oct. 28,1864,on expiration of term of service.
Daniel McDaniels.........	...do...	43	Oct. 22, 1861	3 yrs.	Appointed Sept.1,1863,discharged Aug.16,1865,on Surgeon's certificate of disability; veteran.
William Lambert..........	...do...	24	Dec. 18, 1861	3 yrs.	Appointed—;killed March 31,1865,at Dinwiddie Court House,Va.;veteran.
Edward Rhodes............	...do...	22	Dec. 26, 1861	3 yrs.	Appointed—;mustered out June 27,1865, at Petersburg,Va.,by order of War Department; veteran.
James M. Canterbury......	...do...	20	Nov. 15, 1861	3 yrs.	Appointed March 1,1865;mustered out with company Aug.7,1865; veteran.
Anthony H. Crawford......	...do...	22	April 9, 1864	3 yrs.	Appointed March 1,1865;mustered out with company Aug.7,1865.
John M. Newman..........	...do...	18	Oct. 22, 1861	3 yrs.	Appointed March 1,1865;mustered out June 27,1865,at Petersburg,Va., by order of War Department; veteran.

Names.	Rank.	Age.	Date of Entering the Service.	Period of Service.	Remarks.
Elmon T. Floyd............	Corporal	19	Nov. 20, 1861	3 yrs.	Wounded May 3,1863,at Chancellorsville,Va.;appointed Corporal March 1,1865;mustered out June 27,1865, at Petersburg,Va.,by order of War Department; veteran.
Albert Shore..............	...do...	19	Mch. 14, 1864	3 yrs.	Appointed March 1,1865;mustered out June 27,1865,at Petersburg,Va.,by order of War Department.
Charles Bonsall..........	Bugler	19	Dec. 23, 1861	3 yrs.	Appointed Dec.30,1861;discharged May 3,1862,on Surgeon's certificate of disability.
Martin H. Kouns..........	...do...	16	Nov. 30, 1861	3 yrs.	Appointed Dec.30,1861;discharged Nov. 4,1862,on Surgeon's certificate of disability.
Seliah H. Farley.........	...do...	19	Dec. 4, 1861	3 yrs.	Appointed April 1,1863;mustered out Dec.2,1864,on expiration of term of service.
Solomon Large............	...do...	32	Dec. 4, 1861	3 yrs.	Appointed ——;mustered out with company Aug.7,1865; veteran.
Andrew J. Stephenson.....	Farrier	45	Dec. 30, 1861	3 yrs.	Appointed Dec.30,1861;mustered out Dec.12,1864,on expiration of term of service.
Ulysses Hamlin...........	...do...	27	Nov. 15, 1861	3 yrs.	Appointed Sept.1,1863;mustered out June 27,1865,at Petersburg,Va., by order of War Department; veteran.
James T. Hardy...........	...do...	20	Dec. 2, 1861	3 yrs.	Appointed Oct.15,1862;mustered out June 27,1865,at Petersburg,Va.,by order of War Department; veteran.
William Goldner..........	...do...	32	Feb. 12, 1864	3 yrs.	Appointed ——;mustered out June 27, 1865,at Petersburg,Va.,by order of War Department.

191

SIXTH REGIMENT OHIO VOLUNTEER CAVALRY.

Names.	Rank.	Age.	Date of Entering the Service.	Period of Service.	Remarks.
Stephen Munday...........	Saddler	34	Oct. 28, 1861	3 yrs.	Appointed Corporal Dec.30,1861;reduced to ranks and appointed Saddler Sept.1,1862;mustered out Nov.3,1864, on expiration of term of service.
George M. Booth..........	...do...	21	Oct. 22, 1861	3 yrs.	Appointed Dec.30,1861;killed June 16, 1862,near Mt.Jackson,Va.
William Reis.............	...do...	43	Dec. 4, 1861	3 yrs.	Appointed ——;mustered out June 27, 1865,at Petersburg,Va.,by order of War Department; veteran.
John Fox.................	Wagoner	44	Oct. 25, 1861	3 yrs.	Appointed Dec.30,1861;discharged Nov. 26,1862,on Surgeon's certificate of disability.
Charles Clutts...........	...do...	28	Dec. 5, 1861	3 yrs.	Appointed Dec.1,1862;mustered out Dec. 2,1864,on expiration of term of service.
Adams, George W..........	Private	38	Jan. 26, 1864	3 yrs.	Mustered out June 27,1865,at Petersburg,Va.,by order of War Department.
Adams, James.............	...do...	29	Dec. 3, 1861	3 yrs.	Captured Aug.25,1863,near Salem,Va.; died Nov.17,1863,in prison at Richmond, Virginia.
Adams, Samuel............	...do...	18	Feb. 2, 1864	3 yrs.	Wounded July 28,1865;mustered out June 27,1865,at Petersburg,Va.,by order of War Department.
Akers, William...........	...do...	33	Nov. 6, 1861	3 yrs.	Wounded June 17,1863,at Aldie,Va.; mustered out June 27,1865,at Petersburg,Va.,by order of War Department; veteran.
Arthur, William..........	...do...	24	Nov. 9, 1861	3 yrs.	Mustered out June 27,1865,at Petersburg,Va.,by order of War Dept.;veteran.
Bagley, Richard..........	...do...	36	Oct. 23, 1861	3 yrs.	Died Nov.18,1864,at Washington,D.C.; veteran.

Names.	Rank.	Age.	Date of Entering the Service.	Period of Service.	Remarks.
Bisel, John.............	Private	19	Dec. 10, 1861	3 yrs.	Discharged Aug.8,1862,on Surgeon's certificate of disability.
Blowers, Uriah.........	...do...	28	Dec. 4, 1861	3 yrs.	Mustered out June 27,1865,at Peters- burg,Va.;by order of War Department; veteran.
Boggs, Charles L.......	...do...	23	Oct. 28, 1861	3 yrs.	Discharged July 16, 1863,on Surgeon's certificate of disability.
Bradford, Patrick H....	...do...	18	Dec. 5, 1861	3 yrs.	Died April 21,1863,at Aquia Creek,Va.
Bruce, Wilson S........	...do...	19	Dec. 4, 1861	3 yrs.	Died June 22,1863,of wounds received in action June 17,1863,at Aldie,Va.
Buck, James...........	...do...	38	Mch. 3, 1864	3 yrs.	Transferred to Co.A,14th Regiment Veteran Reserve Corps,from which dis- charged Jan.3,1865,on Surgeon's cer- tificate of disability.
Burbank, Henry G.......	...do...	28	Dec. 2, 1863	3 yrs.	Mustered out June 27, 1865,at Peters- burg,Va.,by order of War Department.
Byard, George L.......	...do...	18	Oct. 24, 1861	3 yrs.	Captured Nov.9,1862,at Fredericksburg, Va.;wounded Aug.21,1864,at Weldon Railroad;died Oct.11,1864, at Phila- delphia, Pa.
Cooper, David G.......	...do...	22	Nov. 2, 1861	3 yrs.	Mustered out June 27, 1865,at Peters- burg,Va.,by order of War Department; veteran.
Corbin, Martin........	...do...	18	Dec. 11, 1861	3 yrs.	Mustered out June 27,1865,at Peters- burg,Va.,by order of War Department; veteran.
Cornwell, Silas.......	...do...	38	Dec. 16, 1861	3 yrs.	Discharged Feb.23,1863,on Surgeon's certificate of disability.
Dalton, William.......	...do...	18	Jan. 3, 1864	3 yrs.	Wounded June 24,1864,at St. Mary's Church,Va.;died June 10,1865,at Petersburg,Virginia.

193

SIXTH REGIMENT OHIO VOLUNTEER CAVALRY.

Names.	Rank.	Age.	Date of Entering the Service.	Period of Service.	Remarks.
Day, James..............	Private	22	Oct. 22, 1861	3 yrs.	Mustered out June 27,1865,at Petersburg,Va.,by order of War Dept.;veteran.
Donohoe, William H.......	...do...	21	Dec. 11, 1861	3 yrs.	Reduced from 1st Sergeant at his own request Feb.10,1862;transferred to Signal Corps,U.S.A.,Jan.1,1864.
Duke, James W...........	...do...	29	Oct. 22, 1861	3 yrs.	Wounded Oct.27,1864,at Hatcher's Run, Va.;mustered out June 27,1865, at Petersburg,Va.,by order of War Department; veteran.
Farnam, Darwin...........	...do...	19	Mch. 26, 1864	3 yrs.	Mustered out June 27,1865,at Chester, Pa.,by order of War Deparment.
Fleming, Isaiah..........	...do...	28	Dec. 30, 1861	3 yrs.	Mustered out March 22,1865,by order of War Department; veteran.
Foster, Bartlett.........	...do...	42	Nov. 18, 1861	3 yrs.	Transferred to Co.K,17th Regiment Veteran Reserve Corps,Feb.15,1864, from which mustered out Nov.26,1864, on expiration of term of service.
Foster, Hector P.........	...do...	23	Nov. 19, 1861	3 yrs.	Discharged March 27,1865,on Surgeon's certificate of disability; veteran.
Frampton, Isaac G........	...do...	23	Oct. 22, 1861	3 yrs.	Captured June 16,1862,near Mt.Jackson, Va.;mustered out Oct.21,1864,on expiration of term of service.
Frank, Conrad...........	...do...	19	Mch. 3, 1864	3 yrs.	Wounded Oct.27,1864,at Hatcher's Run, Va.;mustered out with company Aug. 7, 1865.
Freeman, Moses A.,Jr.....	...do...	19	Nov. 2, 1861	3 yrs.	Mustered out Nov.3,1864,on expiration of term of service.
Freeman, Moses A.,Sr.....	...do...	44	Oct. 29, 1861	3 yrs.	Reduced from Corporal at his own request Dec.31,1862;wounded June 21, 1863,at Upperville,Va.;died Jan. 23, 1864,at Washington, D.C.

Names.	Rank.	Age.	Date of Entering the Service.	Period of Service.	Remarks.
Gillett, Urban J........	Private	18	Dec. 5, 1861	3 yrs.	Mustered out Dec.2,1864,on expiration of term of service.
Hall, John N........	...do...	24	Oct. 25, 1861	3 yrs.	Never joined the company.
Hallock, Nathan D........	...do...	31	Dec. 11, 1861	3 yrs.	Reduced from Corporal;mustered out June 27,1865,at Petersburg,Va.,by order of War Department; veteran.
Hamilton, Henry........	...do...	27	Jan. 14, 1864	3 yrs.	Never joined the company.
Hamilton, Thomas........	...do...	16	Nov. 10, 1861	3 yrs.	Appointed Sergeant Dec.30,1861; wounded June 24,1864,at St.Mary's Church,Va.; mustered out Nov. 3, 1864,at Petersburg,Va.,on expiration of term of service.
Hamlin, McThomas........	...do...	23	Oct. 22, 1861	3 yrs.	Mustered out Oct.21,1864,on expiration of term of service.
Harmon, John F........	...do...	28	Oct. 22, 1862	3 yrs.	Transferred from Co.E March 15,1863; mustered out May 8,1865,on expiration of term of service.
Hileman, Joseph........	...do...	....	Jan. 17, 1864	3 yrs.	Never joined the company.
Hill, John C........	...do...	22	Dec. 18, 1863	3 yrs.	
Holderly, William R........	...do...	18	Feb. 29, 1864	3 yrs.	Mustered out June 27,1865,at Petersburg,Va.,by order of War Department.
Hood, Francis M........	...do...	25	Nov. 15, 1861	3 yrs.	Mustered out Nov.16,1864,on expiration of term of service.
Hoskins, James........	...do...	23	April 1, 1864	3 yrs.	Mustered out June 27,1865,at Petersburg,Va.,by order of War Department.
Imes, George........	...do...	25	Nov. 2, 1861	3 yrs.	Mustered out with company Aug.7,1865; veteran.
Irwin, William........	...do...	34	Dec. 16, 1863	3 yrs.	

SIXTH REGIMENT OHIO VOLUNTEER CAVALRY.

Names.	Rank.	Age.	Date of Entering the Service.	Period of Service.	Remarks.
James, Benjamin N........	Private	29	Dec. 2, 1861	3 yrs.	Reduced from Corporal at his own request Dec.31,1862;mustered out Dec.2,1864,on expiration of term of service.
Johnson, Francis.........	...do...	22	Jan. 15, 1864	3 yrs.	
Kavanaugh, Patrick.......	...do...	29	Dec. 9, 1861	3 yrs.	Mustered out June 27,1865,at Petersburg,Va.,by order of War Department; veteran.
Kearns, Jesse............	...do...	44	Oct. 22, 1861	3 yrs.	Mustered out June 27,1865,at Petersburg,Va.,by order of War Department; veteran.
Kelvey, John.............	...do...	26	Feb. 29, 1864	3 yrs.	Mustered out June 27,1865,at Petersburg,Va.,by order of War Department.
King, James.............	...do...	18	Nov. 20, 1861	3 yrs.	Never reported to company,but joined the 5th Regiment Virginia Infantry, and was subsequently killed in action in West Virginia.
Kopish, Herman...........	...do...	19	Dec. 14, 1863	3 yrs.	
Lambert, Thornton........	...do...	41	Nov. 2, 1861	3 yrs.	Mustered out May 30,1865,on expiration of term of service.
Layne, William F.........	...do...	36	Oct. 31, 1861	3 yrs.	Reduced from Corporal at his own request Dec.31,1862;mustered out Nov. 3,1864,on expiration of term of service.
Little, James E..........	...do...	22	Nov. 6, 1861	3 yrs.	
McCoy, Charles...........	...do...	26	Oct. 3, 1862	9 mos.	Drafted;mustered out July 29,1863, on expiration of term of service.
McNight, George..........	...do...	18	Dec. 12, 1861	3 yrs.	Mustered out June 27,1865,at Petersburg,Va.,by order of War Department; veteran.
Mahan, James............	...do...	41	Aug. 2, 1864	3 yrs.	Mustered out June 17,1865,at Petersburg,Va.,by order of War Department.

ROSTER OF OHIO TROOPS.

Names.	Rank.	Age.	Date of Entering the Service.	Period of Service.	Remarks.
Miller, Fritz..........	Private	35	Mch. 1, 1865	1 yr.	Mustered out June 6,1865,by order of War Department.
Miller, William R........	...do...	22	Mch. 30, 1864	3 yrs.	Mustered out June 27,1865,at Petersburg,Va.,by order of War Department.
Mills, William..........	...do...	19	Aug. 31, 1864	3 yrs.	Mustered out with company Aug.7,1865.
Mock, Isaac N..........	...do...	33	Oct. 1, 1862	9 mos.	Drafted;mustered out July 29,1863,on expiration of term of service.
Morris, William.........	...do...	31	Nov. 4, 1861	3 yrs.	Mustered out Nov.3,1864,on expiration of term of service.
Mowray, S........	...do...	34	Oct. 28, 1861	3 yrs.	Mustered out Nov.3,1864,on expiration of term of service.
Nagle, Conrad..........	...do...	29	Dec. 2, 1861	3 yrs.	Mustered out June 27,1865,at Petersburg,Va.,by order of War Department; veteran.
Neff, Hugh..........	...do...	25	Dec. 13, 1861	3 yrs.	Mustered out June 27,1865,at Petersburg,Va.,by order of War Department; veteran.
Newman, John..........	...do...	41	Oct. 23, 1861	3 yrs.	Captured Nov.14,1863,near Fayetteville,Va.;mustered out Oct.21,1864, on expiration of term of service.
Noble, Samuel..........	...do...	20	Dec. 6, 1861	3 yrs.	Mustered out June 27,1865,at Petersburg,Va.,by order of War Department; veteran.
O'Rafferty, John.........	...do...	38	Jan. 2, 1862	3 yrs.	Captured May 9,1864,on Sheridan's Raid,Va.;died Oct.1,1864,in Andersonville Prison, Ga.
Peterson, George F........	...do...	21	Mch. 2, 1865	1 yr.	Mustered out June 27,1865,at Petersburg,Va.,by order of War Department.
Pickle, Joseph W.........	...do...	18	Oct. 1, 1862	9 mos.	Drafted;mustered out July 29,1863,on expiration of term of service.

197

SIXTH REGIMENT OHIO VOLUNTEER CAVALRY.

Names.	Rank.	Age.	Date of Entering the Service.	Period of Service.	Remarks.
Rhodes, James............	Private	36	Mch. 31, 1864	3 yrs.	Mustered out June 27,1865,at Petersburg,Va.,by order of War Department.
Rhodes, Joshua..........	...do....	19	Dec. 6, 1861	3 yrs.	Captured Oct.21,1862;discharged Feb. 13,1863,by reason of enlistment in Regular Army.
Rickert, Joseph.........	...do....	31	Dec. 2, 1861	3 yrs.	Discharged March 10,1862,on Surgeon's certificate of disability.
Robinson, John A........	...do....	44	Dec. 2, 1861	3 yrs.	Discharged May 26,1862,on Surgeon's certificate of disability.
Scovel, Matthew L.......	...do....	18	Oct. 22, 1861	3 yrs.	Captured Oct.7,1862,near Hartwood Church,Va.;mustered out Oct.25,1864, on expiration of term of service.
Smith, Oliver..........	...do....	35	Jan. 13, 1864	3 yrs.	Mustered out June 27,1865,at Petersburg,Va.,by order of War Department.
Smith, Warren..........	...do....	26	Oct. 1, 1862	9 mos.	Drafted;mustered out July 29,1863,on expiration of term of service.
Smith, William G........	...do....	22	Nov. 2, 1861	3 yrs.	Mustered out Nov.3,1864,on expiration of term of service.
Spear, Charles W........	...do....	18	Dec. 5, 1861	3 yrs.	Reduced from Corporal at his own request Dec.31,1862;mustered out June 27,1865,at Petersburg,Va.,by order of War Department;veteran.
Sperry, James..........	...do....	23	Dec. 5, 1861	3 yrs.	Reduced from Corporal at his own request Sept.1,1862;died Oct.8,1864, at City Point,Va.; veteran.
Spotz, Philip..........	...do....	30	Feb. 25, 1865	1 yr.	Mustered out June 27,1865,at Petersburg,Va.,by order of War Department.
Stanley, William........	...do....	39	Aug. 11, 1864	1 yr.	Mustered out June 27,1865,at Petersburg,Va.,by order of War Department.

Names.	Rank.	Age.	Date of Entering the Service.	Period of Service.	Remarks.
Stepleton, Lawson.........	Private	18	Dec. 10, 1861	3 yrs.	Mustered out Dec. 12,1864,on expiration of term of service.
Stewart, Middleton H.....	...do...	21	Oct. 31, 1861	3 yrs.	Mustered out Nov. 3, 1864,on expiration of term of service.
Stewart, Rufus C..........	...do...	31	Oct. 31, 1861	3 yrs.	Died March 29,1862,in Lawrence County, Ohio.
Tatem, William E..........	...do...	30	Nov. 2, 1861	3 yrs.	Mustered out June 17,1865,at Petersburg,Va.,by order of War Department; veteran.
Thomas, John...............	...do...	19	Oct. 4, 1862	9 mos.	Drafted; died April 17,1863,at Potomac Creek Station, Va.
Thomas, James.............	...do...	18	Feb. 14, 1864	3 yrs.	Died March 20,1864,at Columbus, Ohio.
Turvey, Isaac.............	...do...	29	Dec. 9, 1861	3 yrs.	Discharged May 27,1862,on Surgeon's certificate of disability.
Ward, John E.............	...do...	19	Nov. 14, 1861	3 yrs.	Reduced from Corporal at his own request Aug.31,1863;died Oct.26,1864, at Point Lookout,Md.; veteran.
Wilds, Joseph.............	...do...	19	April 8, 1864	3 yrs.	Mustered out with company Aug.7,1865.
Winters, Amaziah..........	...do...	20	Dec. 10, 1861	3 yrs.	Wounded June 6,1864;mustered out Dec.12,1864,on expiration of term of service.
Zigler, Emanuel..........	...do...	18	Oct. 2, 1862	9 mos.	Drafted;mustered out July 29,1863, on expiration of term of service.
Zimmerman, Jeremiah......	...do...	23	Oct. 2, 1862	9 mos.	Drafted;captured Jan. 13,1862,near Garrisonville,Va.;mustered out July 29,1863,on expiration of term of service.

SIXTH REGIMENT OHIO VOLUNTEER CAVALRY.

COMPANY I.

Mustered in from October 9, 1861, at Camp Hutchins, Warren, Ohio, by James S. Abell and Elias Shepherd,
U. S. Mustering Officers. Mustered out August 7, 1865, at Petersburg, Va., by L. H. Bowen,
1st Lieutenant and Acting Commissary of Musters. Mustering Officer Department
of Virginia.

Names.	Rank.	Age.	Date of Entering the Service.	Period of Service.	Remarks.
James S. Abell...........	Captain	34	Oct. 9, 1861	3 yrs.	Mustered as 2d Lieutenant;promoted to Captain Dec.16,1861;commissioned Major May 9,1864,but not mustered, as he was killed same day in action at Hawe's Shop,Va.
John L. Miller...........	...do...	27	Oct. 7, 1861	3 yrs.	Promoted from 1st Lieutenant Co.C July 25,1864;mustered out Oct.6, 1864,on expiration of term of service.
Reuben E. Osgood.........	...do...	34	Nov. 1, 1861	3 yrs.	Promoted from 1st Lieutenant Co.K Nov.12,1864;commissioned Major July 30,1865,but not mustered;mustered out with company Aug.7,1865.
William J. Haight........	1st Lieut.	44	Oct. 15, 1861	3 yrs.	Mustered as private;promoted to 1st Lieutenant Dec.16,1861;discharged Oct. 2,1862,on Surgeon's certificate of disability.
Elias Shepherd..........	...do...	45	Oct. 8, 1861	3 yrs.	Appointed 2d Lieutenant from civil life;promoted to 1st Lieutenant Oct. 6,1862;captured Sept.1,1863,at Barber's Cross Roads,Va.;mustered out April 25,1865,by order of War Dept.
Jeremiah H. Phillips.....	2d Lieut.	42	Oct. 15, 1861	3 yrs.	Mustered as private;appointed 1st Sergeant Dec.16,1861;captured Nov. 10,1862,in action;promoted to 2d Lieutenant Aug.11,1864,but not mustered;died Sept.19,1864,at City Point, Va.

ROSTER OF OHIO TROOPS.

Names.	Rank.	Age.	Date of Entering the Service.	Period of Service.	Remarks.
Max Elben................	Sad.Ser.	33	Oct. 9, 1861	3 yrs.	Promoted from Saddler Co. I Jan. 1, 1862; discharged Sept. 17, 1862, by order of War Department.
Joseph Young.............	...do...	22	Nov. 28, 1861	3 yrs.	Promoted from Saddler Co. C May 1, 1863; mustered out June 27, 1865, at Petersburg, Va., by order of War Department, veteran.
Shattuck, Charles........	Private	21	Oct. 12, 1861	3 yrs.	Mustered out Oct. 12, 1864, on expiration of term of service.
Smith, Henry.............	...do...	24	Jan. 31, 1864	3 yrs.	Mustered out June 27, 1865, at Petersburg, Va., by order of War Department.
Spring, Rudolpheus L.....	...do...	28	Mch. 7, 1865	1 yr.	Mustered out June 12, 1865, at Baltimore, Md., by order of War Department.
Stone, Wilber H..........	...do...	21	Oct. 12, 1861	3 yrs.	Discharged Aug. 12, 1862, on Surgeon's certificate of disability.
Stroud, Henry............	...do...	22	Oct. 12, 1861	3 yrs.	Discharged Nov. 9, 1862, at Centerville, Va., on Surgeon's certificate of disability.
Thompson, Richard........	...do...	35	Oct. 5, 1861	3 yrs.	Mustered out Oct. 5, 1864, on expiration of term of service.
Tibbs, Sidney............	...do...	26	Oct. 5, 1861	3 yrs.	
Treat, William H.........	...do...	28	Oct. 5, 1861	3 yrs.	Mustered out Oct. 5, 1864, on expiration of term of service.
Walling, Hiram A.........	...do...	21	Oct. 5, 1861	3 yrs.	Wounded June 24, 1864, at St. Mary's Church, Va.; promoted to Hospital Steward Dec. 1, 1864; veteran.

Names.	Rank.	Age.	Date of Entering the Service.	Period of Service.	Remarks.
Jacob B. Templin.........	2d Lieut.	19	Oct. 31, 1861	3 yrs.	Promoted from 1st Sergeant Co.L July 25,1864;wounded Oct.27,1864,at Hatcher's Run,Va.;commissioned as 1st Lieutenant Nov.12,1864;Captain April 8,1865,but not mustered on either commission;discharged April 4,1865,on Surgeon's certificate of disability.
Ezra Faunce..............	1st Sergt.	23	Oct. 12, 1861	3 yrs.	Appointed Corporal Dec.16,1861; Sergeant May 1,1862;1st Sergeant April 14,1864;captured Oct.1,1864, at Davis' Farm,Va.;promoted to 1st Lieutenant Co.G Jan.31,1865;veteran.
Orville M. Bunnell.......	Q.M.S.	36	Oct. 15, 1861	3 yrs.	Mustered as private;appointed Q.M. Sergeant Dec.16,1861;discharged March 27,1863,on Surgeon's certificate of disability.
William K. Kneal.........	...do...	20	Oct. 20, 1861	3 yrs.	Appointed Corporal May 1,1862;Q.M. Sergeant March 27,1863;promoted to Regt.Com.Sergeant Dec.1,1864;veteran.
Edward Sodan.............	...do...	25	Oct. 29, 1861	3 yrs.	Appointed Corporal ——;wounded May ——; 1863,at Chancellorsville,Va.;appointed Q.M.Sergeant Dec.1,1864;mustered out June 27,1865,at Petersburg,Va.,by order of War Department; veteran.
James Stewart............	Com.Ser.	21	Dec. 11, 1861	3 yrs.	Appointed Corporal April 1,1862;Com. Sergeant April 14,1864;died May 30, 1864,of wounds received May 28,1864, at Hawe's Shop,Va.; veteran.

SIXTH REGIMENT OHIO VOLUNTEER CAVALRY.

Names.	Rank.	Age.	Date of Entering the Service.	Period of Service.	Remarks.
James Chaffee............	Com.Ser.	18	Oct. 21, 1861	3 yrs.	Appointed Corporal Dec.16, 1861; wounded Oct.14,1862,at Manassas Junction,Va.;also wounded Oct.14, 1863,near Auburn,Va.;appointed Com. Sergeant July 1,1864;mustered out Nov. 2,1864,on expiration of term of service.
Benjamin F. Bloomer.......	...do...	35	Nov. 14, 1861	3 yrs.	Appointed Corporal—;Com.Sergeant Dec.1,1864;mustered out June 17, 1865,at Petersburg,Va.,by order of War Department; veteran.
Milton O. Jaryen..........	Sergeant	39	Oct. 15, 1861	3 yrs.	Mustered as private;appointed Sergeant Dec.16,1861;discharged Nov. 19,1862,on Surgeon's certificate of disability.
Samuel Castle.............	...do...	26	Oct. 18, 1861	3 yrs.	Mustered as private;appointed Sergeant Dec.16,1861;promoted to Regt. Q.M.Sergeant Aug.1,1862.
Franklin A. Basford.......	...do...	24	Oct. 14, 1861	3 yrs.	Mustered as private;appointed Sergeant Dec.16,1861;discharged March 26,1863,on Surgeon's certificate of disability.
Peter H. Dubendorf........	...do...	27	Oct. 9, 1861	3 yrs.	Mustered as private;appointed Sergeant Dec.16,1861;shot by provost guard at Camp Stoneman,June 9,1864; died June 10,1864,at Washington, D.C., veteran.
George C. Shepherd........	...do...	21	Dec. 10,1861	3 yrs.	Mustered as private;appointed Sergeant Oct.15,1863;captured May 6, 1863,at Louisa Court House,Va.; commissioned 2d Lieutenant July 30, 1865,but not mustered;mustered out June 27,1865,at Petersburg,Va.,by order of War Department; veteran.

ROSTER OF OHIO TROOPS.

Names.	Rank.	Age.	Date of Entering the Service.	Period of Service.	Remarks.
Byron A. Crandall........	Sergeant	26	Nov. 9, 1861	3 yrs.	Mustered as private;appointed Sergeant Oct.15,1862;discharged May 9, 1864,at Cleveland,O.,on Surgeon's certificate of disability.
Emery H. Dice............	...do...	20	Oct. 29, 1861	3 yrs.	Appointed Corporal Dec.16,1861;Sergeant April 1,1863;captured Oct.1, 1864,at Davis'Farm,Va.;died Jan.18, 1865,in Salisbury Prison,N.C.:veteran.
Francis B. Minor.........	...do...	24	Oct. 14, 1861	3 yrs.	Appointed Corporal Dec.16,1861;Sergeant April 1,1863;mustered out Oct. 15,1864,on expiration of term of service.
John Robertson..........	...do...	27	Nov. 1, 1861	3 yrs.	Appointed Corporal May 1,1863;Sergeant April 18,1864;killed May 28, 1864,at Hawe's Shop,Va.;veteran.
Jacob Mesner............	...do...	19	Dec. 5, 1861	3 yrs.	Appointed Corporal April 1,1863;Sergeant July 1,1864;mustered out June 27,1865,at Petersburg,Va.,by order of War Department; veteran.
Michael Stenner.........	...do...	21	Oct. 30, 1861	3 yrs.	Appointed Corporal May 1,1862;Sergeant July 1,1864;mustered out Nov. 2,1864,on expiration of term of service.
Edwin Gale..............	...do...	29	Oct. 22, 1861	3 yrs.	Appointed Corporal April 1,1863;Sergeant Dec.1,1864;mustered out with company Aug.7,1865; veteran.
James Trimble...........	...do...	20	Oct. 28, 1861	3 yrs.	Appointed Corporal April 1,1863;Sergeant Dec.1,1864;mustered out June 27,1865,at Petersburg,Va.,by order of War Department; veteran.

SIXTH REGIMENT OHIO VOLUNTEER CAVALRY.

Names.	Rank.	Age.	Date of Entering the Service.	Period of Service.	Remarks.
Josiah J. Kistler........	Sergeant	22	Nov. 14, 1861	3 yrs.	Mustered as private;appointed Sergeant—;discharged Jan.30,1864,at Washington,D.C.,on Surgeon's certificate of disability.
Jeremiah Morey...........	Corporal	32	Oct. 27, 1861	3 yrs.	Appointed Dec.16,1861;discharged Feb.19,1863,by order of War Dept.
Irwin Warner.............	...do...	30	Oct. 27, 1861	3 yrs.	Appointed Dec.16,1861;transferred to Veteran Reserve Corps May 4,1864.
Dwight H. Petra..........	...do...	35	Nov. 5, 1861	3 yrs.	Appointed Dec.16,1861;discharged June 5,1862,on Surgeon's certificate of disability.
Ithames Haskins.........	...do...	45	Oct. 30, 1861	3 yrs.	Appointed May 1,1862;discharged Sept.27,1862,on Surgeon's certificate of disability.
Pomeroy E. Bancroft......	...do...	23	Dec. 9, 1861	3 yrs.	Appointed June 1,1862;discharged June 4,1862,on Surgeon's certificate of disability.
John Stroup..............	...do...	35	Nov. 13, 1861	3 yrs.	Appointed Aug.1,1862;killed Oct.14, 1863,at Auburn, Va.
Henry Boneham...........	...do...	27	Oct. 25, 1861	3 yrs.	Appointed Jan.1,1864;mustered out June 27,1865,at Petersburg,Va.,by order of War Department; veteran.
Parmenus Faunce..........	...do...	18	Dec. 9, 1861	3 yrs.	Appointed July 1,1864;wounded Oct. 1,1864,at Davis'Farm,Va.; discharged Dec.9,1864,on Surgeon's certificate of disability; veteran.
Henry Beaker.............	...do...	18	Nov. 4, 1861	3 yrs.	Appointed July 1,1864;wounded Oct.1, 1864,at Davis'Farm,Va.;discharged Dec.18,1864,on Surgeon's certificate of disability; veteran.

Names.	Rank.	Age.	Date of Entering the Service.	Period of Service.	Remarks.
Moses Cole..........	Corporal	32	Oct. 28, 1861	3 yrs.	Appointed July 1,1864;mustered out June 27,1865,at Petersburg,Va.,by order of War Department; veteran.
Charles Stark..........	...do...	25	Dec. 7, 1861	3 yrs.	Appointed Dec.1,1864;mustered out June 27,1865,at Petersburg,Va.,by order of War Department; veteran.
Isaac Faunce..........	...do...	18	Oct. 27, 1861	3 yrs.	Appointed Feb.1,1865;mustered out June 27,1865,at Petersburg,Va.,by order of War Department; veteran.
Mowery Shafer..........	...do...	20	Oct. 27, 1861	3 yrs.	Appointed Feb.1,1865;mustered out June 27,1865,at Petersburg,Va.,by order of War Department; veteran.
John G. Schmidt..........	...do...	26	Dec. 6, 1861	3 yrs.	Appointed Feb.1,1865;mustered out June 27,1865,at Petersburg,Va.,by order of War Department; veteran.
Thomas McKritchie..........	...do...	27	Nov. 4, 1861	3 yrs.	Appointed Feb.1,1865;mustered out June 27,1865,at Petersburg,Va.,by order of War Department; veteran.
Gilbert L. Waldorf..........	...do...	22	Oct. 21, 1861	3 yrs.	Appointed Feb.1,1865;mustered out June 27,1865,at Petersburg,Va.,by order of War Department; veteran.
John Morey..........	Bugler	32	Oct. 21, 1861	3 yrs.	Appointed Dec.16,1861;promoted to Chief Bugler Dec.31,1861.
Ira H. Morey..........	...do...	28	Oct. 21, 1861	3 yrs.	Appointed Dec.24,1861;promoted to Chief Bugler ——.
James N. Wade..........	Farrier	43	Nov. 5, 1861	3 yrs.	Appointed Dec.16,1861;discharged June 17,1864,on Surgeon's certificate of disability; veteran.
John McKellep..........	...do...	23	Nov. 6, 1861	3 yrs.	Appointed Dec.24,1861;discharged June 15,1862,on Surgeon's certificate of disability.

SIXTH REGIMENT OHIO VOLUNTEER CAVALRY.

Names.	Rank.	Age.	Date of Entering the Service.	Period of Service.	Remarks.
Ely Fenstermaker........	Farrier	23	Dec. 6, 1861	3 yrs.	Appointed —;wounded Sept.14,1863, at Culpeper,Va.; mustered out June 27,1865,at Petersburg,Va.,by order of War Department; veteran.
John Park...............	..do...	20	Dec. 4, 1861	3 yrs.	Appointed —;mustered out June 27, 1865,at Petersburg,Va.,by order of War Department; veteran.
Max Elben..............	Saddler	33	Oct. 9, 1861	3 yrs.	Appointed —;promoted to Regt. Saddler, Jan.1,1862.
Wash'n A. McCormick......	..do...	24	Nov. 25, 1861	3 yrs.	Appointed —;wounded June 21,1863, at Upperville,Va.;captured Oct.1, 1864,at Davis'Farm,Va.;died Dec.25, 1864,in Salisbury Prison,N.C.;veteran.
Frank J. Goldsmith.......	Wagoner	26	Nov. 14, 1861	3 yrs.	Appointed Dec.16,1861;mustered out June 27,1865,at Petersburg,Va.,by order of War Department; veteran.
Allen, William..........	Private	33	Mch. 3, 1865	1 yr.	Mustered out with company Aug.7,1865.
Ayers, Charles D........	..do...	18	Feb. 13, 1864	3 yrs.	Mustered out June 27,1865,at Petersburg,Va.,by order of War Department.
Bale, George N..........	..do...	27	Oct. 14, 1861	3 yrs.	Wounded June 30,1862,at Luray,Va.; discharged Sept.22,1862,on Surgeon's certificate of disability.
Barker, Charles H.D......	..do...	18	Oct. 14, 1861	3 yrs.	Mustered out Oct.15,1864,at Columbus, O.,on expiration of term of service.
Bradford, Philip W.......	..do...	25	Feb. 19, 1864	3 yrs.	Died March 25,1864,at Cleveland,O.
Brennan, James..........	..do...	18	Feb. 22, 1864	3 yrs.	Mustered out with company Aug.7,1865.
Brown, Charles H........	..do...	25	Feb. 14, 1864	3 yrs.	Also borne on rolls as "Charles Brum"; discharged, date unknown.
Burnett, Milo...........	..do...	23	Dec. 6, 1863	3 yrs.	Mustered out June 27,1865,at Petersburg,Va.,by order of War Department.

Names.	Rank.	Age.	Date of Entering the Service.	Period of Service.	Remarks.
Burns, James..............	Private	23	Oct. 9, 1861	3 yrs.	Wounded June 30,1862,at Luray,Va.; discharged Sept.27,1862,on Surgeon's certificate of disability.
Burns, Joseph.............	...do...	30	Jan. 30, 1864	3 yrs.	Transferred to Navy April 27,1864.
Canfield, Richard.........	...do...	45	Nov. 19, 1861	3 yrs.	Captured Dec.19,1862,at Occoquan,Va.; discharged June 14,1863,on Surgeon's certificate of disability.
Carpenter, Cyrus..........	...do...	19	Feb. 13, 1864	3 yrs.	Mustered out with company Aug.7,1865.
Chaffee, Sherburn H.......	...do...	26	Oct. 30, 1861	3 yrs.	Captured Dec.19,1862,at Occoquan,Va.; mustered out June 27,1865,at Petersburg,Va.,by order of War Dept.;veteran.
Cook, Andrew.............	...do...	21	Aug. 31, 1864	1 yr.	Mustered out May 30,1865,at Petersburg,Va.,by order of War Department.
Cook, Curtis..............	...do...	19	Oct. 15, 1864	1 yr.	Mustered out with company Aug.7,1865.
Cook, Seth................	...do...	19	Sept. 7, 1864	1 yr.	Mustered out May 30,1865,at Petersburg,Va.,by order of War Department.
Covert, Seymore..........	...do...	18	Oct. 29, 1861	3 yrs.	Mustered out June 27,1865,at Petersburg,Va.,by order of War Dept.;veteran.
Craig, Isaiah.............	...do...	36	Oct. 18, 1861	3 yrs.	Transferred to Co.D,20th Regiment Veteran Reserve Corps,Feb.15,1864, from which discharged to date Aug.4, 1865,by order of War Department.
Crooks, Asa..............	...do...	18	Feb. 9, 1864	3 yrs.	Mustered out with company Aug.7,1865.
Crooks, Frank L..........	...do...	25	Oct. 30, 1861	3 yrs.	Died Dec.26,1862,at Fairfax Court House,Va.
Crooks, James H..........	...do...	18	Oct. 1, 1862	9 mos.	Drafted;mustered out July 29,1863,on expiration of term of service.
Crooks, Samuel...........	...do...	28	Nov. 11, 1861	3 yrs.	Mustered out June 27,1865,at Petersburg,Va.,by order of War Dept.;veteran.

SIXTH REGIMENT OHIO VOLUNTEER CAVALRY.

Names.	Rank.	Age.	Date of Entering the Service.	Period of Service.	Remarks.
Curtis, Bennett..........	Private	33	Oct. 1, 1862	9 mos.	Drafted;mustered out July 29,1863, on expiration of term of service.
Davis, Evan.............	...do...	22	Feb. 11, 1864	3 yrs.	Mustered out June 6,1865,at Phila-delphia,Pa.,by order of War Dept.
Davison, Theodore F......	...do...	18	Jan. 30, 1865	1 yr.	Died May 18,1865,at Petersburg,Va.
Deitrick, Delormey.......	...do...	23	Nov. 28, 1861	3 yrs.	Mustered out Dec.3,1864,at Columbus, O.,on expiration of term of service.
Dice, Warren J...........	...do...	20	Oct. 30, 1861	3 yrs.	Mustered out May 29,1865,at Washing-ton,D.C.,by order of War Dept.;veteran.
Dilley, John H...........	...do...	19	Dec. 2, 1861	3 yrs.	Mustered out Dec.2,1864,on expiration of term of service.
Dwyre, Dennis...........	...do...	27	Jan. 11, 1864	3 yrs.	Mustered out July 11,1865,at Columbus, O.,by order of War Department.
Ensminger, Lloyd W.......	...do...	18	Feb. 14, 1864	3 yrs.	Also borne on rolls as "Lloyd W. Irwinger";discharged Dec.28,1864,at Columbus,O.,on Surgeon's certificate of disability.
Fenstermaker, Peter......	...do...	18	Dec. 6, 1861	3 yrs.	Discharged Nov.28,1862,on Surgeon's certificate of disability.
Fenton, John R..........	...do...	20	Oct. 17, 1863	3 yrs.	
Ferris, John............	...do...	18	Oct. 21, 1863	3 yrs.	
Flemming, Horace........	...do...	29	Dec. 31, 1863	3 yrs.	
Fox, Henry.............	...do...	23	Mch. 21, 1865	1 yr.	
Glasgow, Samuel.........	...do...	43	Sept. 9, 1864	1 yr.	Mustered out June 27,1865,at Peters-burg,Va.,by order of War Department.
Gower, Madison..........	...do...	25	Mch. 21, 1865	1 yr.	Mustered out with company Aug.7,1865.
Graves, William.........	...do...	22	Dec. 28, 1863	3 yrs.	Mustered out May 30,1865,at Peters-burg,Va.,by order of War Department.
Frank, Gray.............	...do...	33	Jan. 16, 1864	3 yrs.	Mustered out July 3,1865,at Peters-burg,Va.,by order of War Department.
Green, Bartholomew......	...do...	37	Feb. 20, 1865	1 yr.	Mustered out with company Aug.7,1865.

ROSTER OF OHIO TROOPS

Names.	Rank.	Age.	Date of Entering the Service.	Period of Service.	Remarks.
Green, Charles A.........	Private	18	Feb. 24, 1864	3 yrs.	Mustered out with company Aug.7,1865.
Griffith, John...........	...do...	29	Nov. 29, 1861	3 yrs.	Mustered out June 27,1865,at Peters-burg,Va.,by order of War Dept.;veteran.
Hammel, John.............	...do...	18	Oct. 29, 1861	3 yrs.	Transferred to Co.E,10th Regiment Veteran Reserve Corps,July 1,1863, from which mustered out Oct.29,1864, on expiration of term of service.
Hank, Frank.............	...do...	43	Feb. 28, 1864	3 yrs.	Killed May 28,1864,at Aenon Church, Va.
Hayhusk, James..........	...do...	23	Oct. 29, 1861	3 yrs.	Discharged Sept.1,1862,on Surgeon's certificate of disability.
Hiliard, Daniel M.......	...do...	34	Oct. 24, 1861	3 yrs.	Discharged April 3,1863,on Surgeon's certificate of disability.
Hill, William E.........	...do...	23	Feb. 13, 1864	3 yrs.	Mustered out June 27,1865,at Peters-burg,Va.,by order of War Department.
Hively, Christopher C....	...do...	20	Feb. 25, 1864	3 yrs.	Mustered out June 27,1865,at Peters-burg,Va.,by order of War Department.
Hoffman, George.........	...do...	27	Feb. 29, 1864	3 yrs.	Mustered out June 27,1865,at Peters-burg,Va.,by order of War Department.
Hogue, Albert...........	...do...	35	Nov. 26, 1861	3 yrs.	Arm broken by fall from horse Aug. 24,1863;transferred to Vet.Reserve Corps Sept.20,1864.
Hosmer, Perry...........	...do...	20	Oct. 2, 1862	9 mos.	Drafted;captured June 9,1863,at Stevensburg,Va.;mustered out July 29,1863,on expiration of term of service.
Jacobs, Peter...........	...do...	20	Sept. 8, 1864	3 yrs.	Mustered out May 30,1865,at Peters-burg,Va.,by order of War Department.
Jordon, Orlo............	...do...	24	Mch. 21, 1865	1 yr.	Mustered out July 19,1865,at Peters-burg,Va.,by order of War Department.

SIXTH REGIMENT OHIO VOLUNTEER CAVALRY.

Names.	Rank.	Age.	Date of Entering the Service.	Period of Service.	Remarks.
Keefer, Baley D..........	Private	22	Oct. 1, 1862	9 mos.	Drafted;wounded June 17,1863,at Aldie, Va.;mustered out July 29,1863,on expiration of term of service.
Kegan, Michael..........	...do...	40	Nov. 2, 1861	3 yrs.	Transferred to 101st Co.,2d Battalion Veteran Reserve Corps,Feb.15,1864, from which mustered out Nov.1,1864, on expiration of term of service.
Kellogg, Henry........	...do...	26	Oct. 28, 1861	3 yrs.	Transferred to 243d Co.,1st Battalion Veteran Reserve Corps,Nov.1,1864, from which mustered out Oct.28,1864, on expiration of term of service.
Kilby, William S.........	...do...	21	Dec. 7, 1861	3 yrs.	Died July 23,1862,at Luray, Va.
Kraus, George..........	...do...	29	Feb. 27, 1865	1 yr.	Mustered out with company Aug.7,1865.
Leach, Enord...........	...do...	23	Oct. 15, 1861	3 yrs.	Mustered out Oct.15,1864,on expiration of term of service.
Leaney, Thomas.........	...do...	29	Nov. 19, 1861	3 yrs.	Discharged May 7,1863,on Surgeon's certificate of disability;re-enlisted Jan.2,1864,for 3 years;wounded —; discharged March 21,1865,on Surgeon's certificate of disability.
Leap, Nelson P.........	...do...	32	Nov. 13, 1861	3 yrs.	Sent to U.S.General Hospital June —, 1862;no further record found.
Lee, Thomas.............	...do...	21	Feb. 16, 1864	3 yrs.	Mustered out May 30,1865,at Peters-
Liese, Jacob.............	...do...	35	Aug. 26, 1864	1 yr.	burg,Va.,by order of War Department.
McDonald, John..........	...do...	18	Oct. 11, 1861	3 yrs.	Transferred to Co.I,18th Regiment Veteran Reserve Corps,Sept.1,1863, from which mustered out Nov.16,1865, by order of War Department;veteran.
McMannis, Miles.........	...do...	40	Nov. 14, 1861	3 yrs.	Captured Nov.21,1863,at Fayetteville, Va.;perished by explosion of steamer "Sultana"on Mississippi River near Memphis,Tenn.,April 27,1865.

211

Names.	Rank.	Age.	Date of Entering the Service.	Period of Service.	Remarks.
Mackey, Robert H.........	Private	26	Feb. 25, 1864	3 yrs.	Mustered out with company Aug.7,1865.
Martin, Andrew...........	...do...	22	Nov. 16, 1861	3 yrs.	Discharged June 26,1863,on Surgeon's certificate of disability.
Mason, Charles E.........	...do...	18	Oct. 25, 1861	3 yrs.	Discharged Dec.3,1862,on Surgeon's certificate of disability.
Mason, Henry.............	...do...	44	Oct. 24, 1861	3 yrs.	Discharged June 26,1863,by order of War Department.
Meacham, Adelbert H......	...do...	20	Sept. 6, 1864	1 yr.	Mustered out May 30,1865,at Petersburg,Va.,by order of War Department.
Miner, Erwin B...........	...do...	19	Feb. 29, 1864	3 yrs.	Mustered out May 29,1865,at Washington,D.C.,by order of War Department.
Morgan, Sylvester........	...do...	26	Aug. 30, 1864	1 yr.	Mustered out May 30,1865,at Petersburg,Va.,by order of War Department.
Morse, Porter L..........	...do...	18	Nov. 28, 1861	3 yrs.	Mustered out June 27,1865,at Petersburg,Va.,by order of War Dept.;veteran.
Mummert, John............	...do...	18	Jan. 28, 1864	3 yrs.	Mustered out with company Aug.7,1865.
Near, William............	...do...	23	Nov. 23, 1861	3 yrs.	Mustered out June 27,1865,at Petersburg,Va.,by order of War Dept.;veteran.
Oppenlander, Jacob.......	...do...	25	Dec. 7, 1861	3 yrs.	Killed June 24,1864,in action at St. Mary's Church, Va.;veteran.
Palmer, William H........	...do...	35	Oct. 9, 1861	3 yrs.	Transferred from Captain Stanhope's Co.;discharged Sept.29,1862,on Surgeon's certificate of disability.
Parke, John.............	...do...	20	Dec. 4, 1861	3 yrs.	Mustered out June 17,1865,by order of War Department;veteran.
Pelton, Winthrop.........	...do...	40	Dec. 11, 1861	3 yrs.	Transferred from Captain Stanhope's Co. ——;mustered out Oct.15,1862,by order of War Department.
Randolph,Taylor..........	...do...	21	Oct. 24, 1861	3 yrs.	Prisoner of war;died July 11,1862, in hospital at Winchester,Va.,while a prisoner of war.

SIXTH REGIMENT OHIO VOLUNTEER CAVALRY.

Names.	Rank.	Age.	Date of Entering the Service.	Period of Service.	Remarks.
Reed, Amos C...........	Private	22	Oct. 22, 1861	3 yrs.	Mustered out Oct.26,1864,at Columbus, O.,on expiration of term of service.
Reifinger, Joseph.......	...do....	36	Oct. 9, 1861	3 yrs.	Transferred from Captain Stanhope's Co.May 1,1862;captured May 1,1863, at Warrenton Junction,Va.;mustered out June 27,1865,at Petersburg,Va., by order of War Department;veteran.
Rhodes, Isaac N........	...do....	18	Feb. 18, 1864	3 yrs.	Mustered out with company Aug.7,1865.
Richardson, Levi J......	...do....	28	Oct. 14, 1861	3 yrs.	Transferred to 1st Independent Co. Veteran Reserve Corps May 14,1864, from which mustered out Nov.30,1865, by order of War Department; veteran.
Rose, William..........	...do....	18	Mch. 24, 1865	1 yr.	Mustered out with company Aug.7,1865.
Ropke, Albert..........	...do....	20	Sept. 8, 1864	1 yr.	Mustered out May 30,1865,at Petersburg,Va.,by order of War Department.
Schoville, Sylvester M..	...do....	27	Mch. 24, 1865	1 yr.	Mustered out with company Aug.7,1865.
Schwitz, Christopher....	...do....	40	Oct. 15, 1861	3 yrs.	Mustered out Oct.15,1864, on expiration of term of service.
Shoffer, Quimley........	...do....	18	Feb. 9, 1864	3 yrs.	Captured Oct.1,1864,at Davis'Farm, Va.;mustered out June 22,1865,at Camp Cleveland,O.,by order of War Department.
Shoffer, Samuel........	...do....	33	Oct. 14, 1861	3 yrs.	Mustered out June 27,1865,at Petersburg,Va.,by order of War Dept.;veteran.
Sharp, Samuel..........	...do....	18	Mch. 10, 1864	3 yrs.	Mustered out with company Aug.7,1865.
Shepard, John C........	...do....	22	Feb. 29, 1864	3 yrs.	Mustered out with company Aug.7,1865.
Shepardson, John........	...do....	18	Nov. 9, 1863	3 yrs.	Mustered out with company Aug.7,1865.
Sirrine, James.........	...do....	42	Nov. 18, 1861	3 yrs.	Discharged June 14,1862,on Surgeon's certificate of disability.

ROSTER OF OHIO TROOPS.

Names.	Rank.	Age.	Date of Entering the Service.	Period of Service.	Remarks.
Smith, Charles D.........	Private	18	Oct. 27, 1861	3 yrs.	Discharged "winter of 1862" by civil authority.
Smith, Daniel............	...do...	18	Mch. 10, 1864	3 yrs.	Mustered out with company Aug. 7, 1865.
Smith, George...........	...do...	22	Feb. 21, 1864	3 yrs.	Transferred to Navy April 27, 1864.
Smith, William..........	...do...	21	Jan. 10, 1864	3 yrs.	Mustered out June 17, 1865, at Washington, D.C., by order of War Department.
Stark, Gottleib..........	...do...	29	Oct. 15, 1861	3 yrs.	Discharged Feb. 20, 1863, on Surgeon's certificate of disability.
Stevens, Calvin..........	...do...	38	Nov. 15, 1861	3 yrs.	Discharged Oct. 30, 1862, on Surgeon's certificate of disability.
Stone, William..........	...do...	18	Jan. 18, 1864	3 yrs.	Mustered out with company Aug. 7, 1865.
Struble, Nelson..........	...do...	24	Oct. 1, 1862	9 mos.	Drafted; mustered out July 29, 1863, on expiration of term of service.
Swager, Isaac...........	...do...	42	Nov. 13, 1861	3 yrs.	Discharged June 9, 1863, on Surgeon's certificate of disability.
Templeton, Ira..........	...do...	20	Oct. 1, 1862	9 mos.	Drafted; mustered out July 29, 1863, on expiration of term of service.
Truesdell, Henry S.......	...do...	22	Nov. 11, 1861	3 yrs.	Wounded March 17, 1863, at Kelly's Ford, Va.; mustered out Nov. 11, 1864, on expiration of term of service.
Ulp, William............	...do...	23	Oct. 3, 1862	9 mos.	Drafted; mustered out July 29, 1863, on expiration of term of service.
Urich, William..........	...do...	19	Nov. 1, 1861	3 yrs.	Discharged April 20, 1863, on Surgeon's certificate of disability.
Wade, James N...........	...do...	44	Jan. 5, 1864	3 yrs.	Captured Oct. 1, 1864, at Davis' Farm, Va.; died March 25, 1865, at Erie, Pa.
Wakeman, Melvin G.......	...do...	26	Feb. 29, 1864	3 yrs.	Mustered out June 19, 1865, at Washington, D.C., by order of War Department.
Wakeman, William S......	...do...	22	Feb. 29, 1864	3 yrs.	Mustered out with company Aug. 7, 1865.

214

SIXTH REGIMENT OHIO VOLUNTEER CAVALRY.

Names.	Rank.	Age.	Date of Entering the Service.	Period of Service.	Remarks.
Webber, James M............	Private	26	Oct. 23, 1861	3 yrs.	Mustered out June 27,1865,at Petersburg,Va.,by order of War Dept.;veteran.
Weaver, Andrew............	...do...	18	Sept. 6, 1864	1 yr.	Mustered out May 30,1865,at Petersburg,Va.,by order of War Department.
Wheeler, John............	...do...	41	Oct. 30, 1861	3 yrs.	Discharged Jan.31,1862,on Surgeon's certificate of disability.
White, Isaac N............	...do...	18	Sept. 6, 1864	1 yr.	Mustered out May 30,1865,at Petersburg,Va.,by order of War Department.
Wilber, Edward............	...do...	23	Nov. 6, 1861	3 yrs.	Discharged Sept.29,1862,on Surgeon's certificate of disability.
Wright, Leman T............	...do...	18	Nov. 1, 1861	3 yrs.	Discharged Nov.16,1863,on Surgeon's certificate of disability.
York, Oliver H............	...do...	26	Oct. 28, 1861	3 yrs.	Discharged Dec.17,1861,on Surgeon's certificate of disability.

COMPANY K.

Mustered in December 16, 1861, at Camp Hutchins, Warren, Ohio, by C. R. Bowe, A. Bingham, and James Wyatt, U. S. Mustering Officers. Mustered out August 7, 1865, at Petersburg, Va., by L. H. Bowen, 1st Lieutenant and Acting Commissary of Musters. Mustering Officer Department of Virginia.

Names.	Rank.	Age.	Date of Entering the Service.	Period of Service.	Remarks.
Charles R. Bowe..........	Captain	31	Oct. 9, 1861	3 yrs.	Mustered as 2d Lieutenant;promoted to Captain Dec.16,1861;wounded Oct.14, 1863,at Auburn Mills,Va.;died of wounds Nov. 4,1863.
John E. Wyatt............	...do...	35	Oct. 8, 1861	3 yrs.	Mustered as private;promoted to 1st Lieutenant Dec.16,1861;to Captain Feb.27,1864;captured Oct.1,1864,near Petersburg,Va.;mustered out March 3, 1865,by order of War Department.

ROSTER OF OHIO TROOPS.

Names.	Rank.	Age.	Date of Entering the Service.	Period of Service.	Remarks.
Reuben E. Osgood.........	1st Lieut.	34	Nov. 1, 1861	3 yrs.	Mustered as private;appointed Sergeant Dec.16,1861;promoted to 2d Lieutenant May 16,1862;wounded June 2,1862,at Woodstock,Va.;promoted to 1st Lieutenant July 25,1864;to Captain Co.I Nov.12,1864.
Wallace H. Bullard.......	...do...	33	Oct. 7, 1862	3 yrs.	Promoted from Regt.Q.M.Sergeant April 8,1865;mustered out with company Aug.7,1865.
Mark W. Goss.............	...do...	.....	Sept.26, 1862	3 yrs.	Assigned to company Feb.20,1863,on special duty in office of Military Commander at Columbus,O.;resigned July 29,1864.
Josiah D. Freer..........	2d Lieut.	45	Oct. 26, 1861	3 yrs.	Mustered as private;promoted to 2d Lieutenant Dec.16,1861;resigned May 15,1862.
Hiram G. Suiter.........	...do...	23	Dec. 11, 1861	3 yrs.	Promoted from 1st Sergeant Co.H July 25,1864;to Captain Co.C April 8, 1865.
William H. Smith.........	1st Sergt.	36	Nov. 15, 1861	3 yrs.	Mustered as private;appointed 1st Sergeant Dec.16,1861;died Sept.20, 1862,at Washington, D.C.
Simon D. Young..........	...do...	23	Oct. 28, 1861	3 yrs.	Mustered as private;appointed Sergeant Dec.16, 1861;1st Sergeant Dec. 10,1862;captured Sept.20,1863;promoted to 2d Lieutenant Co.H May 9, 1864.
William F. Tousley.......	...do...	21	Oct. 9, 1861	3 yrs.	Mustered as private; appointed Sergeant July 9,1862;1st Sergeant May 14,1864;died Jan.9,1865,at Alexandria,Va.;veteran.

SIXTH REGIMENT OHIO VOLUNTEER CAVALRY.

Names.	Rank.	Age.	Date of Entering the Service.	Period of Service.	Remarks.
Jerome Pickett..........	1st Sergt.	18	Oct. 29, 1861	3 yrs.	Appointed Corporal Jan.1,1864;Sergeant Dec.1,1864;1st Sergeant Jan. 15,1865;commissioned 2d Lieutenant May 31,1865;1st Lieutenant July 30, 1865,but not mustered on either commission;mustered out June 27,1865, at Petersburg,Va.,by order of War Department; veteran.
George M. St. John........	Q.M.S.	27	Oct. 24, 1861	3 yrs.	Mustered as private;appointed Q.M. Sergeant Dec.16,1861;promoted to Regt.Q.M.Sergeant Dec.31,1861.
Thomas S. Bark............	...do...	36	Oct. 10, 1861	3 yrs.	appointed Corporal Dec.16,1861;Sergeant Jan.1,1862;Q.M.Sergeant Dec. 31,1862;mustered out Oct.12,1864,on expiration of term of service.
Newton J. Allen..........	...do...	28	Oct. 29, 1861	3 yrs.	Appointed Corporal Jan.1,1864;Sergeant July 1,1864;Q.M.Sergeant ——; mustered out June 27,1865,at Petersburg,Va.,by order of War Dept.;veteran.
David Johnston..........	...do...	21	Dec. 11, 1861	3 yrs.	Appointed Corporal Dec.16,1861;Sergeant Jan.1.1863;Com.Sergeant ——; Q.M.Sergeant ——;wounded May 9,1864, on Sheridan's Raid,Virginia;transferred to Veteran Reserve Corps April 12,1865;from which mustered out Aug.25,1865,at Washington,D.C.,by order of War Department;veteran.
Harry A. Young..........	Com.Ser.	31	Nov. 13, 1861	3 yrs.	Appointed Corporal Dec.16,1861;Com. Sergeant Aug.31,1862;mustered out Dec.25,1864,on expiration of term of service.

Names.	Rank.	Age.	Date of Entering the Service.	Period of Service.	Remarks.
Horace Cole.............	Com.Ser.	18	Nov. 26, 1861	3 yrs.	Appointed Corporal Jan.1,1863;Com. Sergeant —;captured July 28,1864, at Malvern Hill,Va.;mustered out Dec.19,1864,on expiration of term of service.
Elhanan W. Grover........	Sergeant	27	Oct. 24, 1861	3 yrs.	Mustered as private; appointed Sergeant Dec.16,1861;discharged Sept. 29,1862,on Surgeon's certificate of disability.
Andrew M. Basquin........	...do...	19	Oct. 29, 1861	3 yrs.	Appointed Corporal Dec.16,1861;Sergeant Sept.1,1862;wounded June 17, 1863,at Aldie,Va.;mustered out Nov. 2,1864,on expiration of term of service.
Jabez H. Hunt...........	...do...	34	Oct. 28, 1861	3 yrs.	Appointed Corporal Dec.16,1861;Sergeant Jan.1,1863;mustered out Nov. 2,1864,on expiration of term of service.
Frank M. Arnold..........	...do...	21	Nov. 30, 1861	3 yrs.	Appointed Corporal Sept.17,1862;Sergeant March 1,1863;mustered out Nov. 7,1864,on expiration of term of service.
Charles B. Blakesley.....	...do...	31	Oct. 17, 1861	3 yrs.	Appointed Corporal Jan.1,1863;Sergeant Dec.1,1864;wounded —;discharged Sept.6,1865,on Surgeon's certificate of disability; veteran.
Jesse Willshire..........	...do...	30	Oct. 15, 1861	3 yrs.	Appointed Corporal Set.30,1862; wounded and captured June 24,1864, at St. Mary's Church,Va.;appointed Sergeant Dec.1,1864;mustered out June 27,1865,at Petersburg,Va.,by order of War Department; veteran.

SIXTH REGIMENT OHIO VOLUNTEER CAVALRY.

Names.	Rank.	Age.	Date of Entering the Service.	Period of Service.	Remarks.
William Dunlap............	Sergeant	20	Dec. 10, 1861	3 yrs.	Appointed Corporal Dec.1,1864,Sergeant Jan.15,1865;killed April 6, 1865,at Sailor's Creek,Va.;veteran.
Daniel S. Robertson......	...do...	18	Dec. 25, 1861	3 yrs.	Appointed Corporal April 1,1863;Sergeant Feb.1,1865;mustered out June 27,1865,at Petersburg,Va.,by order of War Department; veteran.
Cassius C. Starr..........	...do...	19	Nov. 9, 1861	3 yrs.	Wounded May 4,1863,near Ely's Ford, Va.;appointed Corporal Dec.1,1864; Sergeant Feb.1,1865;died April 22, 1865,at Arlington,Va.; veteran.
Martin Oviatt.............	...do...	23	Oct. 25, 1861	3 yrs.	Appointed Corporal from Bugler Feb. 1,1865;Sergeant May 1,1865;mustered out June 27,1865,at Petersburg,Va., by order of War Department; veteran.
Almon A. Sheffield.......	...do...	20	Dec. 11, 1861	3 yrs.	Appointed Corporal Jan.15,1865;Sergeant May 1,1865;mustered out June 27,1865,at Petersburg,Va.,by order of War Department; veteran.
Williard B. Warriner.....	...do...	21	Dec. 11, 1861	3 yrs.	Wounded June 17,1863,at Aldie,Va.; appointed Corporal Feb.1,1865;Sergeant May 1,1865;mustered out June 27,1865,at Petersburg,Va.,by order of War Department; veteran.
Horace J. Edgerton.......	Corporal	18	Oct. 18, 1861	3 yrs.	Appointed March 1,1865;mustered out June 27,1865,at Petersburg,Va.,by order of War Department; veteran.
William Elliott..........	...do...	23	Nov. 1, 1861	3 yrs.	Appointed May 1,1865;mustered out June 27,1865,at Petersburg,Va.,by order of War Department; veteran.

Names.	Rank.	Age.	Date of Entering the Service.	Period of Service.	Remarks.
James Mullen............	Corporal	18	Oct. 13, 1861	3 yrs.	Captured July 12,1862,at Luray,Va.; appointed Corporal May 1,1865;mustered out June 27,1865,at Petersburg,Va., by order of War Department; veteran.
Edwin Prentice..........	...do....	24	Oct. 26, 1861	3 yrs.	Captured July 20,1862,at Luray,Va.; appointed Corporal May 1,1865;mustered out June 27,1865,at Petersburg,Va., by order of War Department; veteran.
Oren N. Wilcox..........	...do....	30	Nov. 29, 1861	3 yrs.	Appointed May 1,1865;mustered out June 27,1865,at Petersburg,Va.,by order of War Department; veteran.
George Cutchaw..........	...do....	20	Dec. 20, 1861	3 yrs.	Appointed Jan.1,1863;killed June 17, 1863,at Aldie,Va.
Harvey Bartram..........	...do....	28	Nov. 10, 1861	3 yrs.	Appointed Dec.16,1861;mustered out Dec.3,1864,on expiration of term of service.
Enoch Morse.............	...do....	30	Nov. 15, 1861	3 yrs.	Appointed Sept.7,1862;captured Oct.1, 1864,near Petersburg,Va.;died Dec.12, 1864,in Salisbury Prison,N.C.;veteran.
Charles L. Murray.......	...do....	18	Oct. 25, 1861	3 yrs.	Appointed Dec.31,1861;died April 25, 1863.
Dallas M. Ware.........	...do....	19	Mch. 30, 1864	3 yrs.	Appointed May 1,1865;wounded—;mustered out June 27,1865,at Petersburg, Va.,by order of War Department;veteran.
Alonzo Hannam..........	...do....	19	Oct. 29, 1861	3 yrs.	Appointed—;wounded and captured June 24,1864,at St. Mary's Church,Va.;died in Rebel Prison, date and place un- known; veteran.
Isaiah, McConkey.......	...do....	18	Feb. 13, 1864	3 yrs.	Appointed June 1,1865;mustered out with company Aug.7,1865.
Lucius Hollenbeck......	...do....	30	Nov. 20, 1861	3 yrs.	Appointed Dec.16,1861;discharged Jan. 3,1863,on Surgeon's certificate of disability.

SIXTH REGIMENT OHIO VOLUNTEER CAVALRY.

Names.	Rank.	Age.	Date of Entering the Service.	Period of Service.	Remarks.
Adelbert McEuen..........	Corporal	18	Dec. 4, 1861	3 yrs.	Appointed June 1,1865;mustered out with company Aug.7,1865; veteran.
Sumner Stoughton..........	Bugler	25	Oct. 29, 1861	3 yrs.	Appointed Dec.16,1861;discharged Aug.9,1862,on Surgeon's certificate of disability.
Morris Root..............	...do....	19	Nov. 4, 1861	3 yrs.	Appointed Dec.16,1861;wounded May 4, 1863,near Ely's Ford,Va.;also wounded May 5,1864,at Todd's Tavern,Va.;transferred to Veteran Reserve Corps April 25,1865;discharged from same Aug.3, 1865,at Washington,D.C.,on Surgeon's certificate of disability; veteran.
Albert J. Criss..........	...do....	18	Nov. 15, 1861	3 yrs.	Transferred from Co.G May 20,1862; discharged Dec.1,1862,on Surgeon's certificate of disability.
Nelson Brown.............	...do....	19	Oct. 28, 1861	3 yrs.	Appointed—;mustered out Nov.2,1864, on expiration of term of service.
George Hopkins..........	Farrier	31	Nov. 8, 1861	3 yrs.	Appointed Dec.16,1861;mustered out June 27,1865,at Petersburg,Va.,by order of War Department; veteran.
Christopher House........	...do....	27	Nov. 21, 1861	3 yrs.	Appointed Dec.16,1861;discharged Jan. 29,1863,on Surgeon's certificate of disability.
John S. Case.............	...do....	23	Dec. 12, 1861	3 yrs.	Appointed—;mustered out June 27, 1865,at Petersburg,Va.,by order of War Department; veteran.
Charles Irish...........	...do....	40	April 4, 1864	3 yrs.	Appointed—;discharged Dec.12,1864, on Surgeon's certificate of disability.
James W. Covert..........	Saddler	29	Oct. 19, 1861	3 yrs.	Appointed Dec.16,1861;discharged Sept.1,1862,on Surgeon's certificate of disability.

ROSTER OF OHIO TROOPS.

Names.	Rank.	Age.	Date of Entering the Service.	Period of Service.	Remarks.
Roswell G. Thomas.........	Saddler	38	Dec. 11, 1861	3 yrs.	Appointed March 1,1863;discharged Aug.12,1864;on Surgeon's certificate of disability.
Luman S. Holt..............	...do....	27	Oct. 15, 1861	3 yrs.	Appointed—;mustered out June 27, 1865,at Petersburg,Va.,by order of War Department; veteran.
Gould Nickerson..........	Wagoner	45	Oct. 29, 1861	3 yrs.	Appointed Dec.16,1861;mustered out Nov.2,1864;on expiration of term of service.
Allen, Justin............	Private	23	Oct. 29, 1861	3 yrs.	
Amos, George W...........	...do....	18	Mch. 29, 1864	3 yrs.	Mustered out with company Aug.7,1865.
Basquin, Oliver..........	...do....	42	Dec. 6, 1861	3 yrs.	Discharged Dec.16,1862,on Surgeon's certificate of disability.
Billington, Azariah......	...do....	21	Dec. 9, 1861	3 yrs.	
Blood, Lester............	...do....	25	Oct. 29, 1861	3 yrs.	Killed June 21,1863,in battle of Upperville, Va.
Boyd, Newton D............	...do....	18	Dec. 10, 1861	3 yrs.	Mustered out June 28,1865,at Petersburg,Va.,by order of War Dept.;veteran.
Bratten, Joseph K.........	...do....	39	Dec. 8, 1861	3 yrs.	Mustered out June 27,1865,at Petersburg,Va.,by order of War Dept.;veteran.
Brown, Seymore...........	...do....	42	Nov. 26, 1861	3 yrs.	Discharged Sept.20,1862,on Surgeon's certificate of disability.
Brown, Daniel............	...do....	20	Oct. 23, 1861	3 yrs.	Killed May 28,1864,in action at Hawe's Shop,Va.; veteran.
Brown, Hiram.............	...do....	28	Nov. 28, 1861	3 yrs.	Discharged June 2,1863,on Surgeon's certificate of disability.
Brown, John..............	...do....	46	Nov. 7, 1861	3 yrs.	Reduced from Sergeant at his own request Jan.1,1862;discharged Sept.11, 1864,on Surgeon's certificate of disability; veteran.

SIXTH REGIMENT OHIO VOLUNTEER CAVALRY.

Names.	Rank.	Age.	Date of Entering the Service.	Period of Service.	Remarks.
Campbell, Henry L.........	Private	19	Oct. 12, 1861	3 yrs.	Discharged Aug. 9,1862,on Surgeon's certificate of disability.
Clark, Wallace............	...do...	18	Mch. 31, 1864	3 yrs.	Mustered out June 27,1865,at Petersburg,Va.,by order of War Department.
Combs, Henry.............	...do...	44	Oct. 19, 1861	3 yrs.	Discharged Sept.11,1862,on Surgeon's certificate of disability.
Cowles, Hiram W..........	...do...	39	Dec. 8, 1861	3 yrs.	Discharged Sept.4,1862,on Surgeon's certificate of disability.
Day, James J.............	...do...	19	Oct. 2, 1862	9 mos.	Drafted;mustered out July 29,1863,on expiration of term of service.
Day, William H...........	...do...	23	Oct. 1, 1862	9 mos.	Drafted;mustered out July 29,1863,on expiration of term of service.
Fairbanks, Joseph W.......	...do...	31	Nov. 19, 1861	3 yrs.	Discharged Oct.22,1862,on Surgeon's certificate of disability.
Fenton, Ambrose..........	...do...	37	Oct. 24, 1861	3 yrs.	Discharged Aug.30,1862,on Surgeon's certificate of disability.
Fieldhouse, Henry........	...do...	22	Dec. 10, 1861	3 yrs.	Died Sept.4,1863,at Washington, D.C.
Gould, Simon H...........	...do...	20	Oct. 25, 1861	3 yrs.	Reduced from Sergeant April 1, 1863; promoted to 1st Lieutenant 116th Regiment U.S.Colored Troops Sept.16, 1864;to Captain March 16,1865;from which mustered out with company July 17,1867; veteran.
Green, William...........	...do...	21	Nov. 13, 1863	3 yrs.	Mustered out with company Aug.7,1865.
Hale, Ralph..............	...do...	37	Oct. 29, 1861	3 yrs.	Dishcarged Dec.20,1862,on Surgeon's certificate of disability.
Halen, Henry.............	...do...	22	Oct. 19, 1861	3 yrs.	Mustered out with company Aug.7,1865.
Hamilton, William S......	...do...	32	Jan. 20, 1864	3 yrs.	Mustered out with company Aug.7,1865.
Hammond, William.........	...do...	32	Jan. 20, 1864	3 yrs.	
Hardin, George..........	...do...	22	Jan. 19, 1864	3 yrs.	

ROSTER OF OHIO TROOPS.

Names.	Rank.	Age.	Date of Entering the Service.	Period of Service.	Remarks.
Harmon, Cyrus P...........	Private	18	Dec. 16, 1863	3 yrs.	Wounded Feb.5,1865,at Hatcher's Run, Va.;discharged June 5,1865,on Surgeon's certificate of disability.
Harris, William H.........	...do...	19	Oct. 18, 1861	3 yrs.	Captured June 21,1863,at Upperville, Va.;killed May 28,1864,at Hawe's Shop,Va.;veteran.
Hayward, Thomas...........	...do...	23	Feb. 27, 1864	3 yrs.	Captured May 20,1864;mustered out June 27,1865,at Petersburg,Va.,by order of War Department.
Hoffmire, Francis G.......	...do...	19	Feb. 13, 1864	3 yrs.	Mustered out with company Aug.7,1865.
Hubbard, Chancy M.........	...do...	40	Feb. 29, 1864	3 yrs.	
Hubbard, Simon H..........	...do...	22	Oct. 19, 1861	3 yrs.	Discharged Aug.20,1862,on Surgeon's certificate of disability.
Jackson, Thomas H.........	...do...	28	Feb. 8, 1864	3 yrs.	
Kent, John................	...do...	21	Oct. 1, 1862	9 mos.	Drafted;mustered out July 29,1863, on expiration of term of service.
Kelsey,Philip.............	...do...	42	Oct. 23,1861	3 yrs.	Died July 8,1862,at Baltimore,Md.
King, John................	...do...	26	Dec. 12, 1863	3 yrs.	Mustered out with company Aug.7,1865.
Knopp, Lester.............	...do...	19	Oct. 1, 1862	9 mos.	Drafted;mustered out July 29,1863,on expiration of term of service.
Lally, Michael............	...do...	38	Dec. 9, 1861	3 yrs.	Wounded July 1,1862,while on picket near Strasburg,Va.;discharged July 30,1862,on Surgeon's certificate of disability.
Lamb, Andrew J............	...do...	19	Nov. 28, 1861	3 yrs.	Discharged Oct. 7,1862,on Surgeon's certificate of disability.
Lane, Peter...............	...do...	24	Jan. 21, 1864	3 yrs.	Mustered out with company Aug.7,1865.
Larr, John................	...do...	37	Oct. 1, 1862	9 mos.	Drafted;mustered out July 29,1863,on expiration of term of service.
Loomis, Nelson............	...do...	18	Feb. 23, 1864	3 yrs.	Mustered out with company Aug.7,1865.

SIXTH REGIMENT OHIO VOLUNTEER CAVALRY.

Names.	Rank.	Age.	Date of Entering the Service.	Period of Service.	Remarks.
Leopold, Henry............	Private	22	Dec. 4, 1861	3 yrs.	Wounded June 17,1863,at Aldie,Va.; captured Oct.1,1864,near Petersburg, Va.;died Feb.15,1865,in Salisbury Prison,N.C.; veteran.
Lindsay,Louis............	...do...	18	Jan. 19, 1864	3 yrs.	Mustered out with company Aug.7,1865.
Littledale, Joseph.......	...do...	31	Dec. 20, 1863	3 yrs.	
Lyman, Carlos P..........	...do...	23	Nov. 15, 1861	3 yrs.	Wounded June 21,1863,at Upperville, Va.;promoted to Captain 100th Regiment U.S.Colored Troops July 11, 1864;from which mustered out with regiment Dec.26,1865; veteran.
McConkey, Elijah.........	...do...	28	Feb. 27, 1864	3 yrs.	Mustered out June 27,1865,at Petersburg,Va.,by order of War Department.
McGee, Patrick...........	...do...	30	Dec. 8, 1863	3 yrs.	Died Aug.18,1864,at New York City.
Martin, David...........	...do...	30	Oct. 22, 1861	3 yrs.	Transferred to Veteran Reserve Corps Feb.15,1864;from which mustered out Aug.14,1865,at Harrisburg,Pa.,by order of,War Department.
Meacham, Reuben..........	...do...	20	Jan. 11, 1864	3 yrs.	Mustered out with company Aug.7,1865.
Mehrling, John..........	...do...	32	Oct. 1, 1862	9 mos.	Drafted;mustered out July 29,1863,on expiration of term of service.
Mitchell, John J.........	...do...	18	Oct. 25, 1861	3 yrs.	Discharged Jan.2,1862,by civil authority.
Morrell, Henry W.........	...do...	20	Feb. 12, 1864	3 yrs.	Captured Oct.1,1864,near Petersburg, Va.;mustered out June 16,1865,at Camp Chase,O.,by order of War Dept.
Murray, William.........	...do...	27	Feb. 24, 1864	3 yrs.	Drafted;mustered out July 29,1863,on expiration of term of service.
Myers, Thomas J.........	...do...	20	Oct. 1, 1862	9 mos.	
O'Connor, John..........	...do...	44	Jan. 8, 1864	3 yrs.	Mustered out June 27,1865,at Petersburg,Va.,by order of War Department.

Names.	Rank.	Age.	Date of Entering the Service.	Period of Service.	Remarks.
Olcott, Charles B........	Private	31	Feb. 28, 1864	3 yrs.	Mustered out July 11,1865,by order of War Department.
Orrindorff, Hezekiah.....	..do...	36	Jan. 5, 1864	3 yrs.	Discharged March 26,1864,on Surgeon's certificate of disability.
Orrindorff, Peter W......	..do...	23	Feb. 2, 1864	3 yrs.	Mustered out with company Aug.7,1865.
Osgood, James S..........	..do...	24	Sept.27, 1862	3 yrs.	Mustered out May 30,1865,at Petersburg,Va.,by order of War Department.
Palmer, David...........	..do...	19	Feb. 14, 1864	3 yrs.	Mustered out with company Aug.7,1865.
Parker, Wellington.......	..do...	21	Nov. 28, 1861	3 yrs.	Killed by accidental discharge of gun Oct.2,1862.
Pepper, Henry J..........	..do...	21	Nov. 10, 1861	3 yrs.	Wounded June 17,1863,at Aldie,Va.; mustered out Nov.29,1864,on expiration of term of service.
Perry, Phileman..........	..do...	38	Oct. 25, 1861	3 yrs.	Discharged Sept.10,1862,on Surgeon's certificate of disability.
Pierce, John.............	..do...	18	Jan. 19, 1864	3 yrs.	Killed Feb. 19, 1864.
Porter, William N........	..do...	18	Mch. 8, 1864	3 yrs.	Absent sick Aug.7,1865;no further record found.
Porter, John.............	..do...	18	Jan. 19, 1864	3 yrs.	
Quinn, William...........	..do...	23	Jan. 9, 1864	3 yrs.	Discharged June 30,1865,on Surgeon's certificate of disability.
Rice, Daniel.............	..do...	23	Jan. 19, 1864	3 yrs.	
Shephard, Alonzo R.......	..do...	44	Dec. 5, 1861	3 yrs.	
Sprague, Calvin..........	..do...	24	Oct. 14, 1861	3 yrs.	Discharged Oct.29,1863,on Surgeon's certificate of disability.
Sprague, Warren L........	..do...	26	Dec. 10, 1861	3 yrs.	Captured Nov.21,1863,near Fayetteville, Va.;died June 6,1864,in Andersonville Prison, Georgia.
Stafford, William........	..do...	23	Jan. 19, 1864	3 yrs.	
Stewart, William.........	..do...	18	Feb. 24, 1864	3 yrs.	Killed April 6,1865,in action at Sailor's Creek,Virginia.

SIXTH REGIMENT OHIO VOLUNTEER CAVALRY.

Names.	Rank.	Age.	Date of Entering the Service.	Period of Service.	Remarks.
Tanner, Warren.............	Private	31	Dec. 6, 1861	3 yrs.	Killed May 28,1864,in action at Hawe's Shop,Va.; veteran.
Thomas, Jefferson..........	...do...	19	Nov. 1, 1861	3 yrs.	Discharged Feb.5,1863,on Surgeon's certificate of disability.
Thomas, Monroe.............	...do...	18	Oct. 28, 1861	3 yrs.	Discharged Aug.15,1862,on Surgeon's certificate of disability.
Thomas, William H. H......	...do...	21	Dec. 11, 1861	3 yrs.	Discharged Feb.5,1863,on Surgeon's certificate of disability.
Tousley, George H.........	...do...	26	Oct. 13, 1861	3 yrs.	Mustered out Dec.12,1864,on expiration of term of service.
Tracy, Bruce..............	...do...	28	Dec. 11, 1861	3 yrs.	
Trimm, Melmouth D.........	...do...	18	Dec. 10, 1861	3 yrs.	Transferred to Veteran Reserve Corps Sept.30,1864;from which mustered out Jan.10,1865,at Johnson's Island,O., by order of War Department.
Viers, Edwin..............	...do...	26	Feb. 21, 1864	3 yrs.	Mustered out with company Aug.7,1865.
Viers, James E............	...do...	23	Feb. 21, 1864	3 yrs.	Captured May 19,1864;mustered out June 27,1865,at Petersburg,Va.,by order of War Department.
Viers, Nehemiah...........	...do...	25	Mch. 11, 1864	3 yrs.	Mustered out with company Aug.7,1865.
Wheeler, William..........	...do...	18	Dec. 10, 1861	3 yrs.	Discharged May 29,1862,on Surgeon's certificate of disability.
Wing, Napoleon B..........	...do...	18	Oct. 28, 1861	3 yrs.	Discharged Sept.5,1862,on Surgeon's certificate of disability.
Winter, Harrison..........	...do...	21	Dec. 6, 1861	3 yrs.	Discharged Dec.21,1862,on Surgeon's certificate of disability.
Winterstein, Manville.....	...do...	21	Nov. 4, 1861	3 yrs.	Wounded Sept.12,1863,at Culpeper,Va.; mustered out Nov.17,1864,on expiration of term of service.

Names.	Rank.	Age.	Date of Entering the Service.	Period of Service.	Remarks.
Wolcott, Willis A.........	Private	30	Oct. 19, 1861	3 yrs.	Discharged Sept.20,1862,on Surgeon's certificate of disability.
Young, Homer..............	...do...	19	Feb. 24, 1864	3 yrs.	Wounded May 13,1864;transferred to Veteran Reserve Corps April 12, 1865; from which mustered out Aug.25,1865, at Washington,D.C.,by order of War Department.

COMPANY L.

Mustered in from October 5 to December 12, 1861, by Chauncey L. Bartlett, and others, U.S.Mustering officers.
Mustered out August 7, 1865, at Petersburg, Va., by L. H. Bowen, 1st Lieutenant and Acting
Commissary of Musters, Mustering Officer Department of Virginia.

Names.	Rank.	Age.	Date of Entering the Service.	Period of Service.	Remarks.
Chauncy L. Bartlett......	Captain	....	Oct. 10, 1861	3 yrs.	Mustered as 2d Lieutenant;promoted to Captain Dec.15,1861,discharged March 16,1863,on Surgeon's certificate of disability.
Richard J. Wright........	...do...	22	Oct. 2, 1861	3 yrs.	Promoted from 1st Lieutenant and Adjutant Feb.17,1863;captured May 17,1864;discharged March 2,1865, by order of War Department.
William H. Bettes........	1st Lieut.	37	Oct. 5, 1861	3 yrs.	Mustered as 2d Lieutenant;promoted to 1st Lieutenant Dec.16,1861;discharged March 23,1863,on Surgeon's certificate of disability.
Andrew H. Smith..........	...do...	24	Oct. 5, 1861	3 yrs.	Appointed Corporal Dec.16,1861;Sergeant Oct.14,1862;Com.Sergeant Sept. 30,1863;1st Sergeant Oct.16,1864; promoted to 1st Lieutenant Jan.31, 1865;commissioned Captain July 30, 1865,but not mustered;mustered out with company Aug.7,1865; veteran.

SIXTH REGIMENT OHIO VOLUNTEER CAVALRY.

Names.	Rank.	Age.	Date of Entering the Service.	Period of Service.	Remarks.
Henry H. Abell.............	2d Lieut.	21	Oct. 18, 1861	3 yrs.	Mustered as private; promoted to 2d Lieutenant Dec.16,1861;commissioned 1st Lieutenant May 9,1864,but declined promotion;mustered out Oct. 25,1864,on expiration of term of service.
Simon Z. Dickinson.......	1st Sergt.	33	Oct. 5, 1861	3 yrs.	Mustered as private;appointed Sergeant Dec.16,1861;1st Sergeant Jan. 1,1863;transferred to Veteran Reserve Corps Sept.1,1863;no further record found.
Jacob B. Templin..........	...do...	19	Oct. 31, 1861	3 yrs.	Mustered as private;appointed Sergeant Dec.16,1861;1st Sergeant Oct. 28,1863;promoted to 2d Lieutenant Co.I July 26,1864.
Isaac W. Kirk.............	...do...	38	Oct. 16, 1861	3 yrs.	Mustered as private;appointed Q.M. Sergeant Dec.16,1861;1st Sergeant Feb.10,1865;wounded April 6,1865, at Sailor's Creek,Va.;commissioned 2d Lieutenant May 31,1865;1st Lieutenant July 30,1865,but not mustered on either commission;discharged Aug. 5,1865,on Surgeon's certificate of disability; veteran.
Michael Eck..............	Q.M.S.	21	Oct. 9, 1861	3 yrs.	Appointed Corporal Oct.31,1862;Sergeant Nov.1,1864;Q.M.Sergeant Feb. 10,1865;mustered out with company Aug.7,1865; veteran.
Silas W. Bettes..........	Com.Ser.	41	Oct. 13, 1861	3 yrs.	Appointed Corporal Dec.16,1861;Sergeant Oct.13,1862;Com.Sergeant—; discharged Feb.18,1863,at Washington, D.C.,on Surgeon's certificate of disability.

ROSTER

OF OHIO TROOPS.

Names.	Rank.	Age.	Date of Entering the Service.	Period of Service.	Remarks.
Thomas E. French.........	Com.Ser.	18	Dec. 11, 1861	3 yrs.	Appointed Corporal May 1,1863;Sergeant May 1,1864;Com.Sergeant Feb. 10,1865;mustered out with company Aug.7,1865;veteran.
Minor J. Dorn............	Sergeant	19	Oct. 30, 1861	3 yrs.	Mustered as private;appointed Dec. 16,1861.
Isaac N. Thayer..........	...do...	27	Oct. 12, 1861	3 yrs.	Mustered as private;appointed Dec. 16,1861;discharged Sept.27,1862,on Surgeon's certificate of disability.
Alfred J. S. Barnes......	...do...	38	Oct. 16, 1861	3 yrs.	Reduced from 1st Sergeant Jan.1, 1862;discharged Oct.26,1862,on Surgeon's certificate of disability.
Addison Bartram..........	...do...	22	Oct. 16, 1861	3 yrs.	Appointed Corporal Aug.31,1862;Sergeant April 1,1863;wounded June 24, 1864,at St.Mary's Church,Va.;died of wounds Aug.2,1864;veteran.
Peter L. Potter..........	...do...	30	Dec. 6, 1861	3 yrs.	Appointed Corporal Oct.17,1862;Sergeant April 1,1863;wounded June 19, 1863,at Middleburg,Va.;captured May 9,1864;mustered out June 27,1865,at Petersburg,Va.,by order of War Dept; veteran.
George A. Joiner.........	...do...	21	Nov. 7, 1861	3 yrs.	Appointed Corporal May 1,1863;Wounded May 28,1864,at Hawe's Shop,Va.;appointed Sergeant Nov.1,1864;discharged July 17,1865,on Surgeon's certificate of disability; veteran.
George H. Shaffer........	...do...	23	Oct. 9, 1861	3 yrs.	Mustered as private;appointed Nov.1, 1864;mustered out with company Aug. 7,1865; veteran.

SIXTH REGIMENT OHIO VOLUNTEER CAVALRY.

Names.	Rank.	Age.	Date of Entering the Service.	Period of Service.	Remarks.
Joseph Andrews............	Sergeant	18	Nov. 11, 1861	3 yrs.	Appointed Corporal Aug.1,1864;Sergeant Nov.1,1864;commissioned 2d Lieutenant July 30,1865,but not mustered;mustered out with company Aug.7,1865; veteran.
Reuben Hawley.............	...do...	25	Oct. 16, 1861	3 yrs.	Appointed Corporal May 1,1863;Sergeant Feb.10,1865;mustered out June 27,1865,at Petersburg,Va.,by order of War Department; veteran.
Henry H. Heisler.........	Corporal	19	Dec. 11, 1861	3 yrs.	Appointed Nov.1,1864;mustered out with company Aug.7,1865; veteran.
Solomon J. Durkee........	...do...	26	Dec. 5, 1861	3 yrs.	Appointed Dec.16,1861;discharged July 11,1862,on Surgeon's certificate of disability.
Aaron Gans...............	...do...	24	Oct. 5, 1861	3 yrs.	Appointed Dec.16,1861;died June 16, 1862,in Stark county, O.
Peter Goothier...........	...do...	25	Nov. 11, 1861	3 yrs.	Appointed Nov.1,1864;mustered out June 27,1865,at Petersburg,Va.,by order of War Department; veteran.
Madison Trail............	...do...	28	Oct. 18, 1861	3 yrs.	Appointed Dec.16,1861;discharged Oct.24,1862,on Surgeon's certificate of disability.
Harley B. Scribner.......	...do...	18	Nov. 12, 1861	3 yrs.	Appointed Nov.1,1864;mustered out with company Aug.7,1865; veteran.
David Elliott............	...do...	19	Oct. 31, 1861	3 yrs.	Appointed Aug.1,1864;mustered out with company Aug.7,1865; veteran.
Bazel Brooke.............	...do...	29	Oct. 31, 1861	3 yrs.	Appointed July 1,1862;transferred to Veteran Reserve Corps March 31,1864.
Jacob Ipes...............	...do...	20	Oct. 18, 1861	3 yrs.	Wounded June 24,1864,at St.Mary's Church,Va.;appointed Nov.1,1864;discharged June 10,1865,on Surgeon's certificate of disability; veteran.

ROSTER OF OHIO TROOPS.

Names.	Rank.	Age.	Date of Entering the Service.	Period of Service.	Remarks.
James A. Hughes..........	Corporal	18	Oct. 16, 1861	3 yrs.	Appointed Nov.1,1864;mustered out with company Aug.7,1865; veteran.
George P. Heintz..........	...do...	18	Feb. 15, 1864	3 yrs.	Appointed May 1,1865;mustered out with company Aug.7,1865.
Robert W. Hills..........	...do...	34	Nov. 22, 1861	3 yrs.	Appointed—;discharged June 16,1863, at Washington,D.C.,on Surgeon's certificate of disability.
Samuel T. Prentice.......	...do...	41	Dec. 2, 1861	3 yrs.	Appointed—;died Sept.17,1862,at New York City.
David A. Musser..........	Bugler	44	Nov. 11, 1861	3 yrs.	Appointed Dec.16,1861;discharged Oct. 30,1862,by order of War Department.
David Potter.............	...do...	21	Dec. 6, 1861	3 yrs.	Appointed—;accidentally wounded; died of wounds Aug.2,1862,at Baltimore, Md.
Luman Hills..............	...do...	19	Nov. 22, 1861	3 yrs.	Appointed Dec.16,1861;died Aug.19, 1862,at Alexandria, Va.
George Wells.............	Farrier	33	Oct. 5, 1861	3 yrs.	Appointed Dec.16,1861;transferred to Veteran Reserve Corps Dec.15,1863, from which mustered out Oct.31,1864, at Indianapolis,Ind.,on expiration of term of service.
Nelson K. Gunder.........	...do...	26	Oct. 31, 1861	3 yrs.	Mustered out Nov.4,1864,on expiration of term of service.
Adam Goothier............	...do...	22	Oct. 9, 1861	3 yrs.	Appointed—;mustered out with company Aug. 7,1865;veteran.
William D. Oswold........	Saddler	27	Dec. 12, 1861	3 yrs.	Mustered out Dec.11,1864,on expiration of term of service.
John G. Carson...........	...do...	27	Nov. 6, 1861	3 yrs.	Appointed Dec.16,1861;promoted to Regt.Q.M.Sergeant Sept.1,1862.

SIXTH REGIMENT OHIO VOLUNTEER CAVALRY.

Names.	Rank.	Age.	Date of Entering the Service.	Period of Service.	Remarks.
Jacob F. Chamberlain....	Saddler	18	Jan. 23, 1864	3 yrs.	Transferred from Co.F Sept.20,1864; appointed—;mustered out June 27, 1865,at Petersburg,Va.,by order of War Department.
George Andrews..........	Wagoner	41	Oct. 9, 1861	3 yrs.	Appointed Dec.16,1861;transferred to Veteran Reserve Corps March 31,1864, from which mustered out Sept.5,1865, by order of War Department.
Adams, John.............	Private	23	Feb. 5, 1864	3 yrs.	
Aldrich, William........	...do...	39	April 7, 1864	3 yrs.	
Andrews, David W........	...do...	28	Oct. 14, 1861	3 yrs.	Reduced from Corporal Feb.4,1862; killed June 24,1864,at St. Mary's Church,Va.; veteran.
Andrews, Lucius G.......	...do...	19	Oct. 9, 1861	3 yrs.	Discharged Jan.31,1863,on Surgeon's certificate of disability.
Anten, Sylvester.......	...do...	32	Mch. 9, 1865	1 yr.	Mustered out June 27,1865,at Petersburg,Va.,by order of War Department.
Arthur, John...........	...do...	18	Dec. 23, 1863	3 yrs.	
Austin, Eusebins S.....	...do...	33	Oct. 5, 1861	3 yrs.	Promoted to Sergt.Major Dec.16,1861.
Barrett, Martin........	...do...	27	Dec. 17, 1653	3 yrs.	
Bazle, John............	...do...	20	Nov. 9, 1861	3 yrs.	Discharged Dec.16,1863,on Surgeon's certificate of disability.
Beans, James...........	...do...	23	Oct. 8, 1861	3 yrs.	Died April 29,1862,at his home in Portage county,O.
Beckwith, Daniel.......	...do...	40	Nov. 4, 1861	3 yrs.	Discharged May 16, 1862,on Surgeon's certificate of disability.
Bissell, Daniel R......	...do...	44	Nov. 17, 1861	3 yrs.	Discharged Sept.25,1864,on Surgeon's certificate of disability.
Bohn, Lewis............	...do...	18	Mch. 9, 1865	1 yr.	Mustered out June 27,1865,at Petersburg,Va.,by order of War Department.
Boyle, John............	...do...	20	Nov. 13, 1861	3 yrs.	Discharged Dec.19,1863,on Surgeon's certificate of disability.

233

Names.	Rank.	Age.	Date of Entering the Service.	Period of Service.	Remarks.
Brennan, James............	Private	23	Jan. 30, 1864	3 yrs.	Drafted;mustered out July 27,1863, on expiration of term of service.
Brooks, Quinton...........	..do...	33	Oct. 2, 1862	9 mos.	
Brown, Patrick............	..do...	22	Feb. 11, 1864	3 yrs.	Mustered out June 29,1865,at Peters-
Carver, James.............	..do...	19	Mch. 7, 1865	1 yr.	burg,Va.,by order of War Department.
Case, Truman..............	..do...	44	Oct. 5, 1861	3 yrs.	Discharged Sept.12,1862,on Surgeon's certificate of disability.
Cassady, James............	..do...	30	Oct. 31, 1861	3 yrs.	
Castner, William H........	..do...	24	Nov. 18, 1861	3 yrs.	Mustered out Nov.4,1864,on expira- tion of term of service.
Chase, Leroy..............	..do...	18	Mch. 31, 1864	3 yrs.	Killed by accidental discharge of his gun March 7,1865.
Clifford, William C.......	..do...	19	Dec. 18, 1863	3 yrs.	
Cobb, Lorenzo A...........	..do...	18	Feb. 4, 1864	3 yrs.	Discharged Aug.22,1864,on Surgeon's certificate of disability.
Cole, William E...........	..do...	20	Dec. 2, 1861	3 yrs.	
Condon, James.............	..do...	25	Feb. 16, 1864	3 yrs.	
Corwin, James.............	..do...	24	Dec. 28, 1863	3 yrs.	
Cox, David................	..do...	20	Dec. 12, 1861	3 yrs.	Discharged Aug.21,1862,at New York City,on Surgeon's certificate of disability.
Cox, William P	..do...	39	Oct. 18, 1861	3 yrs.	Reduced from Sergeant Sept.20,1864; discharged July 17,1865,on Surgeon's certificate of disability; veteran.
Crist, Daniel.............	..do...	29	Dec. 9, 1861	3 yrs.	Died Sept.8,1862,at Columbus, O.
Culler, Jeremiah..........	..do...	28	Oct. 26, 1861	3 yrs.	Mustered out Nov.4,1864,on expira- tion of term of service.
Cummings, William.........	..do...	29	Dec. 3, 1861	3 yrs.	Veteran.
Davis, Frederick..........	..do...	18	Mch. 9, 1865	1 yr.	Mustered out June 27,1865,at Peters- burg,Va.,by order of War Department.

SIXTH REGIMENT OHIO VOLUNTEER CAVALRY.

Names.	Rank.	Age.	Date of Entering the Service.	Period of Service.	Remarks.
Day, Cyrus..............	Private	20	Oct. 2, 1862	9 mos.	Drafted;mustered out July 27,1863, on expiration of term of service.
Dickinson, Luther B......	...do...	27	Nov. 12, 1861	3 yrs.	Transferred to Veteran Reserve Corps July 1,1863.
Farrell, James............	...do...	25	Jan. 6, 1864	3 yrs.	
Folk, James..............	...do...	19	Mch. 31, 1864	3 yrs.	Captured Sept.30,1864,at Arthur's Swamp,Va.;died Jan.22,1865,in Andersonville Prison, Ga.
Fox, Edwin..............	...do...	23	Nov. 18, 1861	3 yrs.	Mustered out June 27,1865,at Petersburg,Va.,by order of War Dept.;veteran.
France, Daniel...........	...do...	18	Feb. 13, 1864	3 yrs.	Discharged March 13,1865,on Surgeon's certificate of disability.
Freeman, George.........	...do...	22	Mch. 9, 1865	1 yr.	Mustered out June 27,1865,at Petersburg,Va.,by order of War Department.
Gibson, James H.........	...do...	22	Oct. 1, 1862	9 mos.	Drafted;mustered out July 27,1863,on expiration of term of service.
Goodhew, William F.......	...do...	29	Oct. 16, 1861	3 yrs.	Died Oct.14,1862,at Washington,D.C.
Goss, Lucius.............	...do...	27	Oct. 5, 1861	3 yrs.	Discharged July 14,1862,at Cumberland, Md.,on Surgeon's certificate of disability.
Gregory, Lafayette.......	...do...	34	Oct. 16, 1861	3 yrs.	Discharged Feb.9,1863,on Surgeon's certificate of disability.
Grim, James.............	...do...	18	Dec. 7, 1861	3 yrs.	Discharged June 21, 1862,on Surgeon's certificate of disability.
Hackett, Warren S........	...do...	32	Oct. 19, 1861	3 yrs.	Discharged Oct.9,1862,at New York City,on Surgeon's certificate of disability.
Hantz, William...........	...do...	23	Feb. 13, 1864	3 yrs.	Mustered out June 27,1865,at Petersburg,Va.,by order of War Department.

Names.	Rank.	Age.	Date of Entering the Service.	Period of Service.	Remarks.
Harley, George............	Private	21	Oct. 2, 1862	9 mos.	Drafted;mustered out June 27,1863, on expiration of term of service.
Harmon, David.............	...do...	20	Dec. 11, 1861	3 yrs.	Transferred to Veteran Reserve Corps May 15,1864;from which mustered out March 2,1865,at St. Louis, Mo.,on expiration of term of service.
Hillman, Jeremiah.........	...do...	28	Oct. 31, 1861	3 yrs.	Transferred to Veteran Reserve Corps —;discharged from same May 8,1865, on surgeon's certificate of disability; veteran.
Hillman, Thomas P.........	...do...	23	Oct. 31, 1861	3 yrs.	Discharged Aug.17,1862,on Surgeon's certificate of disability.
Hills, Ansil W............	...do...	22	Oct. 22, 1861	3 yrs.	Discharged Aug.11,1862,at Columbus, O.,on Surgeon's certificate of disability.
Hills, Henry..............	...do...	23	Dec. 6, 1861	3 yrs.	Mustered out June 27,1865,at Petersburg,Va.,by order of War Dept.;veteran.
Holmes, Thomas............	...do...	21	Oct. 2, 1862	9 mos.	Drafted;mustered out July 27,1863,on expiration of term of service.
Houston, Edward B.........	...do...	19	Mch. 7, 1865	1 yr.	Mustered out June 27,1865,at Petersburg,Va.,by order of War Department.
Hoover, Jacob Z...........	...do...	33	Aug. 27, 1864	1 yr.	Mustered out May 30,1865,at Petersburg,Va.,by order of War Department.
Humphrey, Samuel W........	...do...	39	Oct. 12, 1861	3 yrs.	Transferred to Co.I,5th Regiment Veteran Reserve Corps,Feb.15,1864; from which mustered out Oct.13, 1864, on expiration of term of service.
Ingersoll, Frank S........	...do...	36	Dec. 9, 1861	3 yrs.	
Jenkins, James P..........	...do...	20	Oct. 26, 1861	3 yrs.	Reduced from Corporal Jan.18,1864; mustered out June 27,1865,at Petersburg,Va.,by order of War Dept.;veteran.

SIXTH REGIMENT OHIO VOLUNTEER CAVALRY.

Names.	Rank.	Age.	Date of Entering the Service	Period of Service.	Remarks.
Keener, Charles F........	Private	33	Oct. 16, 1861	3 yrs.	Captured Aug.9,1862,at Sperryville, Va.;transferred to Veteran Reserve Corps March 16,1864;from which mustered out Oct.17,1864,by order of War Department.
McKim, Robert...........	...do...	18	Mch. 29, 1864	3 yrs.	Wounded Dec.10,1864;discharged June 19,1865,on Surgeon's Certificate of disability.
McLaughlin, David C.....	...do...	25	Oct. 2, 1862	9 mos.	Drafted;mustered out July 29,1863, on expiration of term of service.
Mahoney, Charles A......	...do...	18	Sept. 1, 1864	1 yr.	Mustered out May 30,1865,at Petersburg,Va.,by order of War Department.
Mahoney, Charles.......	...do...	35	Mch. 26, 1864	3 yrs.	Mustered out June 27,1865,at Petersburg,Va.,by order of War Department.
Maple, Henry T.........	...do...	25	Mch. 24, 1864	3 yrs.	Mustered out June 27,1865,at Petersburg,Va.,by order of War Department.
Mead, George K.........	...do...	20	Oct. 31, 1861	3 yrs.	Mustered out Nov.4,1864,on expiration of term of service.
Minard, George........	...do...	20	Oct. 28, 1861	3 yrs.	Mustered out with company Aug.7,1865; veteran.
Minard, Harman........	...do...	44	Nov. 7, 1861	3 yrs.	Discharged Aug.18,1862,on Surgeon's certificate of disability.
Moe, Charles..........	...do...	22	Nov. 12, 1861	3 yrs.	Mustered out June 27,1865,at Petersburg,Va.,by order of War Dept;veteran.
Morris, Louis N.......	...do...	32	Oct. 14, 1861	3 yrs.	Discharged Feb.28,1863,on Surgeon's certificate of disability.
O'Neil, Stuart........	...do...	36	April 5, 1864	3 yrs.	Mustered out June 27,1865,at Petersburg,Va.,by order of War Department.
Palmer, John..........	...do...	19	Nov. 19, 1861	3 yrs.	Discharged Jan.31,1863,on Surgeon's certificate of disability.

ROSTER OF OHIO TROOPS.

Names.	Rank.	Age.	Date of Entering the Service.	Period of Service.	Remarks.
Payne, Almon............	Private	41	Nov. 9, 1861	3 yrs.	Transferred to Veteran Reserve Corps March 15,1864; from which mustered out Nov.9,1864,on expiration of term of service.
Peterman, Benjamin F....	...do...	21	Aug. 27, 1864	1 yr.	Mustered out May 30,1865,at Petersburg,Va.,by order of War Department.
Peterman, William.......	...do...	29	Aug. 26, 1864	1 yr.	Mustered out May 30,1865,at Petersburg,Va.,by order of War Department.
Porter, William W.......	...do...	18	Mch. 8, 1864	3 yrs.	Mustered out June 27,1865,at Petersburg,Va.,by order of War Department.
Potter, Daniel H........	...do...	33	Dec. 6, 1861	3 yrs.	Mustered out Dec.6,1864,on expiration of term of service.
Pyle, John.............	...do...	25	Oct. 18, 1861	3 yrs.	Died Aug.16,1862,at Alexandria,Va.
Powers, George D........	...do...	24	April 19,1864	3 yrs.	
Redditt, James.........	...do...	21	Jan. 9, 1864	3 yrs.	Mustered out June 27,1865,at Petersburg,Va.,by order of War Department.
Regal, John S..........	...do...	25	Nov. 23, 1861	3 yrs.	Discharged Feb.23,1863,at Cumberland, Md.,on Surgeon's certificate of disability.
Ring, Daniel...........	...do...	29	Dec. 16, 1863	3 yrs.	Mustered out with company Aug.7,1865.
Ripley, John A.........	...do...	18	Nov. 9, 1861	3 yrs.	Discharged June 7,1862,on Surgeon's certificate of disability.
Robert, Luzem..........	...do...	18	Oct. 8, 1861	3 yrs.	Mustered out Oct.11,1864,on expiration of term of service.
Rodgers, Joseph........	...do...	33	Nov. 16, 1861	3 yrs.	Reduced from Corporal July 1,1864; discharged Feb.18,1864,on Surgeon's certificate of disability.
Sage, Edwin H..........	...do...	26	Oct. 9, 1861	3 yrs.	Reduced from Sergeant May 1,1864; mustered out June 27,1865,at Petersburg,Va.,by order of War Dept.;veteran.

SIXTH REGIMENT OHIO VOLUNTEER CAVALRY.

Names.	Rank.	Age.	Date of Entering the Service	Period of Service.	Remarks.
Santiman, William.........	Private	17	Feb. 5, 1864	3 yrs.	Mustered out June 27,1865,at Petersburg,Va.,by order of War Department.
Schriver, Isaac...........	...do...	18	Oct. 9, 1861	3 yrs.	Mustered out Oct.11,1864,on expiration of term of service.
Sears, David H...........	...do...	22	Oct. 11, 1861	3 yrs.	Discharged Sept.20,1862,at Columbus, O.,on Surgeon's certificate of disability.
Sears, Levi..............	...do...	18	Oct. 8, 1861	3 yrs.	Discharged Feb.23,1863,at Cumberland, Md.,on Surgeon's certificate of disability.
Sharp, Andrew............	...do...	35	Feb. 24, 1864	3 yrs.	Discharged Dec.24,1862,on Surgeon's certificate of disability.
Smith, Garrett J. F......	...do...	41	Nov. 24, 1861	3 yrs.	
Spikler, Henry K.........	...do...	21	Mch. 29, 1864	3 yrs.	Mustered out June 27,1865,at Petersburg,Va.,by order of War Department.
Steadman, Edward E.......	...do...	17	Aug. 14, 1862	3 yrs.	Promoted to Chief Bugler May 1,1865.
Steller, Isaac...........	...do...	23	Feb. 15, 1864	3 yrs.	Killed by shell near Fort Davis,Va., March 25, 1865.
Stewart, Martin E........	...do...	28	Dec. 5, 1863	3 yrs.	Mustered out June 27,1865,at Petersburg,Va.,by order of War Department.
Stratton, William H......	...do...	18	April 18,1864	3 yrs.	
Stutler, David L.........	...do...	18	April 18,1864	3 yrs.	Died Sept.20,1864,at Point Lookout,Md.
Thatcher, John A.........	...do...	40	Dec. 30, 1863	3 yrs.	
Thompson, Addison........	...do...	28	Nov. 12, 1861	3 yrs.	Mustered out June 27,1865,at Petersburg,Va.,by order of War Dept.;veteran.
Thompson, Charles U......	...do...	27	Feb. 17, 1864	3 yrs.	Discharged July 11,1862,at Wheeling, W.Va.,on Surgeon's certificate of disability.
Townsley, Daniel.........	...do...	35	Nov. 9, 1861	3 yrs.	
Underwood, Robert........	...do...	18	Feb. 12, 1864	3 yrs.	Discharged July 20,1865,on Surgeon's certificate of disability,by reason of gun-shot wound.

ROSTER OF OHIO TROOPS.

Names.	Rank.	Age.	Date of Entering the Service.	Period of Service.	Remarks.
Urick, Henry W.	Private	....	Oct. 14, 1861	3 yrs.	Transferred from Captain Stanhope's Co.March 1,1862;mustered out Nov.1, 1864,on expiration of term of service.
Vernon, Henry H.,Jr.	...do...	....	Oct. 28, 1861	3 yrs.	Transferred from Captain Stanhope's Co.March 1,1862;discharged Feb.14, 1863,on Surgeon's certificate of disability.
Ware, William D.	...do...	27	Mch. 29, 1864	3 yrs.	Mustered out with company Aug.7,1865.
Wager, John L.	...do...	37	Mch. 31, 1864	3 yrs.	
Weitzel, Philip.	...do...	35	Oct. 5, 1861	3 yrs.	Mustered out Oct.30,1864,on expiration of term of service.
Wells,John.	...do...	29	Nov. 9, 1861	3 yrs.	Discharged June 7,1862,at Wheeling, W.Va.,on Surgeon's certificate of disability.
Whitecomb, Joseph.	...do...	24	Sept. 6, 1864	1 yr.	Mustered out June 10,1865,at Point Lookout,Md.,by order of War Dept.
White, John.	...do...	33	Nov. 12, 1861	3 yrs.	Discharged Feb.23,1863,at Washington, D.C.,on Surgeon's certificate of disability.
Wilkinson, Richard J.	...do...	19	Oct. 1, 1862	9 mos.	Drafted;mustered out July 27,1863,on expiration of term of service.
Wilson, Henry.	...do...	44	Nov. 2, 1863	3 yrs.	Discharged Jan.14,1865,on Surgeon's certificate of disability.
Winchel, Daniel.	...do...	39	Oct. 7, 1861	3 yrs.	Transferred from Captain Stanhope's Co.March 1,1862;mustered out Oct.11, 1864,on expiration of term of service.
Williams, James.	...do...	27	April 1, 1864	3 yrs.	
Winslow, James.	...do...	22	Dec. 22, 1863	3 yrs.	
Winslow, Thomas.	...do...	22	Dec. 6, 1863	3 yrs.	
Wise, John.	...do...	21	Mch. 31, 1864	3 yrs.	
Wise, Joseph.	...do...	22	Mch. 31, 1864	3 yrs.	
Wooley, David.	...do...	21	Mch. 9, 1865	1 yr.	Mustered out June 27,1865,at Petersburg,Va.,by order of War Department.

SIXTH REGIMENT OHIO VOLUNTEER CAVALRY.

COMPANY M.

Mustered in December 27, 1863, at Cleveland, Ohio, by H. Douglas, Captain 18th Infantry, U.S.A., Mustering Officer. Mustered out August 7,1865,at Petersburg,Va., by L. H. Bowen, 1st Lieutenant and Acting Commissary of Musters, Mustering Officer Department of Virginia.

Names.	Rank.	Age.	Date of Entering the Service.	Period of Service.	Remarks.
John Saxon..............	Captain	24	Dec. 27, 1863	3 yrs.	Mustered as Captain Dec.27,1863;discharged March 20,1865,on Surgeon's certificate of disability.
Matthew H. Cryer.........	1st Lieut.	23	Oct. 16, 1863	3 yrs.	Mustered as 2d Lieutenant;promoted to 1st Lieutenant Dec.23,1863;wounded July 28,1864,at Malvern Hill,Va.; promoted to Captain Co.C Nov.12,1864.
Oliver H. Simmons.........	...do...	20	Nov. 4, 1863	3 yrs.	Promoted from Sergt.Major Nov.12, 1864;commissioned Captain May 31, 1865,but not mustered;mustered out with company Aug.7,1865.
William K. Miller.........	2d Lieut.	23	Dec. 27, 1863	3 yrs.	Mustered as 2d Lieutenant Dec.27,1863; promoted to Captain Co.G Nov.12,1864.
Frank D. Moran...........	...do...	22	Oct. 27, 1862	3 yrs.	Promoted from 1st Sergeant Co.B Nov. 12,1864;to 1st Lieutenant Co.F Jan. 31,1865.
Aaron Wagner.............	...do...	18	Nov. 10, 1862	3 yrs.	Promoted from 1st Sergeant Co.B April 8,1865;commissioned 1st Lieutenant May 31,1865,but not mustered; resigned June 26, 1865.
James E. Darwent.........	1st Sergt.	22	Jan. 2, 1864	3 yrs.	Appointed Corporal Oct.1,1864;1st Sergeant Nov.1,1864;promoted to Sergt.Major Dec.1,1864.

Names.	Rank.	Age.	Date of Entering the Service.	Period of Service.	Remarks.
John W. Wilcox............	1st Sergt.	25	Oct. 25, 1863	3 yrs.	Transferred from 12th Regiment O.V.C. ——;appointed Com.Sergeant Jan.5,1864; wounded July 28,1864,at Malvern Hill, Va.;appointed 1st Sergeant Dec.1,1864; commissioned 2d Lieutenant April 8, 1865;1st Lieutenant May 31,1865,but not mustered on either commission; mustered out with company Aug.7,1865.
John S. Galbraith........	Q.M.S.	19	Dec. 23, 1863	3 yrs.	Mustered as private;appointed Q.M. Sergeant Jan.1,1864;captured June 24, 1864,at Ladd's Farm,Va.;died Nov.15, 1864,in Andersonville Prison, Ga.
John W. Williamson.......	...do...	19	Nov. 1, 1863	3 yrs.	Mustered as private;appointed Ser- geant Jan.1,1864;Q.M.Sergeant Dec.1, 1864;mustered out June 27,1865,at Petersburg,Va.,by order of War Dept.
James C. Boice...........	Com.Ser.	19	Dec. 10, 1863	3 yrs.	Mustered as private;appointed Ser- geant Jan.1,1864;Com.Sergeant Dec.1, 1864;mustered out June 27,1865,at Petersburg,Va.,by order of War Dept.
James T. McCracken.......	Sergeant	18	Dec. 3, 1863	3 yrs.	Mustered as private;appointed Ser- geant Jan.1,1864;mustered out July 5, 1865,at Petersburg,Va.,by order of War Department.
Monroe Kirk.............	...do...	30	Nov. 16, 1863	3 yrs.	Mustered as private;appointed Ser- geant Jan.1,1864;discharged Nov.7, 1864,on Surgeon's certificate of disability.
Euclid M. Suplee........	...do...	21	Dec. 28, 1863	3 yrs.	Appointed Corporal Jan.1,1864;wounded July 28,1864,at Malvern Hill,Va.;ap- pointed Sergeant Dec.1,1864;mustered out with company Aug.7,1865.

SIXTH REGIMENT OHIO VOLUNTEER CAVALRY.

Names.	Rank.	Age.	Date of Entering the Service.	Period of Service.	Remarks.
David Tate...............	Sergeant	27	Nov. 17, 1863	3 yrs.	Appointed Corporal Jan.1,1864;Sergeant Dec.1,1864;mustered out June 27,1865,at Petersburg,Va.,by order of War Department.
Henry H. Holcomb..........	...do...	20	Dec. 22, 1863	3 yrs.	Appointed Corporal Jan.1,1864;Sergeant——;mustered out with company Aug.7,1865.
William J. Donaldson......	...do...	18	Dec. 10, 1863	3 yrs.	Appointed Corporal Dec.10,1863;Sergeant——;mustered out with company Aug.7,1865.
William P. Littell........	Corporal	18	Dec. 10, 1863	3 yrs.	Appointed Jan.1,1864;wounded July 24,1864,at ——;transferred to Veteran Reserve Corps Jan.24,1865.
Thomas B. File............	...do...	18	Jan. 4, 1864	3 yrs.	Appointed Jan.1,1864;killed Sept.30, 1864,at Davis'Farm,Va.
Charles H. Smith..........	...do...	23	Jan. 3, 1864	3 yrs.	Appointed Jan.1,1864.
Henry J. King.............	...do...	18	Dec. 29, 1863	3 yrs.	Appointed Dec.1,1864;died May 13, 1865,at Washington,D.C.,of gun-shot wounds.
George Yanser.............	...do...	19	Oct. 1, 1863	3 yrs.	Appointed Dec.1,1864;mustered out with company Aug.7,1865.
Jacob D. Peterson.........	...do...	18	Nov. 18, 1863	3 yrs.	Appointed Jan.1,1864;captured Oct. 1,1864,at Davis'Farm,Va.;mustered out June 22,1865,at Camp Dennison, O.,by order of War Department.
Andrew Flick..............	...do...	18	Dec. 19, 1863	3 yrs.	Appointed Jan.1,1864;mustered out July 6,1865,at Camp Dennison,O.
Benjamin F. Entriken......	...do...	18	Dec. 18, 1863	3 yrs.	Appointed March 1,1865;mustered out June 27,1865,at Petersburg,Va.,by order of War Department.

ROSTER OF OHIO TROOPS.

Names.	Rank.	Age.	Date of Entering the Service.	Period of Service.	Remarks.
David H. Bricker.........	Corporal	18	Feb. 24, 1864	3 yrs.	Appointed March 1,1865;mustered out June 27,1865,at Petersburg,Va.,by order of War Department.
Charles W. Gardner.......	...do...	18	Nov. 18, 1863	3 yrs.	Appointed Bugler Jan.1,1864;Corporal March 1,1865;mustered out June 27, 1865,at Petersburg,Va.,by order of War Department.
Jacob Thullen............	...do...	18	Jan. 1, 1864	3 yrs.	Appointed May 1,1865;mustered out June 27,1865,at Petersburg,Va.,by order of War Department.
John B. Galbraith........	...do...	18	Nov. 6, 1863	3 yrs.	Appointed May 1,1865;mustered out June 27,1865,at Petersburg,Va.,by order of War Department.
Henry J. Shopley.........	...do...	18	Dec. 17, 1863	3 yrs.	Appointed June 1,1865;mustered out June 27,1865,at Petersburg,Va.,by order of War Department.
George Freeman...........	Bugler	21	Nov. 19, 1863	3 yrs.	Appointed Jan.1,1864;died Nov.30, 1864,at Washington, D.C.
Timothy Burns............	...do...	18	Dec. 1, 1863	3 yrs.	Appointed——;mustered out June 27, 1865,at Petersburg,Va.,by order of War Department.
Richard Stone............	Farrier	21	Oct. 21, 1863	3 yrs.	Transferred from 12th O.V.C.——; appointed Farrier Jan.1,1864;mustered out with company Aug.7,1865.
Egbert D. Ashley.........	Saddler	36	June 5, 1864	3 yrs.	Appointed Saddler Jan.1,1864;mustered out June 27,1865,at Petersburg, Va.,by order of War Department.
Joseph Hively............	Wagoner	40	Nov. 11, 1863	3 yrs.	Appointed——;mustered out June 27, 1865,at Petersburg,Va.,by order of War Department.
Allison, Hamilton K......	Private	18	Dec. 22, 1863	3 yrs.	Died Sept.9,1864,at Philadelphia,Pa.

SIXTH REGIMENT OHIO VOLUNTEER CAVALRY.

Names.	Rank.	Age.	Date of Entering the Service.	Period of Service.	Remarks.
Algier, John A..........	Private	21	Feb. 11, 1865	1 yr.	Mustered out June 27,1865,at Petersburg,Va.,by order of War Department.
Anderson, John..........	...do...	32	Dec. 23, 1863	3 yrs.	Mustered out June 27,1865,at Petersburg,Va.,by order of War Department.
Bailey, Rudd...........	...do...	19	Feb. 16, 1865	1 yr.	Mustered out with company Aug.7,1865.
Baker, James...........	...do...	24	Dec. 24, 1863	yrs.	Missing in action June 24,1864,at St. Mary's Church,Va.;no further record found.
Bell, John S...........	...do...	19	Nov. 12, 1863	3 yrs.	Captured Oct.1,1864,at Davis' Farm, Va.;died Dec.10,1864,in Salisbury Prison,N.C.
Boon, John B...........	...do...	22	Dec. 30, 1863	3 yrs.	Died July 31,1864,at Washington,D.C.
Boyd, Andrew H.........	...do...	18	Dec. 10, 1863	3 yrs.	Captured Oct.1,1864,at Davis'Farm, Va.;died Jan.28,1865,in Salisbury Prison,N.C.
Brown, Amos...........	...do...	27	Nov. 16, 1863	3 yrs.	Captured June 24,1864,at St. Mary's Church,Va.;died Oct.31,1864,at Millen, Ga.,while a prisoner of war.
Burmester, Ernest.......	...do...	18	Dec. 24, 1863	3 yrs.	Died March 20,1864,at Cleveland, O.
Burwell, Daniel E.......	...do...	26	Dec. 3, 1863	3 yrs.	Reduced from Sergeant Dec.10,1864; mustered out July 7,1865,at Columbus, O.,by order of War Department.
Campbell, William.......	...do...	18	Dec. 25, 1863	3 yrs.	Mustered out June 27,1865,at Petersburg,Va.,by order of War Department.
Carey, Philip..........	...do...	27	Dec. 24, 1863	3 yrs.	Mustered out with company Aug.7,1865.
Chambers, John W........	...do...	18	Dec. 26, 1863	3 yrs.	Died Aug.12,1864,at Washington,D.C.
Conway, Peter..........	...do...	19	Dec. 29, 1863	3 yrs.	Mustered out June 27,1865,at Petersburg,Va.,by order of War Department.
Coy, Jacob.............	...do...	22	Dec. 21, 1863	3 yrs.	Mustered out June 27,1865,at Petersburg,Va.,by order of War Department.

ROSTER OF OHIO TROOPS.

Names.	Rank.	Age.	Date of Entering the Service.	Period of Service.	Remarks.
Crawford, Joseph.........	Private	29	Dec. 14, 1863	3 yrs.	Mustered out June 27,1865,at Petersburg,Va.,by order of War Department.
Daniels, Ezra T..........	...do...	19	Jan. 1, 1864	3 yrs.	Captured Oct.1,1864,at Davis'Farm,Va.; mustered out June 27,1865,at Petersburg,Va.,by order of War Department.
Davidson, Joseph W......	...do...	28	Nov. 15, 1863	3 yrs.	Reduced from Sergeant Sept.1,1864; mustered out June 22,1865,at Philadelphia,Pa.,by order of War Dept.
DeVeere, Charles.......	...do...	20	Dec. 26, 1863	3 yrs.	
Donaldson, Richard B.....	...do...	18	Dec. 22, 1863	3 yrs.	Missing in action June 24,1864,at St. Mary's Church,Va;no further record found.
Drager, Frederick.......	...do...	43	Dec. 23, 1863	3 yrs.	Captured Oct.1,1864,at Davis'Farm,Va.; died Nov.28,1864,in Salisbury Prison, N.C.
Eidinise, Almoreen.......	...do...	19	Dec. 24, 1863	3 yrs.	Mustered out June 27,1865,at Petersburg,Va.,by order of War Department.
Eidinise, Adoniga........	...do...	18	Dec. 21, 1863	3 yrs.	Mustered out June 27,1865,at Petersburg,Va.,by order of War Department.
Evans, George G.........	...do...	36	Nov. 2, 1863	3 yrs.	Also known as "William Jones";mustered out June 8,1865,at Petersburg,Va.,by order of War Department.
Everhart, Owen R........	...do...	18	Dec. 22, 1863	3 yrs.	Mustered out with company Aug.7,1865.
Fillorn, Francis M.......	...do...	19	Dec. 15, 1863	3 yrs.	Mustered out with company Aug.7,1865.
Fillson, John N.........	...do...	18	Dec. 26, 1863	3 yrs.	Captured Oct.1,1864,at Davis'Farm,Va.; died Jan.1,1865,in Salisbury Prison, N.C.
Fisher, George W........	...do...	18	Oct. 31, 1863	3 yrs.	Mustered out with company Aug.7,1865.
Folk, John —.............	...do...	18	Oct. 10, 1863	3 yrs.	Killed June 24,1864,at St. Mary's Church,Va.

SIXTH REGIMENT OHIO VOLUNTEER CAVALRY.

Names.	Rank.	Age.	Date of Entering the Service.	Period of Service.	Remarks.
G-ntz, Walter S..........	Private	18	Oct. 29, 1863	3 yrs.	Mustered out with company Aug.7,1865.
Gilson, Robert M..........	...do...	18	Dec. 23, 1863	3 yrs.	Died Dec.16,1864,at Washington,D.C., of wounds received Dec.9,1864,in action at Hatcher's Run,Va.
Handle, John J...........	...do...	34	Dec. 30, 1863	3 yrs.	Mustered out June 27,1865,at Peters-burg,Va.,by order of War Department.
Herrington, Simon E.......	...do...	19	Dec. 22, 1863	3 yrs.	Wounded and captured June 24,1864,at St. Mary's Church,Va.;no further record found.
Hitchcock, Charles........	...do...	19	Jan. 4, 1864	3 yrs.	Transferred to Veteran Reserve Corps ——;from which mustered out May 17, 1865,at Wilmington,Del.,by order of War Department.
Hoover, Horatio...........	...do...	26	Nov. 9, 1863	3 yrs.	Mustered out June 6,1865,at Philadel-phia,Pa.,by order of War Department.
Hunter, George W..........	...do...	18	Jan. 1, 1864	3 yrs.	Mustered out June 27,1865,at Peters-burg,Va.,by order of War Department.
Jones, John D.............	...do...	38	Dec. 14, 1863	3 yrs.	Under medical treatment in Mahoning Co.,Ohio,Aug.14,1865;no discharge furnished.
Kaley, James.............	...do...	19	Nov. 1, 1863	3 yrs.	Captured Oct.1,1864,at Davis'Farm, Va.;mustered out June 27,1865,at Petersburg,Va.,by order of War Dept.
Kincaid, Lemuel...........	...do...	18	Oct. 26, 1863	3 yrs.	Captured Oct.1,1864,at Davis'Farm, Va.;died Jan.13,1865,in Salisbury Prison,North Carolina.
King, William F..........	...do...	18	Oct. 27, 1863	3 yrs.	Mustered out with company Aug.7,1865.
McCanna, James...........	...do...	18	Dec. 10, 1863	3 yrs.	Mustered out June 27,1865,at Peters-burg,Va.,by order of War Department.

247

ROSTER OF OHIO TROOPS.

Names.	Rank.	Age.	Date of Entering the Service.	Period of Service.	Remarks.
McLean, James............	Private	22	Dec. 28, 1863	3 yrs.	Mustered out July 6,1865,at Philadelphia,Pa.,by order of War Dept.
McLain, John P............	...do...	18	Dec. 10, 1863	3 yrs.	Mustered out June 27,1865,at Petersburg,Va.,by order of War Department.
Maddux, Charles E........	...do...	18	Nov. 4, 1863	3 yrs.	Captured Oct.1,1864,at Davis'Farm,Va.;mustered out June 16,1865,at Camp Chase, Ohio,by order of War Dept.
Marietta, Abram...........	...do...	19	Oct. 19, 1863	3 yrs.	Mustered out with company Aug.7,1865.
Miller, Jacob.............	...do...	18	Dec. 29, 1863	3 yrs.	Mustered out with company Aug.7,1865.
Milner, Columbus.........	...do...	20	Nov. 13, 1863	3 yrs.	Died June 13,1864,at Washington,D.C., of wounds received May 28,1864,at Hawe's Shop,Va.
Morehead, Nathan..........	...do...	18	Dec. 21, 1863	3 yrs.	Mustered out July 6,1865,at Columbus, O.,by order of War Department.
Morey, Leman J...........	...do...	20	Jan. 4, 1864	3 yrs.	Mustered out June 27,1865,at Petersburg,Va.,by order of War Department.
Mulvihill, Michael........	...do...	22	Dec. 23, 1863	3 yrs.	Mustered out June 27,1865,at Petersburg,Va.,by order of War Dept.;veteran.
Percy, Nathaniel..........	...do...	25	Dec. 24, 1863	3 yrs.	
Rabshaw, Gideon..........	...do...	43	Dec. 23, 1864	3 yrs.	Mustered out June 27,1865,at Petersburg,Va.,by order of War Department.
Rearding, John...........	...do...	18	Jan. 2, 1864	3 yrs.	Mustered out with company Aug.7,1865.
Rearding, Arthur..........	...do...	20	Jan. 2, 1864	3 yrs.	Mustered out June 27,1865,at Petersburg,Va.,by order of War Department.
Ritter, John.............	...do...	17	Nov. 11, 1863	3 yrs.	Mustered out June 27,1865,at Petersburg,Va.,by order of War Department.
Rundell, Harrison........	...do...	23	Jan. 5, 1864	3 yrs.	Mustered out July 6,1865,at Philadelphia,Pa.,by order of War Department.

Names.	Rank.	Age.	Date of Entering the Service.	Period of Service.	Remarks.
Shaw, William S..........	Private	20	Dec. 30, 1863	3 yrs.	Mustered out June 24,1865,at Point Lookout,Md.,by order of War Dept.
Smith, William K..........	...do...	33	Dec. 26, 1863	3 yrs.	Mustered out June 29,1865,at Petersburg,Va.,by order of War Department.
Smith, William F..........	...do...	19	Dec. 28, 1863	3 yrs.	Mustered out June 27,1865,at Petersburg,Va.,by order of War Department.
Solo, Frank..............	...do...	18	Jan. 5, 1864	3 yrs.	
Stigleman, Thompson.......	...do...	18	Nov. 3, 1863	3 yrs.	Mustered out June 27,1865,at Petersburg,Va.,by order of War Department.
Stine, Elmer.............	...do...	20	Dec. 30, 1863	3 yrs.	Mustered out with company Aug.7,1865.
Stine, William...........	...do...	18	Dec. 30, 1863	3 yrs.	Mustered out with company Aug.7,1865.
Stine, Henry.............	...do...	44	Feb. 8, 1865	1 yr.	Mustered out with company Aug.7,1865.
Stewart, Edward..........	...do...	22	Dec. 23, 1863	3 yrs.	Mustered out June 27,1865,at Petersburg,Va.,by order of War Department.
Stover, John A...........	...do...	21	Feb. 11, 1865	1 yr.	Mustered out June 19,1865,at Baltimore,Md.,by order of War Department.
Thomas, John.............	...do...	18	Jan. 4, 1864	3 yrs.	Died June 27,1864,at City Point,Va.
Tobin, Joseph............	...do...	18	Oct. 31, 1863	3 yrs.	Mustered out June 6,1865,at Philadelphia,Pa.,by order of War Department.
Vaname, William..........	...do...	18	Dec. 9, 1863	3 yrs.	Discharged April 25,1864,on Surgeon's certificate of disability.
Van Fossen, Robert D......	...do...	18	Dec. 26, 1863	3 yrs.	Mustered out June 27,1865,at Petersburg,Va.,by order of War Department.
Webber, George W.........	...do...	18	Oct. 31, 1863	3 yrs.	Captured Oct.1,1864,at Davis'Farm, Va.,mustered out June 27,1865, at Petersburg,Va.,by order of War Dept.
Welch, John..............	...do...	18	Nov. 30, 1863	3 yrs.	Mustered out June 27,1865,at Petersburg,Va.,by order of War Department.

ROSTER OF OHIO TROOPS.

Names.	Rank.	Age.	Date of Entering the Service.	Period of Service.	Remarks.
Whittle, James............	Private	18	Nov. 1, 1863	3 yrs.	Mustered out June 28,1865,at Petersburg,Va.,by order of War Department.
Whittaker, John B.........	..do...	18	Jan. 1, 1864	3 yrs.	Mustered out June 27,1865,at Petersburg,Va.,by order of War Department.
York, Amos...............	..do...	18	Dec. 29, 1863	3 yrs.	

UNASSIGNED RECRUITS.

Names.	Rank.	Age.	Date of Entering the Service.	Period of Service.	Remarks.
Andrew, Andrew...........	Private	21	Aug. 31, 1864	1 yr.	No final record found.
Baker, James.............	..do...	24	Dec. 24, 1863	3 yrs.	No final record found.
Byard, G. R.............	..do...	...	Oct. 23, 1861	3 yrs.	No final record found.
Burt, George M..........	..do...	28	June 27, 1863	3 yrs.	No final record found.
Braggins, James L.......	..do...	21	Oct. 5, 1864	1 yr.	No final record found.
Bartlett, William.......	..do...	18	Mch. 4, 1865	1 yr.	No final record found.
Bliss, George M.........	..do...	23	Jan. 25, 1865	1 yr.	No final record found.
Byrne, Joseph J.........	..do...	28	Jan. 4, 1864	3 yrs.	No final record found.
Bline, George..........	..do...	23	Mch. 10, 1865	1 yr.	No final record found.
Collier, Oliver E......	..do...	19	Oct. 2, 1862	9 mos.	Drafted; no final record found.
Chambers, George W.....	..do...	43	June 12, 1863	3 yrs.	No final record found.
Clark, George.........	..do...	22	May 13, 1864	3 yrs.	No final record found.
Curtis, Alford........	..do...	19	June 22, 1863	3 yrs.	No final record found.
Crookte, Peter........	..do...	18	Oct. 17, 1862	9 mos.	Drafted; no final record found.
Dunn, James..........	..do...	22	May 13, 1864	3 yrs.	No final record found.
Farmer, Henry........	..do...	22	Oct. 2, 1862	9 mos.	Drafted; no final record found.
Fishback, John.......	..do...	18	June 12, 1863	3 yrs.	No final record found.
Goff, John...........	..do...	36	June 12, 1863	3 yrs.	No final record found.
Hines, Francis M.....	..do...	22	Nov. 12, 1862	3 yrs.	Discharged April 27,1863,on Surgeon's certificate of disability.
Helleman, George.....	..do...	...	Oct. 1, 1862	9 mos.	Drafted; no final record found.
Henry, George........	..do...	21	June 24, 1863	3 yrs.	No final record found.
Huston, John W.......	..do...	21	June 9, 1863	3 yrs.	No final record found.
Haver, Sutter........	..do...	23	Aug. 3, 1864	3 yrs.	No final record found.

SIXTH REGIMENT OHIO VOLUNTEER CAVALRY.

Names.	Rank.	Age.	Date of Entering the Service.	Period of Service.	Remarks.
Jones, William........	Private	30	Nov. 2, 1863	3 yrs.	No final record found.
Johnson, William......	...do...	40	June 8, 1863	3 yrs.	No final record found.
Jones, Robert........	...do...	....	....	9 mos.	Substitute; no final record found.
Kilman, Joseph T......	...do...	40	Jan. 1, 1864	3 yrs.	No final record found.
Kendell, Richard M....	...do...	33	June 23, 1863	3 yrs.	No final record found.
Lewis, Israel D.......	...do...	18	Feb. 25, 1864	3 yrs.	No final record found.
McDonald, James.......	...do...	25	June 12, 1863	3 yrs.	No final record found.
McGillen, George W....	...do...	21	June 9, 1863	3 yrs.	No final record found.
McIntyer, Jeremiah....	...do...	23	May 30, 1864	3 yrs.	No final record found.
Mullett, Robert A.....	...do...	21	Oct. 1, 1862	9 mos.	Drafted; no final record found.
Myers, Julias, A......	...do...	21	June 13, 1863	3 yrs.	No final record found.
Monroe, Alfred H......	...do...	27	June 6, 1863	3 yrs.	No final record found.
Moyer, John..........	...do...	24	Aug. 29, 1864	1 yr.	No final record found.
Moore, James.........	...do...	24	Oct. 13, 1864	1 yr.	No final record found.
Murphy, Andrew.......	...do...	18	Nov. 20, 1863	3 yrs.	No final record found.
Muldoon, Edwin.......	...do...	23	May 13, 1864	3 yrs.	No final record found.
Murray, Robert.......	...do...	20	May 13, 1864	3 yrs.	No final record found.
Nolan, John W........	...do...	21	Dec. 6, 1863	3 yrs.	No final record found.
Omahan, John.........	...do...	44	June 9, 1863	3 yrs.	No final record found.
Otter, Ernest........	...do...	22	Oct. 10, 1862	9 mos.	Drafted; no final record found.
Phelix, Jeremiah.....	...do...	26	June 10, 1863	3 yrs.	No final record found.
Page, John..........	...do...	22	Oct. 15, 1864	3 yrs.	No final record found.
Roberts, Samuel......	...do...	19	Feb. 14, 1864	3 yrs.	No final record found.
Rice, Samuel J.......	...do...	39	June 13, 1863	3 yrs.	No final record found.
Raggio, Damerico.....	...do...	34	June 8, 1863	3 yrs.	No final record found.
Rooney, Phelix.......	...do...	32	June 25, 1863	3 yrs.	No final record found.
Rosenborough, Robert..	...do...	26	June 23, 1863	3 yrs.	No final record found.

INDEX:

Carolyn N. Seelink
618 Silver
Delta, Colorado 81416